Writers Under the Rims
A Yellowstone County Anthology

Parmly
Billings
Library
1901-2001

Writers Under the Rims

A Yellowstone County Anthology

edited by: Sue Hart
Donna Davis
Ken Egan Jr.
Joyce Jensen

Published by the Parmly Billings Library Foundation
as a gift to the community, in honor of the Library's 100th anniversary.

ISBN 0-9712850-0-4
© 2001 Parmly Billings Library Foundation
All Rights Reserved.

Front Cover: "Tracks, Yellowstone River at Billings" by Michael Sample.
 Michael S. Sample has lived in Billings since he was six. He is a freelance outdoor photographer whose photos have appeared in *National Geographic, Outdoor Life,* and other major magazines, as well as in many books. He is one of the founders of Falcon Press.

Back Cover: "The Comet Hale-Bopp Photographed over the Billings
 Rimrocks on March 25, 1997" by Larry Mayer.
 Larry Mayer, chief photographer for *The Billings Gazette,* has been with the newspaper since 1977. His photography has also appeared in *The New York Times, Life, Time, Newsweek, U.S. News and World Report, Montana Magazine,* and more than twenty books.

Assistance with book design by Bob Morrison.

Reprinted with the permission of Scribner, a Division of Simon & Schuster from *Ride with Me, Mariah Montana* by Ivan Doig. Copyright 1990 by Ivan Doig.

Kelly, Luther S. *"Yellowstone Kelly": The Memoirs of Luther S. Kelly* edited by M. M. Quaife. New Haven: Yale University Press, 1926. Reprinted by permission of Yale University Press.

Linderman, Frank B. *Pretty-Shield: Medicine Woman of the Crows.* (Originally *Red Mother.)* New York: The John Day Co., 1932.

Nabokov, Peter. *Two Leggings: The Making of a Crow Warrior* New York: HarperCollins, 1987.

Printed in the United States of America
by Artcraft, Billings, Montana

Acknowledgments

How do we say thank you? Very early in this book's history, an author said, "You know no committee ever wrote a book." The committee grew in size as the project grew, and thanks to these many wonderful volunteers, this committee wrote a book!

First are the contributors. Without all 132 of them, this book simply could not exist. Submissions came from books and articles sent by the authors or their heirs. In some cases others made submissions. Thank you, authors, photographers and artists! Without the graphics, this book would be much less interesting. Thanks to Don Miller, who did a fabulous job making prints of our graphics, made wonderfully clean copies, and for the story his mother told him about the meadowlark song. We are extremely grateful to Michael Sample and Larry Mayer for the cover photos celebrating the beauty of our Rims. We also appreciate the Hawkins Collection, the Parmly Billings Library, the Western Heritage Center, the Yellowstone Art Museum and the Montana State University-Billings Library Special Collections for permitting use of some graphics. Thank you to all who submitted works we would otherwise have missed: each editor, Marie Armstrong, John James, Kathy Jones, Kevin Kooistra-Manning, Louise McDonald, Rich Pittsley, Dee Ann Redman, Shirley Steele, Gary Svee, and Marilyn Wade.

Next are the editors. Thousands of hours of work, all volunteer, were donated by these editors, each of whom has a real life, which they put on hold for this project. Sue Hart, Donna Davis, and Ken Egan, thank you.

The idea of a county anthology celebrating the 100th birthday of the Parmly Billings Library came from Don Allen of the Library Centennial Planning Committee. That Committee, co-chaired by Steven Fenter and Diane Cross, followed each step with great interest and enthusiasm and cheered this project along. Bill Cochran, Library Director, and some of the staff—Jim Curry, Kathy Jones, Sandy Raymond, Dee Ann Redman, and Karen Stevens—provided some of the loudest cheers, as did Lydia Diakakis, Carol Drum, Carol Green, Jane Howell, Jan Jelinek, Lise McClendon Webb and Leila Wright. Thanks to all our cheerleaders! An Anthology Committee picked the size of the book, searched for authors and passages, discussed marketing, and performed other important tasks. Thanks to each of you: Don Allen, Marie Armstrong, Kathy Jones, Louise McDonald, Suzanne Sandridge, Marilyn Wade and Lise McClendon Webb. A special thanks to Gary Svee for his assistance and support.

Many people willingly read parts of this book and because of them there are fewer mistakes. Several evaluators read and chose a particular passage; proofreaders made their eyeballs spin by reading every punctuation mark and paragraph line; and index readers made sure each entry was valid. The editors read and re-read selections numerous times. Marie Armstrong, Adeline Bartle, Rosanne Bos, Jane Howell, the Chad Martin family, Louise McDonald, Berta Morrison, Pam Muskett, Chris Rubich, Shirley Steele, Gary Svee, Marilyn Wade, and Richard S. Wheeler, your help was so very needed. Thank you everyone.

We needed written permission—no reprint permission meant no selection from that author. We certainly thank each author, heir and publisher who sent us permission. But we also thank those who helped find addresses and phone numbers, who wrote e-mails and letters, or who made phone calls: each editor, David and Marie Armstrong, Rosanne Bos, Eileen Melby, Rich Pittsley, Gary Svee, and Marilyn Wade.

Producing the book was a fascinating process. Thanks to Bob Morrison, Jon Lodge, and Keith Keller for their assistance and hard work. They gave extremely valuable advice and out of it came a fine-looking book. Bob, thanks for the stunning cover layout.

Funding is necessary. Because of generous donations from First Interstate Bank, Billings and First Interstate Bank Foundation, the Parmly Billings Library Foundation, Friends of the Library, M. & J. Jensen, C. & K. O'Brien and others, this book exists. Thanks to the officers of the Parmly Billings Library Foundation Board: Donna Davis, President; Lise McClendon Webb, Vice President; Norma Buchanan, Secretary; Chris Lindstrand, Treasurer; and to each member of the Board for being the publisher and for paying the bills! Thanks Kelly Addy, Don Allen, Bette Bohlinger, Carol Drum, Carol Green, Lynette Kerbel, Greg McDonald, Ann Miller, and David North.

Know that everyone who helped, even if I forgot to name you, is gratefully appreciated. Each and every one of you deserves a pat on the back for a job well done and for a book to be proud of. Thank you, thank you, thank you one and all.

No book can be properly launched without a rousing party. Thanks, Lise McClendon Webb, for that and for the Centennial Logo on page iii.

An unknown author/illustrator left his "story," one of the first permanent writings of Yellowstone County. We say thanks as we use his "story" as the dingbat between selections in this book.

 Joyce Jensen, managing editor

Joyce Jensen, of course, is too modest and self-effacing to give herself credit for the tremendous job she has done as Managing Editor for this endeavor. She has been absolutely tireless in tracking down materials and people, organizing meetings, sending out inquiries and permission to reprint letters, and taking care of the endless details that are the major—and most time-consuming—part of an undertaking of this sort. Without Joyce, there would be no *Writers Under the Rims*—and that is not an overstatement.

In addition to everything else she took on to ensure the success of this project, she also had to ride herd on the editorial board, nagging us along—in the nicest possible way!—when we needed prodding to meet deadlines; providing us with every possible sort of assistance; and, in general, making this at times seemingly overwhelming task fun and rewarding. Largely as a result of her efforts, you are holding a book of which we are very proud, and we hope you will be, too.

Thanks, Joyce. We truly could not have done it without you!

Sue, Donna, and Ken

Contents

Personalities, Places, Ponies

Beginnings

Later Voices

Graphics

To/
The Parmly Billings Memorial Library

Being on a library shelf will be a mighty small range for these two hosses, after being used to so much freedom and before I corralled 'em into these pages.

The air and sunshine they'll get now will be only from friendly faces, and I hope they get much of that in this secure shelter of their home ranges.

WILL JAMES
'39

Will James said it all in this 1939 dedication to *The Dark Horse*. The editors echo his sentiments and hope you feel that the Parmly Billings Library (PBL) is your "home range," too.

See page 43 for biographical information about **Will James**.

Epigraphs

History of the Parmly Billings Memorial Library
author unknown [written about 1965]

Before there was a public library in Billings, there was a library club whose constitutional purpose was to keep men, young and old, off the streets. It did so well that a committee waited on Frederick Billings, Junior, who agreed to give $35,000.00 to build a library on land granted by the Northern Pacific Railroad for 99 years. This lease expires in 1999. The Library was built and named for his brother, Parmly, who had represented the family's interests in Billings and who had died at the age of 25. (Parmly was Mrs. Billings' maiden name—a well-known one in Vermont.)

Mabel Collins, the first librarian, was the very model of a modern librarian, although no one knew that sixty-four years ago. She knew her books— they were both a stimulus and an inspiration to the reader. She knew "Public Relations" long before the phrase was coined and she practiced it. At the end of her first year, books had circulated 12,250 times or 3.7% per capita, and the cost to operate the library was $3,644.00. She resigned in 1916.

Parmly Billings Memorial Library [1909]
by Miss Mabel Collins, Librarian
Billings, Montana: Metropolis of the Great Yellowstone Valley

Mabel Collins, the first librarian, was hired in 1901 and resigned in 1916.

Billings possesses one of the finest library buildings and one of the best equipped libraries in the west, the Parmly Billings Memorial Library. The building, a gift to the city of Billings by Frederick Billings, Jr., of New York, was given in memory of his brother, Parmly Billings, at one time a resident of this city. It was dedicated October 1, 1901, and since that time has been maintained by the city, which levies a tax of one mill on the dollar for its maintenance. The building cost in excess of $25,000 and is very well furnished with books, possessing more than 6,000 volumes. Additions are being made to this collection every day. It is in charge of Miss Mabel Collins as librarian and her two assistants. During the past year 27,250 books were issued to patrons. Thousands took advantage of the reading room, where are kept all the latest periodicals.

The large, well lighted reading room, the collection of best books, all of the standard periodicals in the way of daily newspapers and magazines are an attraction, especially to the men who are temporarily out of work, and the noon hour finds many young men and women spending the time at their disposal in the reading room. The library answers many questions over the telephone and so far as it is within its power it is always glad to be of service in this way. The value of any library does not consist in the number of volumes possessed but in the use to which they have been put.

Yellowstone County

Landmarks Volume III reprint of the 1883 City Directory,
Billings, Montana Territory

Landmarks, Inc. was formed in 1974 to prepare for the 1976 Montana celebration of the U.S. Bicentennial, but its work has extended far beyond that original goal. Among other accomplishments, it has helped establish Crime Stoppers, entered sites and buildings on the National Registry of Historic Places, launched Bright 'N Beautiful Billings, and promoted oral history of the region.

The county bearing the name of the famous, almost classic, Yellowstone River was organized but a few weeks ago. A great part of its area, including the town of Billings and the prosperous settlement adjoining, was formerly comprised with all the mammoth county of Custer, with the county seat—Miles City—from 100 to 175 miles away. The inconvenience and expense incident to the transaction of judicial and official business at such a distance from their homes made the erection of a new county an apparent necessity to the people of Billings and vicinity. They, therefore, applied by their representative to the territorial legislature, and on the 23rd of March last their request was granted, and the bill for the establishment of Yellowstone County, with Billings as its county seat, became a law. Her election of county officers was held a little later. The county starts its new career with small debt—a proportion of the liabilities of Custer County—with a careful and diligent official corps, and under the most favorable auspices in every respect.

Yellowstone County stretches westward from the mouth of the Big Horn River, along the Yellowstone River to a distance of 110 miles, and from the

Yellowstone River northward to the boundary of Meagher County, a distance of over fifty miles. It thus comprises an area of nearly 6,000 square miles—almost equal in size to the State of Massachusetts, and greater than Connecticut and Rhode Island combined. Not one acre of its surface is barren or unproductive. The Musselshell Valley in the north of the county, and that of Yellowstone in the south, form two parallel belts of agricultural fertility. Between the two rivers lie the Yellowstone and Musselshell sheep and cattle ranges, universally acknowledged to be the best in the territory. The Clark's Fork Bottom—a beautiful agricultural valley—is entirely within the boundaries of Yellowstone County, as are the vast coal fields of the Bull Mountains.

Billings, the county seat, is situated midway along the length of the county. Junction City, near the eastern boundary of the county, and opposite the mouth of the Big Horn River, is a lively village of about 150 inhabitants. It is a freighting point for goods consigned to Forts Custer and McKinney on the south, and Assiniboine on the north.

Park City, a village of about the same size, is 23 miles west of Billings. It was settled in the spring of 1882 by a party from Wisconsin, commonly called the "Ripon colony." Huntley, Canyon, Stillwater and Merrill are other trading points within the county, situated along the Yellowstone Valley. They are all yet in their infancy, but are destined to grow and prosper with the development of the country surrounding them. Separated from Yellowstone County by the river of the same name lies a portion of the great Crow Reservation—a region rich in gold, silver and coal, and possessing fine agricultural and grazing lands. That portion of the Reservation west of the Big Horn river will be retroceded and opened for settlement within the next two years. It will then be incorporated with Yellowstone County, and will go to swell the extent and resources of this banner county of Montana.

Foreword

Through the years since their foundings, Billings and the smaller communities that grace the surrounding Yellowstone County have been known as agricultural, business, and railroad centers. The area has not, however, acquired a reputation for the literature produced here or for the number of writers who spent their formative years in the region or who moved here as adults and became enamored of their surroundings, and who have set their stories in Montana, often specifically here in Montana, as a result. We hope that *Writers Under the Rims* will remedy this oversight as readers are introduced to a number of authors and works that they may not have known existed. Obviously, we have often had to limit the selections in this volume to excerpts from longer works—tantalizing tastes, we hope, which will tempt you to visit the Parmly Billings Library to check out the novels or collections of stories, essays or poems from which we have chosen an example of an author's body of work.

Readers of this volume will, we suspect, be pleasantly surprised— even amazed—at the quality and variety of the works they will encounter here. Some of the pieces will make them laugh; some may bring tears to their eyes. Some will inform, and others will simply entertain, but whether readers are learning something new about the history or geology or people of the place they call home—or once called home—or chuckling over the adventures (or misadventures) of some of the characters they will meet in these pages, we are confident they will be enjoying their reading experience.

The editors have chosen to divide the book into three sections: People, Places, Ponies; Beginnings; and Later Voices. A fussy—or more orderly-minded—reader might point out that it would make better sense to—well, begin with "Beginnings," instead of having that be the center section. Some, however, will have already noticed that the divisions in the order noted above begin with the letters PBL, an abbreviation for the institution this volume honors on its 100th anniversary of serving Billings and the surrounding area, the Parmly Billings Library.

It is customary for gifts to be given in celebration of a birthday or anniversary, but, as it has done since its earliest years, the Parmly Billings Library is the giver rather than the recipient of this wonderful gift. *Writers Under the Rims* is the library's gift to the people of Billings and of Yellowstone County—a portable miniature of the library itself, which has served as a repository of books and papers and other works which tell—and preserve—our history. In *Writers Under the Rims,* we have collected bits and pieces of history, of fiction, of nonfiction, of art work, of poetry, of scholarly (and decidedly unscholarly) writings—all chosen to reflect who we are as the lucky residents of Billings and Yellowstone County, who and where we have been, and even what we have yet to be.

And what could be a more fitting recognition of the importance of a community's library than a collection of work in large part produced by authors who no doubt have made use of the resources found there, whether during its early years on Montana Avenue, in what is now the Western Heritage Center (a fitting transition, since libraries are, by their very nature, heritage centers as well) or in its present location on North Broadway. There are even references to the library in some of the selections, including an account in the excerpt from Dale Eunson's wonderful story of his growing-up years near Acton, *Up on the Rim,* of having to take refuge on the library steps while a thousand-some sheep crowded Montana Avenue.

Some of the authors represented here will be familiar to readers, especially those found in the L (Later Voices, or Last) section. Sandra West Prowell and Lise McClendon, for example, have each created a popular mystery series; Gary Svee and Terry C. Johnston are well-known, award-winning writers of western historicals; John Potter and Mark Henckel are popular *Gazette* columnists—as is Addison Bragg, whose contribution appears in an earlier section because of its subject matter. (*The Gazette,* in fact, is well represented, and some readers may be surprised to discover that a news writer [Svee] and an entertainment writer [Christene Meyers] write in other fields as well.)

It's that kind of surprise, as well as the discovery of writers whose names are perhaps not so familiar—Dan Aadland, Wilbur Wood, Kathy Mosdal O'Brien, Tami Haaland, Willem Wildschut, Kenneth Feyhl, Gary Leppart, W. H. Banfill, the Rev. Benjamin Shuart, May Vontver, and Gwendolen Haste, among many others—that makes *Writers Under the Rims* a true treasure. We have no doubt that the few hours spent perusing this volume will lead readers to countless more hours of enjoyment as they "follow up" on the adventures of a Teddy Blue Abbott, learn more about the life of Crow Medicine Woman Pretty-Shield, as told by Frank Linderman, visit Pompeys Pillar for the first time after reading Captain Clark's own account of his time there, or enjoy an outing to the Indian Caves to view the rock paintings of shield warriors described in Lawrence Loendorf's essay.

May this collection inspire readers to tell their own Yellowstone County stories to family and friends. May it help us all appreciate the talent and the dedication of Yellowstone County writers, past, present, and future. And may it especially make us all even more aware of the marvelous gift that was made to the City of Billings 100 years ago by the Billings family to honor the memory of their son and brother, the Parmly Billings Library.

Sue Hart, Montana State University-Billings
Donna Davis, Parmly Billings Library Foundation Board
Ken Egan Jr., Rocky Mountain College
Joyce Jensen, Parmly Billings Library Centennial Committee

Personalities, Places, Ponies

Horses Round the Bend
J. K. Ralston
pen and ink drawing (1968)
from The Hawkins Collection

Rock Painting of Shield Warriors at Pictograph Cave, Montana

by Lawrence L. Loendorf

Billings native **Lawrence L. Loendorf** is professor of archaeology at New Mexico State University. His research focuses on the Great Plains, the U.S. Southwest, ethnography, and rock art. He serves as the President of the American Rock Art Research Association and recently initiated a multi-year project to document the condition of thousands of rock paintings in Canyon de Chelly, Arizona. He was also selected as a member of an international team of scholars studying the paintings in Chauvet Cave, France.

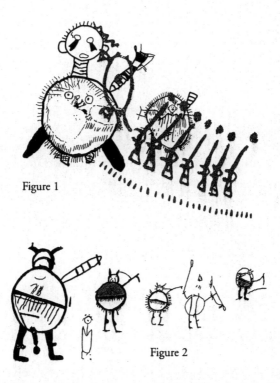

Figure 1

Figure 2

Figure 1. Two shield warriors from Pictograph Cave, Montana, with a row of muskets and an abstract ovoid form superimposed upon them. The large shield warrior to the left remains more than a meter in height. The illustration, made from an original scale drawing, is a tracing by Linda Olson to learn about juxtaposition and superimposition.

Figure 2. A row of shield warriors in Pictograph Cave, Montana. One small v-shouldered figure is found below the shield warriors. The largest figure at the left is about 50 cm in height. Mulloy (1958) made the illustration from original scale drawings; information on juxtaposition from a Linda Olson tracing.

Introduction

Pictographs and petroglyphs of shields and shield warriors represent an important component of the rock art in western North America. They are found from Alberta to Texas but the number of these figures varies considerably from region to region. In south central Montana they can be the most common motif and represent more than half of the figures at a site. In other areas such as northern Utah or eastern New Mexico the figures are often prominent but they rarely represent more than ten percent of the total number of rock art images at a site and in southeastern Colorado, western Kansas, or Texas only a few isolated examples are known. Shield and shield warrior pictographs and petroglyphs were made over a long period of time. One type in Montana was made about 750 years ago while others were made in the historic period less than 150 years ago. At Fremont Culture sites in Utah there are shield warriors that apparently date to more than 1000 years of age.

From the outset it should be clear that the shield and shield warrior motif, made across western North America over a time span of 1000 years, was the product of different cultural groups. These groups spoke several different languages. Some had a farming subsistence, others were big game hunters, and some were apparently gatherers with a greater reliance on small animals and plants than big game. Furthermore, some of these groups may have changed their means of subsistence, like the Crow Indians of Montana, during the time they made the shield and shield warrior motif. With these caveats in mind, in this essay I examine the shield warrior figures at Pictograph Cave southeast of Billings, Montana.

Shield Warriors at Pictograph Cave

Three different types of shields are recognized in rock art: (1) Free-standing shields or circular forms that have designs or figurative motifs on them; (2) shield warriors or human figures hidden behind large shields that also frequently have designs or figurative forms on them; and (3) shields held in the hand of a human character or in some other auxiliary position, perhaps on a stand near a teepee. It is the second of these types, the shield warriors, that are discussed in this essay. Identified in the literature as shield-bearing warriors, shield-anthropomorphs, or shield warriors, these human figures have been illustrated and reported for many years as round body figures that "look much as if they were standing behind great shields." They are believed to be representations of pre-horse, pedestrian warriors who used large shields to cover their bodies in combat. Encounters with pedestrian warriors carrying large shields or accounts of actual battles where large shields were used are found in the historical literature for the northwestern Plains, the northern Plains and the southern Plains. An excellent example of painted shield warriors, on foot, defending their stronghold against horse-riding warriors with shields, is found on an old hide painting. In addition there are rock art scenes of pedestrian warriors hiding behind large shields while defending themselves against horse-riding warriors with hand-held shields…[apparently] the shields of Plains Indian warriors [were] reduced in size by at least half their diameter when they began using them on horseback.

William Mulloy reported fifteen shield warrior paintings from Pictograph Cave, a large sandstone overhang a few kilometers east of the Yellowstone River near Billings, Montana, and compared them to other sites in the region. He described the figures as the

> …front view of a man almost entirely obscured by a large circular shield.…Most prominent is the shield from which the head, which is circular or ovoid, projects at the top and the legs at the bottom of the shield. In only two cases are the arms shown. [One] looks as though it might have a shield on his back as well as in front. Five have some object which expands upward obliquely on the right side from behind the shield. It might be a spear or club and it always has something on its end. Legs are standardized and shown in profile or three-quarter view. A peculiar stylized way of representing the knees consists of adding a projection to the front or curving them in a peculiar way. Six have horned headgear or hair arrangement and six [are] phallic.

Mulloy included scale with the illustrations of these figures, but the scale is hard to read and incorrect in some places; he failed to present data on the juxtaposition of the figures and the information he offered on superimposition was incorrect. In 1993 and again in 1996, Linda Olson completed tracings of the remaining pictographs in the cave and although many of the figures are badly eroded or covered with minerals, considerable information was obtained on size, juxtaposition, and superimposition of the shield warriors (Figure 1).

The largest figure is painted in black and white and although it is eroded and missing its feet, the painting measures more than a meter in height. This pictograph has a round head, round eyes, with the weeping eye motif, semi-round ears attached to each side of the head, spiked hair, and a long neck with v-shaped chevron designs. The shield has fringe around its perimeter and an eroded design that has eyes and may have been some kind of animal or human form. A club-like object with parallel barlines across it is protruding from behind the shield on its upper right side. Based on stylistic evidence, this shield warrior is thought to be part of the Castle Garden Shield style and dated between A.D. 1100 to 1200.

Immediately to the right of this figure there is another shield warrior about half the size of its larger neighbor. Its head and one leg are missing but the shield is fringed and there is a club-like object with parallel bars on it protruding from its upper right side. There is a human form with a rectangular body, straight legs, v-shoulders and upraised arms superimposed on the shield. The round head, round eyes, and bulbous ears are characteristic of Spring Boy, a Hidatsa culture hero found in ledger drawings. The figure is also very similar to painted figures on the actual rawhide shields of several important Crow Indian chiefs. Spring Boy is an Hidatsa hero who was also important to the Crow Indians as Thrown in the Spring Boy. This character together with his twin brother, Lodge Boy, engaged in many exploits that are related in Hidatsa and Crow tales. Other representations of Spring Boy and/or Lodge Boy have been found as pictographs and petroglyphs in Wyoming and Montana. It is not known when these figures were introduced to the region but the Crow, who separated from the Hidatsa, are not believed to have moved to the Pictograph Cave area until circa A.D. 1550.

Both of these shield warrior paintings are superimposed by a row of guns or flintlock muskets and an abstract design, painted in red. Thus we know the shield warriors predate the historic period, a conclusion that is obvious because the figures are faint and eroded, missing legs, heads and other parts.

Another group of shield warriors in Pictograph Cave is found in a position that was very near the cave fill when the excavations were undertaken. Five of the figures in this group face to the right in a row that makes them appear as though they were marching warriors (Figure 2). The leftmost of the group stands about 23 centimeters in height; it has straight legs, knobby knees, and a rounded head with horn-like appendages. Three more of the shield warriors in the group have a similar dividing line on their shields. These figures are somewhat smaller than the leftmost but they are stylistically similar in other ways as well. All have knobby knees, all have horned-headgear, and all have clubs or rakes sticking out from behind their shields. These shield warriors are painted combinations of red and black, all black, and white and black. This group, including the leftmost, appears to be related and probably made at about the same time.

Other shield warrior figures in Pictograph Cave were apparently made by simply using a charred stick to create the outline of the shield warrior with occasional fringe or feathers depicted around the shield but no other decoration added to them. One of these figures is unusual in that it has its arms depicted and in one hand it holds a bow or a bow lance while in the other it has a straight object that might be an arrow. Similar figures in a charcoal-based pigment are found throughout the Bighorn Basin of northern Wyoming where it is not uncommon for a parallel-sided body to be shown through the shield, in x-ray fashion. Horses and riders, made in the same black pigment, are found with these figures, suggesting they are all contemporary, and the horses indicate they date to the historic period, after A.D. 1750, and probably more likely have an age in the A.D. 1800s.

Summary

In this short essay I have described the shield warriors in Pictograph Cave. These vestiges of the past were a popular motif that apparently played an important role in the lives of the former hunting and gathering peoples who occupied the region. The small sample from Pictograph Cave displays considerable variation in the size, paint colors, and the technique by which the figures were made. But this variation is not inclusive of the differences in shield warriors across the region. In southern Montana the figures are made by pecking the outlines, pecking the complete figure, incising the outlines, filling an incised outline of a figure with paint, and simply painting them on the wall. Some of the latter are painted in one color while others, like some in Pictograph Cave, are in two or three colors. This variation is probably related to change in the artists through time and the different groups who made the motif. It illustrates the complicated nature of the shield warrior motif.

When William Mulloy reported the figures from Pictograph Cave, he assumed that the shield warrior motif, in and of itself, was a discreet typological entity and a shield warrior in Montana was comparable to a shield warrior in Utah or New Mexico. We now know that this typology is far too inclusive and future archaeologists will need to concentrate on dividing the motif into subsets for more refined analyses.

Chief Arapooish's Speech

The Adventures of Captain Bonneville U.S.A. in the Rocky Mountains and the Far West digested from his journal by Washington Irving

Arapooish (Sore Belly, Rotten Belly) was a prominent chief among the River Crows. He received instruction in the art of war from his guardian spirit, the thunderbird. He refused to sign the 1825 Peace Treaty between the Americans and the Crows. Death took him in a battle with the Blackfeet in 1834.

Born in New York City in 1783, **Washington Irving** established himself as a Founding Father of American Literature through *The Sketch Book* (1820), a collection of stories that included "Rip Van Winkle" and "The Legend of Sleepy Hollow." Arapooish's speech appears in Irving's *The Adventures of Captain Bonneville* (1837).

Before we accompany Captain Bonneville into the Crow country, we will impart a few facts about this wild region, and the wild people who inhabit it. We are not aware of the precise boundaries, if there are any, of the country claimed by the Crows; it appears to extend from the Black Hills to the Rocky Mountains, including a part of their lofty ranges, and embracing many of the plains and valleys watered by the Wind River, the Yellowstone, the Powder River, the Little Missouri, and the Nebraska. The country varies in soil and climate; there are vast plains of sand and clay, studded with large red sandhills; other parts are mountainous and picturesque; it possesses warm springs, and coal mines, and abounds with game.

But let us give the account of the country as rendered by Arapooish, a Crow chief, to Mr. Robert Campbell, of the Rocky Mountain Fur Company.

"The Crow country," said he, "is a good country. The Great Spirit has put it exactly in the right place; while you are in it you fare well; whenever you go out of it, whichever way you travel, you fare worse.

"If you go to the south, you have to wander over great barren plains; the water is warm and bad, and you meet the fever and ague.

"To the north it is cold; the winters are long and bitter, with no grass; you cannot keep horses there, but must travel with dogs. What is a country without horses?

"On the Columbia they are poor and dirty, paddle about in canoes, and eat fish. Their teeth are worn out; they are always taking fish-bones out of their mouths. Fish is poor food.

"To the east, they dwell in villages; they live well; but they drink the muddy water of the Missouri—that is bad. A Crow's dog would not drink such water.

"About the forks of the Missouri is a fine country; good water; good grass; plenty of buffalo. In summer, it is almost as good as the Crow country; but in winter it is cold; the grass is gone; and there is no salt weed for the horses.

"The Crow country is exactly in the right place. It has snowy mountains and sunny plains, all kinds of climates and good things for every season. When the summer heats scorch the prairies, you can draw up under the mountains, where the air is sweet and cool, the grass fresh, and the bright streams come tumbling out of the snowbanks. There you can hunt the elk, the deer, and the antelope, when their skins are fit for dressing; there you will find plenty of white bears and mountain sheep.

"In the autumn, when your horses are fat and strong from the mountain pastures, you can go down into the plains and hunt the buffalo, or trap beaver on the streams. And when winter comes on, you can take shelter in the woody bottoms along the rivers; there you will find buffalo meat for yourselves, and cottonwood bark for your horses; or you may winter in the Wind River valley, where there is salt weed in abundance.

"The Crow country is exactly in the right place. Everything good is to be found there. There is no country like the Crow country."

Such is the eulogium on his country by Arapooish.

Clark's Exploration of the Yellowstone

Vol. 8, The Journals of the Lewis & Clark Expedition
June 10-September 26, 1806, Gary E. Moulton, Editor

Born in Virginia in 1770, **William Clark** served as the expedition co-commander with Meriwether Lewis on their Voyage of Discovery to the American Northwest. Clark was subsequently appointed Superintendent of Indian Affairs for the Louisiana Territory and Governor of Missouri Territory. He was a most inventive speller.

Gary E. Moulton, a professor of history at the University of Nebraska–Lincoln, is the author of several books. In 1990 he won the J. Franklin Jameson Prize for Outstanding Editorial Achievement, awarded by the American Historical Association for his work on the Lewis and Clark journals.

[Excerpts from Clark's journals during his time in present-day Yellowstone County.]

Wednesday July 23, 1806 [Canoe camp near present-day Park City, Montana] ...I gave Sergt Pryor his instructions and a letter to Mr. Haney and directed that he G. Shannon & Windser take the remaining horses to the Mandans, where he is to enquire for Mr. H. Heney...with a view to engage Mr. Heney to provale on some of the best informed and most influential Chiefs of the different bands of Sieoux to accompany us to the Seat of our Government....in the evening had the two Canoes put into the water and lashed together ores and everything fixed ready to Set out early in the morning, at which time I have derected Sergt. Pryor to Set out with the horses and proceed on to the enterance of the big horn river [NB: which we suppose to be at no great distance] at which place the Canoes will meat him and Set him across the Rochejhone below the enterance of that river.

Thursday 24th July 1806
...at 8 A M. we Set out and proceeded on very well to a riffle about mile above the enterance of Clarks fork or big horn river [downstream from present-

day Laurel, Montana]…The Indians call this—or "The lodge where all danc" at this riffle the Small Canoes took in a good deel of water which obliged us to land a little above the enterance of this river…to dry our articles and bail the Canoes. I also had Buffalow Skin tacked on So as to prevent the waters flacking in between the Two canoes.…I deturmined to wait for Sergt. pryor and put him across the river at this place. on this Island I observd a large lodge the Same which Shannon informed me of a fiew days past. this Lodge a council lodge, it is of a Conocil form 60 feet diamuter at its base built of 20 poles each pole 2 1/2 feet in Secumpheranc and 45 feet Long built in the form of a lodge & covered with bushes. in this Lodge I observed a Cedar bush Sticking up on the opposit side of the lodge fronting the dore, on one side was a Buffalow head, and on the other Several Sticks bent and Stuck in the ground. a Stuffed Buffalow skin was Suspended from the Center with the back down. (on) the top of those poles were deckerated with feathers of the Eagle & Calumet Eagle also Several Curious pieces of wood bent in Circleler form with sticks across them in form of a Griddle hung on tops of the lodge poles others in form of a large Sturrip. This Lodge was errected last Summer. It is Situated in the Center of a butifull Island thinly Covered with Cotton wood under which the earth which is rich is Covered with wild rye and a Species of grass resembling the bluegrass, and a mixture of Sweet grass which the Indian plat and ware around their necks for its cent which is of a Strong sent like that of the Vinella after Dinner.…I met with Sergt. Pryor, Shannon & Windser with the horses they had but just arived at that place. Sergt. Pryor informed me that it would be impossible for the two men with him to drive on the horses after him without tireing all the good ones in pursute of the more indifferent to keep them on the Course. that in passing every gangue of buffalo Several of which he had met with, the loos horses as Soon as they Saw the Buffalow would imediately pursue them and run around them. All those that Speed suffient would head the buffalow and those of less Speed would pursue on as fast as they Could. he at length found that the only practiacable method would be for one of them to proceed on and when ever they Saw a gang of Buffalow to Scear them off before the horses got Up. This disposition in the horses is no doubt owing to their being frequently exercised in chasing different animals by their former own-ers the Indians I had the horses drove across the river and Set Sergt. Pryor and his party across. [downstream from present Blue Creek at Billings, Montana]. H. Hall who cannot Swim expressed a Willness to proceed on with Sergt. Pryor…but observed he was necked, I gave him one of my two remaining Shirts a par of Leather Legins and 3 pr. of mockersons which equipt him Completely and Sent him on with the party by land to the Mandans. I proceeded on the river much better than above the enterance of the Clarks fork deep and [NB: more navigable] the Current regularly rapid from 2 to 300 yards in width where it is all together, much divided by islands maney of which are large and well Supplyed with Cotton wood trees, Some of them large, Saw emenc number of Deer Elk and buffalow on the banks. Some beaver.... for me to mention or give an estimate of the differant Spcies of wild animals on this river particularly Buffalow, Elk Antelopes & Wolves would be increditable. I shall therefore be silent on the Subject further....Camped a little below Pryers river...[near present-day Pryor Creek, downstream from Billings, Montana]

Friday 25th July 1806

...at 4 P M arived at a remarkable rock Situated in an extensive bottom on the Stard. Side of the river & 250 paces from it. [present-day Pompeys Pillar] this rock I ascended and from it's top had a most extensive view in every direction. This rock which I shall Call Pompy's Tower is 200 feet high and 400 paces in secumphrance and only axcessable on one Side which is from the N. E the other parts of it being a perpendicular Clift of lightish Coloured gritty rock on the top there is a tolerable Soil of about 5 or 6 feet thick Covered with Short grass. The Indians have made 2 piles of Stone on the top of this Tower. The nativs have ingraved on the face of this rock the figures of animals &c. near which I marked my name and the day of the month & year....after Satisfying my Self Sufficiently in this delightfull prospect of the extensive Country around, and the emence herds of Buffalow, Elk and wolves in which it abounded, I decended and proceeded on a fiew miles, Saw a gang of about 40 Big horn animals fired at them and killed 2...dureing the time the men were getting the two big horns...to the river I employed my Self in getting pieces of the rib of a fish which was Semented within the face of the rock   this rib is [NB: about 3 inchs (diame) in Secumpherance about the middle...it is 3 feet in length tho a part of the end appears to have been broken off I have Several peces of this rib   the bone is neither decayed nor petrified but very rotten.* the part which I could not get out may be Seen, it is about 6 or 7 Miles below Pompys Tower...emence herds of Buffalow about our camp as it is now running time with those animals the bulls keep Such a grunting nois which is very loud and disagreeable Sound that we are compelled to Scear them away before we can Sleep. the men fire Several Shot at them and Scear them away.

* Clark found the fossilized rib in the uppermost Cretaceous Hell Creek Formation; the rib probably came from a terrestrial dinosaur....

...Sunday 8th August 1806 [Pryor joined Clark several days later on the Missouri River]

...at 8 A. M. Sergt. N. Pryor Shannon, hall & Windsor Came down the river in two Canoes made of Buffalow skins. Sergt. Pryor informed me that the Second night after he parted with me on the river Rochejhone he arived about 4 P M on the banks of a large Creek which contained no running water. he halted to let the horses graze dureing which time a heavy Shower of rain raised the Creek so high that Several horses which had Stragled across the Chanel of this Creek was obliged to Swim back....In the morning he could See no horses. in lookg about their Camp they discovered Several tracks within 100 paces of their Camp, which they pursued found where they had Caught and drove off all the horses. they prosued on five miles the Indians there divided into two parties. they Continued in pursute...finding that there was not the Smallest Chance of overtakeing them, they returned to their Camp and packed up their baggage on their backs and Steared a N. E. course to the River Rochejhone which they Struck at pompys Tower, there they killed a Buffalow Bull and made a Canoe in the form and shape of the mandans & Ricares...Sergt. Pryor informs me that the Cause of his building two Canoes was for fear of ones meating with Some accedent in passing down the rochejhone a river entirely unknown to either of them by which means they might loose their guns and amunition and be left entirely destitute of the means of precureing food. he informed me that they passed through the worst parts of the rapids & Shoals in the river without takeing a drop of water, and waves raised from the hardest winds dose not effect them. on the night of the 26th ulto: the night after the horses had been stolen a Wolf bit Sergt. Pryor through his hand when asleep, and this animal was So vicious as to make an attempt to Seize Windsor, when Shannon fortunately Shot him. Sergt. Pryers hand has nearly recovered....

[Pryor parted with Clark on July 24, 1806, near present-day Billings, Montana. The incident...occurred on the night of July 25-26.]

Pompeys Pillar
Signature Rock on the Yellowstone
by Gary Leppart

Gary Leppart is a full-time professional wildlife photographer and writer who lives near Billings. His works have been published in numerous national and regional publications, such as *Sports Afield* and *Montana Magazine*. He has traveled extensively throughout the northern United States and Canada to capture wildlife images.

When the evening clouds cast shadows across the irregular sandstone faces of Pompeys Pillar, some observers say they can see the spirits of long-departed travelers who stopped briefly at this spot. The list of Native Americans, explorers, fur trappers, homesteaders, and others is indeed a lengthy one.

Long before the first Euro-American walked the banks of the Yellowstone River, the Crow Indians called the monolith "Where the Mountain Lion Lies." It was also known to the Crows as "Mountain Lion's Lodge."

An Indian legend says the rock that became known as Pompeys Pillar fell from the bluff on the opposite side of the river and rolled to its present location. Modern geologists believe the outcropping was formed by the action of the Yellowstone River washing against a soft sandstone cliff. The river eventually wore an opening through the rock and the large block of sandstone was left isolated on the south bank.

Archaeological evidence suggests that the immediate area surrounding the Pillar was used as a camping spot by Native Americans for at least 5,000 years. The sandstone outcropping was an obvious landmark, a place where the entire village could ford the Yellowstone (also known as Elk) River. Nearly-vertical sandstone cliffs on the north bank impede cross-river travel for a number of miles upstream and downstream. It is not mere happenstance that a bridge now crosses the Yellowstone a short distance west of Pompeys Pillar.

A Record of Visitors

The first Euro-American explorer to describe Pompeys Pillar was François-Antoine Larocque, a French fur trader with the North West Company. Larocque and a party of Crow Indians visited Crow country during the late summer of 1805. On September 15, on the return leg of his journey down the Yellowstone River, Larocque noted in his journal that he had come to "a Whitish perpendicular Rock on which is painted with Red earth a battle between three persons on horseback and 3 on foot."

Since 1806, the pillar has been closely associated with the Lewis and Clark Expedition. Captain William Clark and nine members of the Lewis and Clark Expedition (also known as the Corps of Discovery) stopped at the landmark during the afternoon of July 25, 1806. They ascended the landmark and were obviously impressed with the view of distant mountain ranges and the wealth of wildlife present in the valley of the Yellowstone. Clark was particularly impressed with the numbers of bison, elk, and wolves that could be seen from the top.

Before continuing downriver, Clark carved his name and the date on the northeast face of the pillar. He would later refer to the outcropping as Pompy's Tower, named for little Jean Baptiste Charbonneau, son of expedition members Toussaint Charbonneau and his Shoshone wife, Sacagawea. Clark had grown very fond of the infant and often referred to him as "My boy Pomp."

The term Pompy's Tower survived until 1814, when an editor of the expedition journals changed the name to Pompeys Pillar. It has been known as Pompeys Pillar ever since.

Clark noted evidence of previous human visitors when he mentioned finding two piles of stones on the summit. His journal entry for July 25 stated, "The nativs have ingraved on the face of this rock the figures of animals and etc. near which I marked my name and day and month and year." Present-day visitors can still see faint red marks a short distance to the left of Clark's signature, remnants of pictographs—probably the very same paintings Larocque had observed the year before.

Clark's name and the July 25, 1806, date carved into the soft sandstone of the pillar are the only surviving evidence verifying that the Lewis and Clark Expedition passed through here. It is this singular fact that makes Pompeys Pillar a significant landmark today.

Following almost immediately on the heels of the Lewis and Clark Expedition, fur trappers and traders invaded the Yellowstone Valley. Some of them also stopped at Pompeys Pillar and engraved their names in the rock.

There is much more to the story of Pompeys Pillar. That unique geologic feature has served humanity over a long period of time as a signature rock, a lookout point, and as a site of cultural significance. During somewhat more recent historical times, the Pillar served as a stopping point for steamboat traffic, a camping area for military expeditions, and a picnic site favored by Yellowstone Valley settlers.

During the 1860s and 1870s, steamboats traveled the lower and middle reaches of the Yellowstone. The name of the steamboat *Josephine* was engraved on Pompeys Pillar in 1875 by her captain, Grant Marsh. At that time, the mouth of the Bighorn River had been considered the head of navigation on the Yellowstone River, but Marsh managed to pilot his steamboat upriver to the present location of Billings. Marsh was the first individual to raise an American flag atop Pompeys Pillar.

Significant Landmark

More and more Euro-Americans came into the region and began to alienate the native tribes. Hostile activities eventually commenced. Several

U.S. military expeditions passed near the Pillar as the Indian conflicts blossomed into full-scale warfare. One of the more notable incidents occurred in August of 1873, when the 7th Cavalry commanded by Colonel David S. Stanley accompanied surveyors for the Northern Pacific Railroad to the middle Yellowstone Valley (Lieutenant Colonel George Armstrong Custer was also present). The military detachment camped a short distance northwest of Pompeys Pillar on the north bank of the river. While encamped, a number of the men bathed in the river. Six Sioux warriors appeared on the opposite shore and fired a volley into the naked swimmers, causing a frantic scramble for cover. The soldiers weren't injured and the warriors soon withdrew. Although the encounter was brief, it was undoubtedly very humorous to all but those in the direct line of fire.

The "Montana Column," under the command of Colonel John Gibbon, marching from Fort Shaw (near present-day Great Falls) to the vicinity of the Little Bighorn River during the now-famous Indian campaign of 1876, passed within the shadow of Pompeys Pillar during April of 1876. Some of the soldiers added their names to the rock.

During the 1880s, the Northern Pacific Railroad extended its tracks past the monument. In 1882, railroad employees placed a protective screen over Clark's name, the first attempt to provide protection for the famous inscription. At the present time, Clark's name and the date are protected by bulletproof glass and a sophisticated alarm system.

During the first half of the 20th century, white settlers rapidly filled the Yellowstone Valley with farms, houses, roads, and communities. Pompeys Pillar was a popular gathering place for 4th of July celebrations and picnics. More names and dates were added to the rock during this time.

In May of 1928 the Daughters of the American Revolution erected a bronze memorial plaque to honor the Clark party, and in 1938 1,000 Masons assembled at Pompeys Pillar to honor Lewis and Clark, who were Masons. The ceremonies included dedicating another plaque to honor the explorers.

In July 1966, dedication ceremonies were again held at Pompeys Pillar, to designate the site a National Historic Landmark. More than 3,000 visitors participated in the event and floaters paddled a replica pirogue (canoe) down the Yellowstone River to the Pillar.

...The Bureau of Land Management purchased the monument in 1991 and has been busy improving the site since then. In 1994, during the third year of operation by the federal government, more than 44,000 individuals visited the landmark. Future visitation is expected to increase.

Pompeys Pillar, now owned by all Americans, should have a fascinating future, not unlike its historic and unusual past. In time, a visitor's center will likely be constructed, where the complete story of Pompeys Pillar can be told. The story is well worth the telling. [In 2001 this site became Pompeys Pillar National Monument.]

Chief Plenty Coups

Plenty Coups: Great Chief of the Crow Indian People
by Flora Hatheway

Joliet-born in 1905, **Flora Hatheway** ran the Pryor Trading Post with her husband, Sam, for forty years. They were good friends of Chief Plenty Coups. He often told them stories of the Crow Indians and about himself, tales that Hatheway later converted into children's books.

To say that Plenty Coups grew up without trouble would be like saying that the wind did not blow! This great Chief of the Crow Indians had to learn early to endure hardship.

It was only about ten years after his birth in the Crazy Mountains near Mission Creek and Fort Ellis in 1848, that he was left to make his own way in the world. A smallpox epidemic nearly wiped out the tribe. His mother, "Ees-asi" or "Broad-face," was among the many who "crossed the slippery log." His father, "Strikes the Arrow," was killed a short time later by a party of Piegans in the Wolf Mountains.

In spite of these great misfortunes, Plenty Coups remained so cheerful and energetic that he continued to be a favorite of most of the Crows, and thus was always welcome in any teepee in which he chanced to stop. He also was especially welcome because he was a vivid storyteller and a good provider of game.

His name, "Faces Buffalo North," was changed to "Swift Arrow" because his arrows always brought meat to the fires of his hosts.

While he was yet a mere boy, perhaps twelve years of age, it happened that the warriors went on a raiding party, leaving him and his friends at home with the women and children. Rebelliously, eight boys decided to follow the braves at a safe distance while the men hunted for a Cheyenne or Sioux war party, from whom they hoped to seize some horses badly needed at camp.

Although Plenty Coups was usually the leader, his friend Bellrock, an older boy, actually led the rebellious youths that fateful day. They stayed a few miles behind the warriors until evening, when they stopped to consider what their rebellion had done for them. They were far from camp, without food, and with only their death clothes [clean clothes] packed on their backs. They did not have as much as an arrow should they meet an enemy! They even had to admit to each other they were lost and very, very sorry they had followed the warriors early that morning. After some heated discussion, they decided to go on in hopes of finding a Cheyenne camp to raid, or a pony to bring back—anything to help lessen the punishment they knew would be coming to each one on returning to camp!

Bellrock graciously requested Plenty Coups to lead the way. Although Plenty Coups felt this was a trick, he accepted the honor and gave his wolves their orders. These orders were, "Walk in silence, listen always, and like the owl, see all!" The boys slipped on into the twilight. Some time later as the dark night settled over them, they came upon a hidden camp in a deep coulee, framed with cottonwood trees and willows. They could smell the smoke of the hidden camp and the aroma of cooking food.

Hidden, they waited for the unknown camp to get settled for the night, while Plenty Coups slipped off to try to inspect it more closely! When he returned, he told his wolves that the camp was small and the men were asleep. The horses were hidden behind the camp but could be reached if all in the raiding party were careful and quiet.

They stopped long enough to put on their death clothes, leaving their other clothes hidden in the willows.

Finally reaching the horses, they opened the willow corral, each boy silently leading a horse to the edge of a stream that led away from the sleeping camp. After stealthily creeping down the creek a little farther, each boy straddled his horse and drove the rest of the horses ahead of them.

They were joyous at knowing they had accomplished a great feat and left the unsuspecting enemy behind—horseless and afoot!

It was not yet dawn when the boys arrived back in their home camp and were horrified to discover that they had raided the camp of their own warriors! The women sent the boys back with the horses, warning them to accept whatever penalties would be given them by the humiliated warriors. They were frightened, as they knew they had committed one of the most serious of offenses. When they met the grim, sore-footed men a few miles from camp, they were prepared for the worst.

The warriors, having found the boys' clothing hidden in the willows, were ready for them. They tied the boys together like captives, allowed them only scraps to eat, and led them back to camp, where a hasty council was called.

Plenty Coups was chosen to explain their actions.

He said, very simply, "Last night we proved that we are now men. We found that the old warriors sleep soundly! Perhaps they need young wolves to guard their camp! The Cheyenne could have taken them as easily as we took their horses! But we are proud that we did not fail. We now await your punishment."

The old Chief pointed to the Dog Star in the heavens and said, "You will follow as the Dog Star in the sky and speak only when spoken to. You will guard the women from now until the big one, the full moon, returns. You will gather chips for the fires, scrape hides for tanning, and you will help the women in all tasks they point out for you. I have spoken!"

The eight boys, no longer free, but captive prisoners, accepted the punishment which they knew was just. Plenty Coups, too, knew it was a fair punishment. The full moon had just left the sky and many suns would pass before they could again join the camp's conversation and fun.

Whenever in later years he would tell about this adventure, Plenty Coups would say with a rueful smile, "We never again ran off, and the warriors after this did allow one young boy to go along on each raid. This proved to be a hollow victory, as the chosen boy was obliged to guard the horses at night while the warriors slept. He would usually return to camp tired, hungry, and much wiser!"

My First Journey to Washington

in *Exploits of Plenty Coups, Chief of the Crows*

by Willem Wildschut

Dutch immigrant **Willem Wildschut** researched among the Crow people from 1918 to 1928. He became a research associate of the Museum of the American Indian, Heye Foundation. The museum intended to publish his extensive work on Crow religion, art, culture, and history; the Depression, however, thwarted that plan, and Wildschut subsequently moved to Los Angeles, never to return to his beloved Crow country. His original research has furnished source material for important books on Crow culture, including Peter Nabokov's *Two Leggings: The Making of a Crow Warrior.*

[This is as told by Chief Plenty Coups. Their route: from near Mission Creek east of present-day Livingston, Montana, to Butte, south through Idaho to the Union Pacific Railroad in Utah, east to Chicago, then to Washington, D.C.]

It was during the spring of the year [1880]. There was yet no railroad in our country, and we were obliged to travel by stage coach which carried a light at night. We traveled in two coaches, snow was still lying on the ground. We set out from the old agency near Flesh Scraper mountain. The horses were relayed, but we had no rest during these changes of horses. We traveled toward Butte, which took us four nights and five days. The further we came into the mountains, the deeper lay the snow. At Butte we rested for the first time and slept a whole day and night. Here I combed my hair for the first time since leaving our camp.

Early the next morning, we were awakened and told to dress quickly, and eat. The teams were ready and we traveled down the mountain, following Flathead River. Again we were relayed. We continued until we came close to another mountain, where we saw an Indian driving some horses. We called him to us. He was a Bannock. We asked him where the Bannocks were. He told us that they were on the other side of the mountain in the valley. He also told us that their chief, Comes-Out-Of-The-Grease, had gone to Washington.

We again found so much snow and such deep snowdrifts that we sometimes had great difficulty in getting through. The Bannock told us that we should reach his camp early in the morning, but instead, we did not arrive there until about sunset. Early the next morning we took a sweatbath with the Bannocks. They told us that the road from their camp to the next station was hard and rough, and that it would be better to travel by daytime. At that station, however, we should see the "Fast-Wagon" (train). They described it as a big black horse, with his belly nearly touching the ground. This black horse had a big bell on his back, and he ran so fast that every time he stopped, he puffed like everything. When I heard this I was very anxious to see it.

We left about noon, and came to a big barn some time after dark, and here we slept. Early the next morning we started again, and found the snow very deep, but soon it started to rain, which made the roads even worse. It was again after dark before we stopped at a dugout town, where they were building the railroad. Here we had supper. There was a white man with us and he pointed to a clock, and told us that when the hands should be in a certain position, we should start again. We, however, did not know what he meant. Next morning we were awakened, took our bundles, and were escorted to the train. We entered the cars and sat down. We placed our bundles on shelves, and looked out of the window. The train followed the river. Through the windows, we could see many horses, game and mountains. Stewart, who was travelling with us, acted as interpreter. We arrived at the Bannock agency, and many Indians were there. As soon as the train stopped, we wanted to get off, but were told to aty [stay] where we were. That black horse was panting so hard that the bell on his neck was ringing. We thought the train journey was grand. I realized, however, that it was not a horse that pulled and I wondered what made it go so fast. Birds would fly along outside our windows, they were swift, but before long we outdistanced them. We had often been told that the Sioux was a numerous tribe, but it seemed to me that the Bannock was even larger. We halted at a junction, and another train passed going in a different direction. I saw a lake with a mountain rising from its center. We saw many white man's places, and also passed a large number of elk and buffalo carcasses freshly skinned. We passed the snow covered mountains and traveled through still some other mountains. Old-Crow said: "This is the place where Hangs-His-Feet was killed." I did not know anything about this. We came to a big forest and passed it and finally we arrived at the Missouri. Here we met a white man, called Wood Frost, who had been our agent. He invited us to dinner, and gave us some red paint and shells. We had not even finished our meal, when we had to leave, and go back to the train. We crossed the Missouri and were told that we were going to Chicago.

It was the first time that I had even seen so many white people together. It was a strange sight to see so many tall black houses. Here we left the train. There was a big lake, and we spent much time there, watching the ice bump against the shore and breaking to pieces. It was the biggest ice break up I had ever seen, and the waves were very high. There was more travel by train and finally we arrived in Washington in the afternoon. Here wagons were ready awaiting us. They took us to our lodging and we were told to rest, and sleep till the next morning when we should be taken to see President Hayes.

Ledger Art

by Medicine Crow

Medicine Crow was one of the great visionary chiefs of the Crow Tribe during the early reservation days. The name "Medicine Crow" is more properly translated as Sacred or Medicine Raven. His main spirit helpers were the eagle and a large striped-tail hawk.

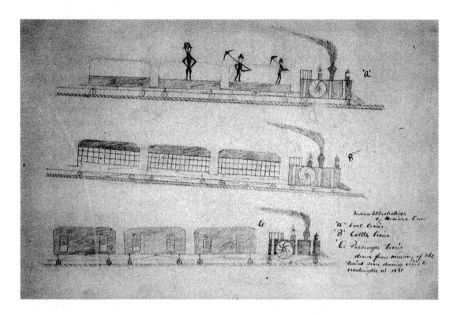

Crow Agency clerk Charles H. Barstow encouraged Medicine Crow to draw, from memory, what he had seen on his trip to Washington, D.C. in 1880. On most of the drawings are brief labels in Barstow's fine penmanship. On this one, the script reads:

Indian Illustrations
by Medicine Crow
"a" coal train
"b" cattle train
"c" passenger train
drawn from memory of the trains seen during visit to Washington, D.C. in 1880.

Courtesy: Barstow Collection, Special Collections, Montana State University-Billings Library.

The Crow Indian Delegation to Washington, D.C., in 1880

by C. Adrian Heidenreich

C. Adrian Heidenreich is professor of Native American Studies at Montana State University-Billings. He has participated in many Native American social and spiritual ceremonial activities, including the sweat lodge and Sun Dance. He is an adopted member of the Heywood and Mary Lou Big Day family in the Crow Tribe and is a Ties the Bundle clan member and a Whistling Waters child. The following excerpt is representative of his extensive publications, public lectures, and consultations on native cultures.

The Crow delegation met...with President Rutherford B. Hayes, who shared certain assumptions of his time about how the so-called "Indian problem" should be handled. The general feeling favored making Indian reservations smaller, consolidating different tribes, confining Indian people to the reservations, and encouraging each Indian to own and farm a piece of private land, until such time as the Indians could be "civilized" and assimilated into the general population. This approach had been initiated as government policy in President Ulysses S. Grant's "Peace Policy" beginning in 1869. The 1877 "Peace Medal" designed for President Hayes illustrated some of these ideas. It pictured an Indian listening to a white farmer who was offering the Indian the "blessings" of the farming life, a man following a horse-drawn plow, and nearby a woman and baby sitting on the porch of a big house. Although the Hayes medal was not minted until after the visit of the Crow delegation, the President urged that they adopt this way of life. Plenty Coups described the President's comments:

> The President said that he had sent for us to talk concerning the future of our people. He said that he wanted us to send our children to school and that they would build a house and barn for each of us. He wanted us to learn how to farm. He said they were going to build a railroad through the Yellowstone Valley, but that they wanted us to make peace with the other tribes in our part of the country.

The most critical purpose of the visit was to convince the Crow to give up their southern Montana reservation, or at least the western portion of it, and allow the Northern Pacific Railroad to build through their country. It was to this effect that agent Keller had brought the Crow to Washington. As Pretty Eagle told the Crow council after his return,

> I went from this (Crow) camp and got in among the whites and stopped. We went out riding one day and went to see the Great Father. He was very good to us, and shook hands with us, so that we all thought him a common white man, till they told us he was our Great White Father who sends us all the things we get every year. We went into his house and

he said, "My children, I want to tell you something. I want a little piece of your land." He wanted from the Boulder to the mountains and all the mountains, and a road cut through our land to drive cattle over, and a railroad to run through our land. The whites got together and talked until it made my heart feel dead.

According to Plenty Coups, President Hayes also suggested giving the Crow another hunting ground in North Dakota, but

> I refused because we did not wish to leave our country. When the President asked my reasons I said that in North Dakota the mountains are low and that I wanted to live where the mountains are high and where there are many springs of fresh water.

The Crow leaders did not approve of these ideas. Plenty Coups remembered,

> My companions told me to make some reply, so I said that we were also glad to see him and that we wished to speak with him, too. I said that he had asked us to do many things, but that before we could give him our answer, we would like time to talk it over among ourselves.

The government did not want the Crow to refuse, of course. Using a technique also used with the Bannocks and other tribes, officials kept the Crow in Washington on an extended visit, for over a month. The Crow leaders felt that the President was holding them hostage and trying to exact a "yes-treaty" from them. Hostages or not, the Crow enjoyed their stay in Washington, D.C. While there, they toured the city, visited the Capitol, which Medicine Crow pictured with flags flying and the Potomac River nearby, and went shopping—each one received $20 spending allowance...

The Crow also visited Mount Vernon and Plenty Coups was inspired.

> I was one among many visitors at Mount Vernon that day, and yet there was no talking, no noise, because people were thinking of the great past and the unknown future. When people think deeply they are helped, and in the silence there I sent my thoughts to the Great White Chief in that other life. I spoke to him, and I believe he heard me. I said: "Great Chief, when you came into power the streams of your country's affairs were muddy. Your heart was strong, and your tongue spoke straight. Your people listened, and you led them through war to the peace you loved. They remember your words even to this day, and are helped and made strong by them. As you helped your people, help me now, an Absarokee chief, to lead my people to peace. I, too, have a little country to save for my children."

Struck by the importance given George Washington's home, he planned then to leave his own land and house as a similar park for the Crow people, and later decided to give it for the benefit of all Montanans.

A Park for All People:
Chief Plenty Coups State Park

by Ken Oravsky and Rich Pittsley

Ken Oravsky has been a writer and freelance photographer for the past twenty years. His stories and photos have appeared in magazines such as *Backpacker, New Jersey Outdoors,* and *Montana Outdoors.* He is currently president of Oravsky Communications, a company that helps rural schools and small businesses to implement modern technologies.

Born in Michigan in 1949, **Rich Pittsley** has lived in Montana since 1954. He served as Park and Museum Director at Chief Plenty Coups Peace Park for nine years.

The most eloquent speaker at the original Veterans Day ceremony held in Washington, D.C., on November 11, 1921, was a man from Montana. This statesman traveled often to Washington, and listed Theodore Roosevelt and World War I leaders U.S. General James G. Harbord and French Field Marshall Ferdinand Foch as his friends. He received gifts from many people all over the world, including a Remington rifle presented by the Prince of Monaco. He also attended Woodrow Wilson's first inauguration in 1913. Though he lived his whole life within the borders of Montana, he was never a citizen of Montana, nor of the United States. Alech-chea-hoos, or Plenty Coups, was Apsaalooke (pronounced Ab sa' lo ga), or Crow. He was the last head chief of the Crow Tribe. During the often-difficult transition from a nomadic lifestyle to the reservation way of life, Chief Plenty Coups often stood alone, leading his people toward a peaceful coexistence with the Euro-Americans moving into Crow country. Plenty Coups was often referred to as the "Chief of Chiefs" for his efforts to preserve his culture through cooperation with the Euro-American culture, rather than military conflict.

Chief Plenty Coups was born in 1848 close to present-day Billings, near the "place that has no pass." As a young man, he fasted in the Crazy Mountains, and the site of his future home was revealed to him in a vision. Many years later, Plenty Coups, speaking with his biographer, Frank Linderman, recounted the vision that led him to build his home at this location:

> I dreamed. I heard a voice at midnight and saw a person standing at my feet, in the east. He said, "Plenty Coups, the Person down there wants you now." He pointed, and from the peaks in the Crazy Mountains I saw a Buffalo-bull standing where we are sitting now. I got up and started to go to the Bull, because I knew he was the Person who wanted me. The other Person was gone.

Plenty Coups' vision continued with the Bull changing into a "Man-person wearing a buffalo robe with the hair outside." Plenty Coups continued to explain that the "Man-person" told him to follow through a hole in the ground to the Arrow Creek Mountains (the Pryors). "At last we came out of the hole in the ground and saw the Square White Butte (Castle Rocks) at the mouth of Arrow Creek."

Plenty Coups then told Linderman how the "Man-person" shook his red rattle and pointed out toward the plains filled with "Spotted-buffalo." These odd looking buffalo were interpreted by the clan's medicine man, Yellow-bear, and other clan men of importance as the cattle that would take over their lands and replace the buffalo. Plenty Coups continued:

> I followed him back through the hole in the ground without seeing anything until we came out right over there (pointing) where we had first entered the hole in the ground. Then I saw the spring down by those trees, this very house just as it is, these trees which comfort us today, and a very old man sitting in the shade, alone.

Plenty Coups was told that he was indeed the old man in the vision. He knew that he was to build his home near the sacred spring. Plenty Coups had his log home built near Pryor Creek, overlooking the Medicine Spring in the early 1890s. He also built a small store near the home, where he sold apples from his orchards and other items in an effort to demonstrate the mercantile system to his people.

During this period, the Crow people, as well as other plains tribes, were being moved onto reservations by the U.S. government, a change that many native people resisted. The government set up schools on the new reservations, but many people refused to attend or to send their children to them. Plenty Coups, although he never learned to read and write in English, was a great proponent of education. At every opportunity, he encouraged his people to pursue a good education. Plenty Coups is well known to Native Americans across the continent for his famous quote: "With education, you are the white man's equal; without it, you are his victim."

Plenty Coups made his first trip to Washington, D.C., in 1880. He also made many subsequent trips. With each successive trip, he became more well known, and was increasingly viewed as a representative of all tribes.

During one trip to the nation's capital, Plenty Coups visited Mount Vernon, the home of George Washington. He later told Frank Linderman how Washington's home inspired him.

...In 1928 Chief Plenty Coups deeded his allotment on 189.2 acres to the U.S. government to be used as "a park for all people." An elaborate ceremony was held the next year at his home, and his friend General Harbord accepted the gift on behalf of the government. The U.S. government, however, could not legally accept title to the land. When the Chief died in 1932, the land was given to the Big Horn County Commissioners to manage. As the Chief had specified, they used income from agricultural leases on the outer 149 acres to maintain the house and 40 acre "park area."

In 1951, because of the friendship between Plenty Coups and Billings Kiwanis president George Snell, the Kiwanis Club became the park's trustee under a court order of August 8, 1951. The Kiwanis Club paid for a caretaker and also restored a log building in which Plenty Coups kept a general merchandise store. The Kiwanis Club also restored the grave site, and operated a museum in the south addition of the Chief's house.

Pretty-Shield:
Medicine Woman of the Crows
by Frank B. Linderman

Frank B. Linderman came to Montana Territory in 1885 at the age of 16. He moved to the Flathead Valley, lived the life of a frontiersman, and began his life-long study of the ways and lore of the Northwestern and Plains Indians. Wishing to communicate with and experience the people around him, Linderman mastered the subtle art of sign language, an ability that led the Crow to name him "Sign Talker."

Foreword

Throughout forty-six years in Montana I have had much to do with its several Indian tribes, and yet have never, until now, talked for ten consecutive minutes directly to an old Indian woman. I have found Indian women diffident, and so self-effacing that acquaintance with them is next to impossible. Even when Indian women have sometimes acted as my interpreters while gathering tribal legends they remained strangers to me. I had nearly given up the idea of ever writing the life of an old Indian woman when Pretty-Shield delighted me by consenting to tell me her story.

Of all the old Indian women I know Pretty-Shield would have been my choice, since in her the three essential qualifications for such story telling are in happy combination, age that permits her to have known the natural life of her people on the plains, keen mentality, and, above all, the willingness to talk to me without restraint. Besides these necessary qualifications Pretty-Shield is a "Wise-one," a medicine woman, of the Crow tribe. She not only belongs to a great Crow clan, the "Sore-lips," that has given her people many leaders and chiefs, but to a prominent Crow family. And there is yet another reason why I should have selected Pretty-Shield, having written *American,* the life of the aged Crow chief [Plenty Coups]; Pretty-Shield's story would be contemporaneous, since she is not more than eleven years younger than the Chief, and of the same tribe; and the tribe itself is ideal. The Crows (Absarokees), who are essentially plainsmen, have inhabited what is now Southeastern Montana for generations. They were constantly at war with the Sioux, Cheyennes, Arapahoes, and Blackfeet, so that nothing need be said of their ability as warriors. Their survival against such enemies, who greatly outnumbered them, is an eloquent proclamation that the Crows were brave.

Like the old men Pretty-Shield would not talk at any length of the days when her people were readjusting themselves to the changed conditions brought on by the disappearance of the buffalo, so that her story is largely of her youth and early maturity. "There is nothing to tell, because we did nothing," she insisted when pressed for stories of her middle life. "There were no buffalo. We stayed in one place, and grew lazy."

Some of her stories are obviously tribal myths, others "grandmother tales," and yet all, to the Indian mind, teach needed truths that may be obscure to others. Nothing is more bewildering to me than recording the dreams of old Indians. Trying to determine exactly where the dream begins and ends is precisely like looking into a case in a museum of natural history where a group of beautiful birds are mounted against a painted background blended so cunningly into reality that one cannot tell where the natural melts to meet the artificial.

Such a story as this, coming through an interpreter laboring to translate Crow thoughts into English words, must suffer some mutation, no matter how conscientious the interpreter may be (and Goes-Together was conscientious). However, in this, as in all my work with Indians, my knowledge of the sign language made it always possible for me to know about what Pretty-Shield said, so that, even though she wished to do so, the interpreter could never get very far afield without my knowing of the divergence.

Anyhow Pretty-Shield was all that I could have wished. If I have failed to let my readers know her, the fault is mine.   F. B. L.

[Chapter] One

"I well remember the first time that the Crow clans gathered after I had left my mother to live with my aunt. It was in the springtime. A crier, on a beautiful bay horse, rode through the big village telling the people to get ready to move to the mountains. His words set thoughts of again seeing my mother and sisters and brothers dancing in my young head. I felt very happy.

Almost at once my aunt began to pack up; and then she took down her lodge.

"How I loved to move, especially when the clans were going to meet at some selected place, always a beautiful one." She turned to look out of the window at the wide plains, screened by the giant cottonwoods that surround Crow Agency, her eyes wistful.

"A crier would ride through the village telling the people to be ready to move in the morning. In every lodge the children's eyes would begin to shine. Men would sit up to listen, women would go to their doors to hear where the next village would be set up, and then there would be glad talking until it was time to go to sleep. Long before the sun came the fires would be going in every lodge, the horses, hundreds of them, would come thundering in, and then everybody was very busy. Down would come the lodges, packs would be made, travois loaded. Ho! Away we would go, following the men, to some new camping ground, with our children playing around us. It was good hard work to get things packed up, and moving; and it was hard, fast work to get them in shape again, after we camped. But in between these times we rested on our traveling horses. Yes, and we women visited while we traveled. There was plenty of room on the plains then, so that many could ride abreast if they wished to. There was always danger of attack by our enemies, so that far ahead, on both sides, and behind us, there were our wolves who guarded us against surprise as we traveled. The men were ever watching these wolves, and we women constantly watched the men.

"I have been dreaming," she said, smiling, "not telling stories. I will try to stay awake after this."

Just here a boy of about sixteen years entered the room with an air of assurance. Decked out in the latest style of the "movie" cowboy, ten-gallon hat, leather cuffs and all, he approached Pretty-Shield, spoke a few words to her in Crow, and then stood waiting while the old woman dug down into a hidden pouch for a silver dollar, which she gave him without a word.

"My grandson," said Pretty-Shield, when the boy had gone. "I have told you that I have raised two families of grandchildren. This one is of the first lot. They never get over needing me, though," she smiled, her kind face again merry.

"I wonder how my grandchildren will turn out," she said, half to herself, a dazed look coming into her eyes. "They have only me, an old woman, to guide them, and plenty of others to lead them into bad ways. The young do not listen to the old ones now, as they used to when I was young. I worry about this, sometimes. I may have to leave my grandchildren any day now."

"Did you ever whip your own children?" I asked.

"No, Sign Talker, you know that my people never did such things. We talked to our children, told them things they needed to know, but we never struck a child, never."

She stopped short, her lips pressed tightly together. "Lately I did strike a child," she said, grimly. "There seemed to be nothing else to do. Times and children have changed so. One of my granddaughters ran off to a dance with a bad young man after I had told her that she must not go. I went after her. It was a long way, too, but I got her, and in time. I brought her home to my place, and used a saddle strap on her. I struck hard, Sign Talker. I hope it helped her, and yet I felt ashamed of striking my grandchild. I am trying to live a life that I do not understand.

"Young people know nothing about our old customs, and even if they wished to learn there is nobody now to teach them.

...'We came from Magah-Hawathus (Man-Alone, or Loneman). He made us, gave us our language, which is different from the others; and He made our enemies, as well. He told us that we should always have to fight to hold our country, but said that He would always be with us, because we would be outnumbered. And He kept His promise, or we should have long ago been wiped out."

Two Leggings:
The Making of a Crow Warrior

based on a field manuscript prepared by William Wildschut
for the Museum of the American Indian, Heye Foundation

by Peter Nabokov

Peter Nabokov is professor in the Department of World Arts & Cultures and American Indian Studies at UCLA. He is the author of *Indian Running, Architectures of Acoma Pueblo,* co-author of *Native American Architectures,* and editor of *Native American Testimony.* His forthcoming book is *A Forest of Time: American Indian Ways of History* (Cambridge University Press).

Before the cold weather we made a few hunting trips as far as the Bull Mountains along the Musselshell River. Then the days began shortening and one morning we woke up in the middle of a freezing blizzard. Everything was covered with snow, but we were safe and warm. Those were the days when we visited each other's tipis and when the old men told tales of our grandfathers. I wanted to show myself as brave as those men. I wanted to make a name for myself which would be spoken by my grandchildren years after I had gone to the Other Side Camp.

Although we count the new year from the time the snow-turned-back [the first snowfall] it was still late-leaf-falling season and a few days later a warm wind blew in. The snow began melting and some places were completely bare. About this time I heard that Bushy Head was going to the Sioux country. I was the first to ask to join.

In the early morning, after Bushy Head's preparations, thirteen of us set out on foot, leading two pack horses to carry our supplies. Bushy Head had dreamed of Sioux horses along Big River and some distance below Plum Creek. We followed Arrow Creek to Elk River, which we crossed at the Mountain Lion's Lodge [Pompeys Pillar], and walked through the hills toward the Musselshell River. Late one night we reached the southern spurs of the Bull Mountains and made camp in a thick pine grove. We had been traveling for some time and our supplies were gone. Two men went looking for buffalo and soon returned with two hides and meat. After cooking and eating the best parts we went to sleep. No guards were placed since we were still far from Sioux country. We slept past sunrise and while we washed in a creek a helper built our cooking fire. Then we ate, roasting some meat to pack with us, and continued north.

The wind was still west and by now almost all the snow was gone. We hoped for colder weather since it was tiring to walk across the soft ground.

Toward evening we arrived at the Musselshell River. The younger men wanted to spend the night here but Bushy Head and I were for crossing and his word was law. Some did not like this but we were on the other side before sundown.

We camped a few miles north of the present town of Roundup at the base of a rimrock with pines on top. The weather was so fine that after eating we fell asleep without making a shelter. Again we placed no guard and the rimrocks protected us from the little wind now coming from the north.

Sometime past the middle of the night I felt that someone slapped my face. Waking up, I did not recognize the country. I felt very cold and noticed my blanket had been blown away. It was snowing hard with a strong east wind rushing around the rimrock edge.

I woke up the others, afraid they would freeze without enough covers. Some of the young men, tired from the long march, had not felt the change and were already numb. Weasel could not feel anything from the knees down and was unable to stand.

We moved about a mile west where a sharp curve in the rimrocks protected us from the wind. After rubbing Weasel's legs with snow we placed him next to a fire and wrapped a blanket around him.

We were afraid to fall asleep and huddled together with our backs to the rimrock. The fire reflected off the rocks and kept us a little warm. Although we were glad to see daylight, it grew colder. We roasted the remaining meat which made us feel better. The snow had stopped just before dawn and Bushy Head gave orders to move. But as we were packing the two horses it fell again and we decided to wait. The wind blew harder and soon there was a blizzard, the snow so thick you could not see an arm's length ahead. We fed that small fire through that day and that night and through the next day and the next night. On the morning of the third day the sun finally appeared, but the air was colder with the clear sky.

We had not eaten anything for two days and saw no game so we decided to try to reach the trader's store at the mouth of Plum Creek. The snow was higher than our knees and higher than a horse in the drifts along the coulees. It would take us about four days to walk to the store, but camp was even farther away and Bushy Head did not want to go back.

I was only wearing a torn pair of buckskin leggings and as we started out my legs grew numb. I took the red blanket from around my shoulders and cut it into leggings. The buffalo hide we had brought was frozen stiff and I cut off its long hair. Pulling the extra leggings over my old pair I tied them at the ankles and stuffed hair in between.

Someone had killed a deer. Bushy Head was roasting the meat and as I walked up he stared. My legs were like young pine trees. When he called me Lots Of Leggings the others laughed, telling me to eat or I would have only extra leggings for my meal.

They teased me for three more days, calling me that name until we reached the trader's store at the mouth of Plum Creek on Big River. In the store the trader saw my leggings and asked a man who spoke a little English my name. When he said Lots Of Leggings the trader did not understand and said Two Leggings; my friend said that was right.

Incident along the Yellowstone: The Story of the Immell-Jones Massacre

by John A. Popovich

Born in Roundup in 1911, **John A. Popovich** had a long, productive career in the oil industry. His fascination with regional history began in his youth and continued until his death in 1997. He helped form the Yellowstone Corral of the Westerners in 1971 and contributed frequently to its publication, *Hoofprints*. He was a friend of J. K. Ralston for 52 years, a relationship reflected in his life of the artist, *The Voice of the Curlew*.

[Robert Jones and Michael Immell were leaders of a fur-trapping party that had an uneasy meeting with 38 Piegan Blackfeet at the Three Forks.]

Apprehension of treachery, however, was still foremost in their minds as they sped with all dispatch for the Yellowstone, being extremely vigilant at night, keeping careful watch over their horses. Only after descending the Yellowstone to a point some miles above the mouth of Pryor's Fork, where a friendly band of Crow were supposedly encamped, did they feel secure for the first time.

...At this particular point the trail wound along a narrow creek bed now called Alkali Creek. It still provides access from the City of Billings to Billings Heights. But the physical features of this trail were greatly altered by cuts and fills when a modern highway was built. Now there are only one or two spots along its way where a vestige of the original terrain can be seen. This natural bottleneck was well known to the Indians and here they set the stage for their ambuscade. The date was May 23rd, 1823.

William Gordon, a Virginian who joined the Company the year before, was in lead of the party. There are conflicting accounts as to why. One source stated he was hunting ahead of the party and another version is that he was scouting ahead to apprise the party of any danger. Even Gordon's report to Pilcher and his own biography are at variance. At any rate, the Indians, undetected, allowed Gordon to pass and leave the scene of ambush. When the remainder of the party approached, they had to break into single file on entering "the narrow defile" as they termed it. When all were in the confines of the defile, between three and four hundred Piegan and Blood Indians began their attack from their place of concealment. Knowing the leaders of the party, they concentrated their main thrust on Immell and Jones.

In his letter to Hempstead, from information he received from survivors at a later date, Pilcher describes the encounter in part: "an Indian supposed to be one of their principals rushed boldly on Immell covering himself with his shield and when Immell with a well directed shot downed him, about 33 Indians descended upon him and cut him to pieces. Jones, already wounded twice, tried to rally the men and collect the scattered horses but the Indians descended on him and lanced him from every side." Another account states that Jones killed two Indians and while drawing his pistol received two spears in his breast. Five others quickly fell in the onslaught: P. Bergy, Bry, Plaude, Leblac and Lemere. There were four wounded. The remaining men and the wounded, under the leadership of Charles Keemle, in some miraculous way during the excitement, extricated themselves and escaped with only their lives to the nearby Crow village.

...While ensconced at the Crow village near Pryor's Fork, the survivors constructed skin canoes. Proceeding down the Yellowstone they picked up their cache of furs from the previous fall's hunt, amounting to 32 packs, and continued by river to Ft. Vanderburgh near the Mandan villages.

...The loss from the encounter with the Blackfeet was staggering to Pilcher. Two of his most valuable men were killed, the entire spring hunt of about 25 packs of beaver, supplies, traps, guns, horses and mules stolen. His initial estimate of the loss was $15,000 to $16,000. In his claim, a final accounting of $13,465 was submitted.

Benjamin O'Fallon, in a letter dated July 3rd, 1823 to William Clark, Superintendent of Indian Affairs in St. Louis, told Clark he was just interrupted by the arrival of a letter from Mr. Pilcher advising him of the Immell and Jones disaster and saying: "The flower of my business is gone & etc., etc." In this letter, O'Fallon also dwelt on the attack made by the Blackfeet on Major Henry's men. O'Fallon further stated he felt both atrocities could be attributed to the Hudson's Bay traders who were inciting the Indians against [them].

...O'Fallon's letter was released to the St. Louis press by Clark and was subsequently featured in other newspapers throughout the country. The British Chargé d'Affaires at Washington sent a clipping of this release to the Secretary of State for Foreign Affairs in London who brought it to the attention of the Hudson's Bay Company in Canada.

...Lieutenant James Bradley, 7th U.S. Infantry, in his manuscript describes a large rock situated at the throat of the portal, mentioned earlier, adjacent to Alkali Creek. On this rock were Indian petroglyphs which aroused Bradley's curiosity as it did for all subsequent visitors over the years. When a road was built in 1902 near where Sixth Avenue now intersects the road crossing Alkali Creek to Billings Heights, the rock was blasted away. It is most unfortunate it could not have been preserved. During the removal of the rock and debris, seven human skulls were found at its base, the identical number as the fatalities in the Immell-Jones incident. To speculate whether these skulls were related to the incident is obviously conjecture. However, the challenge in finding some plausible answer cannot easily be dismissed from one's mind. We do know that Gordon and Keemle returned in 1824 to Crow country on the Yellowstone, the year after the battle. If they were in this vicinity, and it is very possible they were, they would have had a compelling desire to revisit a scene where an event so fresh in their minds had occurred. One can be certain they would have felt duty bound to collect any remaining bones of their comrades and tenderly place them in a common burial....

Old Neutriment

by Glendolin Damon Wagner

Glendolin Damon Wagner, a native of Iowa, moved to Billings from South Dakota in 1921 and remained until her death in 1961.

    The following is an excerpt from her biography of **John Burkman,** a trooper of the Seventh Cavalry, who saddled George Armstrong Custer's horse, Victor, and was one of the last to speak with the general on the day of the Battle of the Little Big Horn. He later took part in the Nez Perce War. He participated in the Sturgis Battle at Canyon Creek, north of Laurel, and was with the troops that captured Chief Joseph in the Bears Paw Mountains. He died in Billings in 1925.

"Oncst we had a fight with the Sioux close to Pompeys Pillar. It might o' turned out purty serious, they bein' about two thousand Redskins agin four hunderd o' us. They tried to lead us into a trap whar we'd o' been completely surrounded but Custer outwitted 'em. It was Bloody Knife fired the fust shot, killin' a Sioux. Custer had his horse shot from under him but he want hurt none hisself. Settin' Bull led the charge agin us and fur a spell looked like they was goin' to have things their own way. Then we charged full tilt agin 'em, regimental colors flyin', band playin' Garry Owen, and they turned and run like hell. Four o' our men was killed. We buried 'em near Pompeys Pillar. Ain't no stone to mark their graves. Funny, settin' in a train, with it rollin' so peaceful along steel rails, to think back on them stirrin' times. Reckon folks nowadays don't allus figger how much they owe to sich men as Varnum and Braden and Moylan and Custer and the army of common privates under 'em. It was in this fight that Tuttle—him that used me fur a card table—was killed.

"Budd, they ain't no better Indian fighter ever lived than Custer was or one that understood Indian warfare better. Time and agin, his forces outnumbered four to one—ten to one—he's licked 'em. He knowed all about their tricks and traps. He knowed you had to take 'em by surprise. That's what he aimed to do up on the Little Big Horn and we'd licked 'em thar too, if Reno and Benteen hadn't turned yellow and left him to fight it out alone. I hear as how some folks say nowadays that he rushed into things pellmell. Why, that's how he won every big battle agin the Redskins aimin', whenever possible fur night or early morning attack. They blame him fur this and they blame him fur that.

"Some say he'd orter found out fust what a big force he was buckin' up agin. Sich folks don't stop to think how things was in them days. Hunderds of miles from telephone or telegraph or railroads. No way to git messages to and fro except by messenger on horseback. Then we was invaders in hostile country which the Indians knowed every inch by heart. Custer was cautious.

He scouted continual hisself. He had Ree scouts and Crows on the lookout every minute. But Montana bein' so rough, what with buttes and coulees, a hull regiment, horses and men, could hide a mile away and never be seen."

Visions of Reno Crossing
Ghosts of the Old West
by Earl Murray

Earl Murray, a third-generation Montanan, is among the most acclaimed of modern-day novelists of the Western frontier. He is a former botanist and rangeland conservationist with a lifelong interest in Indian lore. He now lives in Colorado.

Though quite interesting, the site of the Battle of the Little Bighorn is a tragic place. Indian people call this place the Greasy Grass. On a hot Sunday in June 1876, Lieutenant Colonel George Armstrong Custer and those in his command met a large force of Indian warriors here, mostly Sioux and Cheyenne. Custer and his men were wiped out to the last man.

While Custer was meeting his fate, a battalion of soldiers under the command of Major Marcus Reno fought on an adjacent battlefield some five miles distant. Their fight lasted through that day and into the next. Reno, who actually initiated the fighting, was subsequently joined by a command under Captain Fredrick Benteen, but not before a great number of his men were cut down in a disorderly retreat across the Little Bighorn River and into the surrounding hills.

The crossing on the Little Bighorn where Reno and his men fled the Indian forces, hauling what dead and wounded they could carry with them, is now referred to as the Reno Crossing. On that day it was a scene of madness and blood. Now it stands as silent as infamous Last Stand Hill, where it is said that Custer and what remained of his men were finished by the Indians.

The Indians also suffered the loss of many warriors that day, as well as some women and children. The shock of death hit both sides. To this day, the feel of loss and sorrow has never left the valley.

Though history has seen more monumental battles, the Little Bighorn fight provoked more than its share of discussion. The documented knowledge of the battle continues to increase. Troop and Indian movements throughout the encounter are now better understood. But history will forever hold to herself some of the secrets of that terrible day, for the dead cannot speak . . . or can they?

Christine Hope will always remember her small apartment near the battlefield cemetery. She will never fully understand what happened to her one night in the darkness of that apartment. After that unusual night, which was followed by a day of questioning her sanity, Chris Hope became a believer in the unexplained.

Chris was a student intern at the battlefield during the summer season of 1983. A native of Minnesota and not long out of college, she had come to the battlefield for a change of pace from social work. Tours and talks and seminars were soon a part of her daily routine; she enjoyed her work.

Toward the end of the season, Chris and a park ranger named Tim Bernardis decided they would visit that section of the battlefield known as the Reno Crossing. It was late in the evening and the excursion was planned for the afternoon of the following day.

Chris fell asleep on the sofa in her apartment that night. Some time after midnight she awakened for some reason and began to look around the room. It was pitch black, with only a shaft of moonlight coming in through a window across from the couch. When Chris looked more closely, she could see that the shaft of moonlight bathed a man's face, a man she did not know, who was sitting in one of her living room chairs.

She was immediately confused and frightened. Who was this man and how did he get into her apartment? And what did he want with her? He appeared to be dressed in a form of contemporary clothing, but something about him told Chris he was not a man from modern times. His hair was cut differently from the style she was used to seeing on most men. It alarmed her to realize that the haircut was more in style with the photos she had seen of soldiers who had fought in the Battle of the Little Bighorn.

Chris Hope remembered a lot of things about this intruder. She remembered his light beard and his flowing handlebar mustache. But what reached the deepest into her brain was his face, and the look in his eyes.

"It was his eyes that got to me the most," Chris said later. "It's hard to explain, but those eyes stood out. They were filled with incredible fright. The moon shone on them and they were filled with terror."

Chris could not believe she was actually seeing what was before her. The vision numbed her. Finally she blinked. When she refocused her eyes, the chair was empty.

The darkness seemed to close in now like an immense wall. What else might come out of this black space all around her? It was some time before Chris could move. She finally got to a light switch and flooded the room with light, then turned on the rest of the lights in the apartment. She was alone. There was no one to talk to, to ask if she had been dreaming. But Chris Hope knew when she was awake and when she was dreaming. She had certainly been awake.

When the first light finally entered the apartment, Chris got ready for another day of work. She tried to dispel from her mind what she had seen in the moonlight a few hours before. She looked closely at the chair next to the window. There was nothing about it on this bright fall morning to suggest that anything unusual had occurred the night before. But the vision of the man with the handlebar mustache remained like an indelible inset within her mind, his wide, terror-filled eyes staring at her.

All during that day, Chris kept feeling that those eyes were trying to convey a message. Something behind the unspeakable horror was reaching out to say something. She went about her schedule, her mind drifting at times to what had happened. Finally, she resolved to forget it in whatever way she could.

Around four o'clock that afternoon Chris and Tim Bernardis took their trip to the deep ravines that marked the area where Major Marcus Reno and his troops had fled in retreat from the oncoming warriors. Tim told Chris how the battle had begun at the eastern edge of the Indian encampment, and how, overpowered by overwhelming numbers, Reno turned tail for the cover of the trees along the river. During the fighting, Reno lost control of his command, and the soldiers scrambled through the water and into the hills beyond. Tim pointed out where various segments of the force, dragging what dead and wounded they could take with them, finally dug in and made a desperate stand.

At the bottom of a steep hill, near the edge of the Little Bighorn River, Chris noticed a solitary marker. A soldier had fallen here, Tim explained, one of Reno's men. The particulars about the man could be researched later in the files.

When their tour of the river crossing was complete, Chris and Tim went to the visitors' center. There Tim found a book published some years back and now out of print that detailed the military biographies of the men who died at the battle. The marker at the edge of the river belonged to a soldier who had been assigned to Company B of the Seventh Cavalry. His name was Second Lieutenant Benjamin H. Hodgson.

"Here is his picture," Tim said.

Chris looked and her breath stopped. The man had a long, flowing handlebar mustache. There was no question, she realized, that the photo was of the man she had seen in her apartment the night before.

Canyon Creek

Nez Perce Summer 1877: The U.S. Army and the Nee-Me-Poo

by Jerome A. Greene

Jerome A. Greene, research historian with the National Park Service, has written and edited books and articles about the frontier military experience. His books include *Frontier Soldier: An Enlisted Man's Journal of the Sioux and Nez Perce Campaigns, 1877* and *Yellowstone Command: Colonel Nelson A. Miles and the Great Sioux War, 1876-1877.* He lives in Arvada, Colorado.

The various scouts, both of Sturgis's and Howard's commands (evidently not constrained by the military discipline of the proceedings) ranged about—"bushwhacked around," said [John W.] Redington—during the fighting and got involved in several small-scale skirmishes with the warriors. Redington was incredulous over one of these, in which a dozen or so scouts atop a knoll drew the warriors' attention:

> A shower of hostile bullets went slap-bang right among and through them, zipping and pinging and spitting up little dabs of dust under their horses' feet, and before and behind them. Logically, every one of those scouts was scheduled to get shot. And yet neither man nor horse was hit. Why? Don't know!…Must have been thirteen guardian angels watching over each scout and diverting bullets by inches and half-inches.

Later, while joining his colleagues in a flank attack on a Nez Perce position, Redington received a wound in the knee. "One of my fellow Boy Scouts took his mouthful of tobacco and slapped it onto the wound, making it stay put with a strip of his shirt. It smarted some, but caused hurry-up healing, and the few days' stiffness did not hinder horse riding." Redington further remembered the aftermath of the battle, when "we had to cut steaks from the horses and mules shot during the day. The meat was tough and stringy, for the poor animals had been ridden and packed for months, with only what grass they could pick up at night. But it was all the food we had."

Trooper Jacob Horner recollected the lack of food and water during the day-long fight and the suffering of the wounded soldiers afterwards, many of whom, over objections of medical personnel, drank stagnant alkali water collected from buffalo wallows to relieve their thirst. Horner also recalled Colonel Sturgis's tendency to spit tobacco "in every direction. The other officers moved away to avoid him." On one occasion, Horner acted as a messenger for Sturgis:

> Sturgis noticed that the troops, who were dismounted and firing on their bellies, were removed too far from their horses. He turned to me and ordered me to deliver a verbal message to Major Lewis Merrill to

bring the horses closer....I mounted and headed for the puffs of smoke. When I got into the center of action I suddenly had a strange feeling. I saw that I was the only mounted trooper in sight. What I had to do, had to be done quickly. The bullets were whining over the field. I spurred on to where I thought I might find the major. Suddenly I recognized him in the grass. The sun sparkled on his glasses. I knew it was him. I yelled the order and he acknowledged it with a grunt. I lost no time in wheeling my horse around and heading for headquarters. I escaped being hit.

Horner recalled watching Sturgis when a man was brought to the headquarters area with a severely wounded heel. He saw the colonel wince at the sight of the injured youth, possibly reminded of the loss of his son with Custer the previous year. Horner watched as a buddy was brought in with a badly wounded arm requiring removal. "He asked me if I wanted to watch the amputation. I told him I would rather not."

Most of the personal accounts agree that Benteen displayed great coolness and bravery in the Canyon Creek combat. One stated that after his surrender Joseph asked to see the officer who rode the buckskin horse at Canyon Creek and whom the warriors had tried repeatedly but unsuccessfully to shoot. He was described as having a "trout rod in his hand and a pipe in his mouth." It was Benteen. And although accounts of Goldin and others are quick to condemn Sturgis's management of the engagement (some stated that he was afraid because of what had happened to the regiment at the Little Bighorn), most such judgments are without foundation. Even though Sturgis failed to finally deter the tribesmen at Canyon Creek, Private Horner remembered the colonel as genial, energetic, and cool in battle, and said that he was highly regarded by his soldiers. From all indications, too, some Seventh Cavalry soldiers showed certain compassion for the Nez Perces in their struggle, perhaps because they had but recently joined in the campaign against them, as opposed to Howard's men who had been in the field since June. The men of the Seventh had been reading of their plight in the newspapers for most of the summer, and Goldin not only confessed that "our sympathies were with the Indians," but noted admiringly that "the resourcefulness of those Indians was the cause of much talk among our men."

Chief Joseph Inscription

by Kenneth J. Feyhl

Kenneth J. Feyhl was reared in Wyoming's Big Horn Basin. After serving in the U.S. Army Air Corps during World War II, he earned a degree in geology at the University of Washington-Seattle. His career in oil and gas production allowed time for research on the archaeology and history of this region.

Introduction

Rising from the Sturgis-Nez Perce Battlefield on Canyon Creek north of Laurel, Montana, is a promontory bearing the local name "Horse Cache Butte." On the Two Pine School USGS quadrangle map it is named "Calamity Jane Horse Cache."

In 1953 Ken Feyhl discovered an unusual inscription on a vertical sandstone face of the promontory. The inscription is partly in English and partly in aboriginal petroglyph. The maker of the scratched notation will never be known for sure but circumstantial evidence suggests that it was inscribed by a partially literate person, possibly a Nez Perce participant in the 1877 battle. Even if it is a later production, it has an intrinsic interest.

Calamity Jane Horse Cache Butte

The butte is a triangular mesa capped with massive cliffs of Eagle Sandstone. The table-top bears a half section of native pasture isolated from the valley floor by vertical cliffs and steep talus slopes. Vertical relief is approximately 400 ft.

Until the recent grading of a ranch road to the table top the only access was a winding trail ascending a spur along the northern wall. This access could be blocked to confine herds to the pasture on top. It was used by a colorful early-day character known then and now as Calamity Jane. Charles Zimmerman observed that Calamity lived near the butte and kept her horses on it. The butte was then known as Calamity Jane Hill. After her time the butte was used to hold small bunches of stray horses and the name was changed to "Horse Cache."

Calamity Jane's cabin could be seen until recent years in decaying remnants on the south bank of Canyon Creek near the butte. Zimmerman noted that in 1895, 1896 and 1897 "Nez Perce came from Idaho on their way to South Dakota to visit the Sioux. They always had a herd of horses. They would water at a spring near Calamity Jane's cabin."

Horse Cache Butte is just west of Buffalo Trail....Buffalo Trail ran north from Laurel, Montana, to serve ranches in the Molt-Lake Basin country.

Butte Archaeological Sites

Horse Cache Butte has been designated site 24YE704 under the national numbering system for archaeological sites. In the Archaeological and Historical Values Assessment of the proposed Calamity Jane Reservoir Project field crews from Montana State University conducted an intensive survey and reported two archaeological sites on the butte-top. These were called occupation/lookout sites. A third was termed an "Occupational site." Two petroglyphs, a complete and a partial shield-bearing figure on the south wall of the butte, were deemed of dubious and probably fraudulent origin. They were not given a site number.

The butte has an apex or promontory point at its eastern end. At the base of the talus slope below this apex are several large sandstone blocks which have fallen from the cliff above. In the lee of one of these were found the remains of a small prepared hearth with charred bone, charcoal, and two small side-notched projectile points.

Directly above the fallen sandstone blocks, at the top of the talus, is the inscribed panel. It is 22 in. long and 19 in. high. It contains two groups of horse hoofprints and the words "IN-MUT-TOO-YA-LAT-LAT," twice given. Inscribed in English is "Chief Jos" and "1877."

Discussion

The talus at the place of the inscription is sufficiently wide to allow a platform for a lookout. The author sat here on a cold, windy day, much as it may have been in September 1877. It was uncomfortable on top of the butte but the observation platform was protected and warm, admirably sited to monitor for following troops. From this place one can look south to the Clark's Fork River where it joins the Yellowstone and where William Clark in 1806 described the deserted ceremonial circle "Where They All Dance." Except for an intervening low ridge one could see the place where Joseph and his people, pursued by General Howard and his command, crossed the Yellowstone. On the north side of the river they followed the Canyon Creek drainage northwest, upstream, and one's imagination can trace their route through the likely sags in the low hills and along the flats to Horse Cache Butte itself. A sentry in the petroglyph position would see the first troopers on the low ridge three miles to the south.

Here Colonel Sturgis of Howard's command caught up with the rear guard near the butte, attacked, and retreated. Andrew Garcia accompanied the attacking troops as scout. He revisited the battle site in June 1937 with Max Big Man, a Crow living in Laurel at the time. Garcia recalled that the battle took place September 13, 1877, on his twenty-second birthday. The battle, according to Garcia, began about four o'clock in the afternoon and lasted as long as light remained. While Garcia was exploring the battlefield on his return visit, Max Big Man climbed to the top of Horse Cache Butte and "sang the songs that old war parties sang long ago. The little group below was thrilled by the coincidence."

On the cliffs near the inscription, at head-height and above, are many scars from rifle fire. Some are recent, some have weathered back to the mother-tone of the rock. Could these older ones denote an exchange of fire between a safely ensconced sniper and the troops below? From this position a sniper could be deadly effective. His nest at the top of a long steep talus slope was practically inaccessible and he could turn into a nearby steep, winding crevasse which cuts 30 ft. or so up from the inscription to the top of the cliffs. From the top he could rejoin Joseph's warriors with complete safety as they streamed west and north around either side of Horse Cache Butte.

The Inscription

Petroglyph depictions of horses' hooves are fairly common in rock art and perhaps more so in paintings and drawings in other media. The Nez Perce were particularly oriented toward a horseback lifestyle and were successful in the selective breeding and upgrading of their herds. "Among the Indian tribes the Nez Perces were one of the few that consistently practiced selective breeding; thus, the horses they raised were superior." Three sets of four hooves in the proper anatomical placement are depicted.

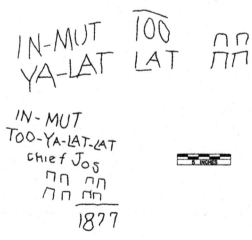

A memorial to Chief Joseph is in the loftiest place on the Canyon Creek Battlefield.
Graphic courtesy Ken Fehyl.

According to Alan G. Marshall, Lewis-Clark State College, Lewistown, Idaho, the inscription "looks like an attempt to spell Chief Joseph's Nez Perce name, 'Hinmatonyalatkaykt'. I have seen some attempts to render it in the same way."

Other renditions of Joseph's Nez Perce name are given as:

Hin-mah-too-yak-lat-kekht (Josephy 1965)
HeinmotTooyalakekt (Brown 1971)
Hin-mah-Too-Yah-lat-kekt (grave marker in Nespelem, Washington)

The identical spelling, IN-MUT-TOO-YA-LAT-LAT, is found at the close of a translated statement of Chief Joseph entitled "An Indian's View of Indian Affairs" published in the April 1879 issue of the *North American Review.* That most likely is the source providing the spelling for the inscription. It also points to a post-1879 inscription date. Any participant of the battle could have returned as Andrew Garcia did. One of the Nez Perce who visited the nearby spring in later years, or any student of the battle, might have climbed to the inscription site for the commanding view. Whoever it was likely knew that one translation of Joseph's Indian name is "Thunder Traveling To Loftier Heights," because, in his own way, he left a memorial to Joseph in the loftiest place on the battlefield.

Bad Land and Lions

The Dark Horse

by Will James

Will James was born Joseph Ernest Nephtali Default in 1892 in Quebec, Canada. He wrote and illustrated 23 books focused on his beloved cowboy life. His later years were spent at his ranch on Pryor Creek and at his Billings home on Smokey Lane.

As much as it had been a puzzle and confusing to Colonel when he'd been loaded in the horse trailer and whizzed away from his home pastures some eight months past, the long scary ride on the train amongst the strange horses afterwards, then the winter at the ranch and all, this which he was now experiencing was near as much of a puzzle and confusing. This being away out, in a wild country and nothing to stop him from roaming on and on.

Little Charro had been the first one to notice the pasture gate being opened. This only left 'em into a big field where stock was kept off and hay would later be cut and stacked for the winter's feeding. But with the colt's natural curiosity, and as they went to exploring and rambling over the big field, Charro found another gate and there he took the lead once more, thru the last opening to the big outside and freedom.

That was the last fence, and the little wild colt, feeling the openness in his blood, the sense any wild creature keeps even tho maybe raised in captivity, stuck his nose in the air, smelled of the earth and looked all around, near like a freedom-loving human released from prison, and even more appreciating, for there was more freedom bred in one drop of his blood than there could be in all of any human being.

The air and warm breezes had been the same in the good green pasture and field he'd just left, but now, out of them, it was like, well, like freedom, and that's all needs to be said, for that can't be described.

Little Charro took the lead in a slow walk, sniffing at near every bush he passed and once in a while stopping to look all around him. He zigzagged considerable as he went, followed none of the plain trails that was along the fence bordering the ranch and went acrost many after leaving it, but with all his aimless-like traveling he was heading straight for one direction, that of his home range and where his wild horse instinct drawed him.

With Colonel there was an entirely different feeling. To him, there really was no home, no range. With his past experiences and like jerked away from where his instinct dwelled, that all had become a blur. The only home he knew now was that of the ranch, and he was going away from there into another strange world, creating in him another strange feeling.

This was one time when, with all his speed, he didn't race ahead of his little pardner, Charro. For in him he not only felt confidence but that he was leading him into a great adventure, and much like one youngster following another braver one thru dark woods to haunted houses and caves, he was curious but glad to only follow.

Every once in a while, when Charro would stop to take a look all around and sniff at the air, Colonel would also do the same, but most always in only one direction, and that was back the way he come, the ranch. It wasn't so much that he wanted to return there as the feeling that he was leaving all touch with humans, the care his breed was so used to, and heading out for the unknown. He sometimes listened as tho Virginia was calling him and would get to wondering if he should go on. But Charro, not at all wondering that way, kept on a-going, and half for fear of being left behind, alone, and again curious as to what might lay ahead he'd catch up with him.

This was something like the time when he was trailed in from the railroad to the ranch. There was the company of humans then, and even tho he couldn't realize very much at the time and he was now much stronger and bigger, the sun was shining instead of a blizzard howling, he had the same feeling of strange adventure, sort of confusing and scary with so much open-ness, and being able to go where he pleased, nothing to stop him was mighty new to him. He'd felt easier if Virginia or Brad had been along.

Or maybe he should of stayed by the saddle horses him and Charro had been pasturing with. Them had been wise and stayed where the good grass was, but Charro and him had gone on, on to where now they was well out in the open and in rough country, on the horse range, and the tall trees of the ranch couldn't be seen no more.

Bunches of horses was now and again sighted when the horse range was reached, and Colonel was for going towards every bunch that was seen, for no reason only maybe to satisfy his curiosity and getting acquainted, but lit-tle Charro wouldn't have none of that, and instead of going near, made a good circle around and past 'em.

But, near of a sudden, they come onto a bunch that Charro hadn't seen and couldn't get to dodge. The bunch was in a steep hollow, a water hole was in the bottom and the horses was watering there. The colts no more than seen the bunch below when Colonel soon learned the reason why his little pardner had dodged such bunches. For at one glance of the colts a wicked-looking, long-maned black stallion left the bunch and came on a high lope to meet 'em. Little Charro, sensing danger, lit out as fast as he could for a wild plum thicket and hid, while Colonel, seeing no more harm in the black than there'd been with the outlaw buckers he'd got to know as being friend-ly, kind of wondered at Charro's actions.

But he didn't get to wonder long. For the black stallion, much against having a strange one even looking at his bunch, charged into Colonel with all his teeth, hoofs and weight, without warning, folded him up like an accordion and sent him a-sailing to roll quite a few times before he come to a dazed footing.

He was still in a daze when the stallion lit into him again, but this time Colonel also got to sensing what little Charro already knew, and instead of holding his ground like in friendly meeting he started to moving, moving as fast as he could and away from that murderous black. But being sort of knocked out of wind he didn't get away fast enough, and this time the stal-lion champed his teeth on the back of his neck. The fact that Colonel was now trying to slip away was all that saved him from a broken neck.

As it was, he was sent a-rolling once more. But not as hard as before, and when he got up it was fairly clear in his mind that he should get to running as quick and as fast as he could. That he did, but the stallion would of got him again, only, maybe it was only by chance but little Charro showed himself about then and attracted the stallion's attention, and that saved Colonel's neck.

The black stopped just long enough to investigate little Charro, which by then had again got in the thick of the thorny plum thicket and where the openings was too low for the big horse to follow, besides, Charro was still too much of a colt for the stallion to get after. By the time the black got thru his investigation, Colonel was well away at a safe distance and still a-going. The stallion looked his direction, shook his head in defiance and warning, and went back to his bunch down by the water hole.

Colonel's size had been his downfall there. He was only a few months past yearling but near as tall if not near as broad as the stallion, where, with little Charro, still a few months short of being a yearling, and with his stunted growth he looked more like a six-month-old colt. But the wild instinct of his past generations wasn't stunted any, neither was his brain, and now with the good care of the past winter he could well follow on the trail of his ancestors again.

With the surprise and scare that Colonel had got he'd kept on running until he begin to tire. When he finally slowed down and then stopped he was quite some distance from where he'd met the stallion and left Charro, and looking around some he seen he was well on his way back to the ranch. He looked around some more, for Charro now, and not seeing him anywhere he was sort of up a stump as to what to do. He missed his little pardner very much right then, for he was still mighty scared. He nickered for him but of course there was no answer.

He stood for a spell, just looking around, then he realized he was thirsty. The run had sweated him up considerable, then there was a big gash on the top of his neck where some of his hide and flesh was missing. Blood was running pretty free from that, making him still thirstier and some weaker.

The last water he'd seen was where the stallion and his bunch had been, but he was far from hankering to go back to that place as yet, and now that he was alone and so well on his way back to the ranch he was kind of debating as to which way to turn. It would be kind of hard to go by his lonesome now, being he was so attached to little Charro. But could he find Charro again? He knew he could find the ranch, and water on the way there.

He sort of circled around a few steps at a time then, like hardly realizing or caring which way he went, he headed back the direction of the water hole and where he'd last seen Charro.

And Charro, also far from wanting to lose his long-legged pardner, had got out of his hiding place after the stud bunch had watered and gone, went to take a drink himself and then, instead of hitting for his home range which had been his intention he went back the way Colonel had gone, towards the ranch. But he wasn't traveling very fast, not near as fast as Colonel had in getting away from the stallion. He just trotted and walked along, sniffing of the brush as wild horses do for the scent and kept looking ahead for sight of him.

Colonel wasn't very fast on his return to the water hole either, and sometimes he'd stop to look back the direction of the ranch, wondering if to go on. But always the thought of little Charro would win him over and he'd poke along towards where he'd last been with him.

He was poking along that way, not at all thinking that Charro would also be on the hunt for him, when coming to the sharp point of a brush-covered ledge and seeing a horse in the shadow heading his way, Colonel lost all thoughts of Charro, snorted his fear that it might be the stallion and, without taking a second look, scampered out into more open country. He'd went on some more, only he heard a loud nicker, and turning in his tracks he then recognized Charro coming out of the brush. It was with great surprise and pleasure as he nickered back and trotted on to meet him. It would be a long time before Colonel would come up in friendly greeting to a strange range horse, but he still had more to learn about that, that all wasn't such as the black stallion.

Now that the two got together again there was a little horse talk as to what next and which way. Colonel, now satisfied and feeling safer with his little pardner being near, thought only of water and took the lead this time, for the water hole, and too thirsty right then to think of what had happened to him there not so long before.

Not a horse was in sight as the two neared the water hole, nor none by it as Colonel now took care of first peeking down into it. He then went down while Charro sort of kept watch up above. Colonel quenched his thirst some, and now he done one thing which he'd never done before and which surprised him as much as how good it felt, he got down to his knees at the edge of the muddy water hole, then on his side and went on rolling in the few inches of water and sticky mud. The flies is what had decided him to do that, they'd been pestering him considerable, especially the raw gash on his neck and where the blood streamed down along it. The water and sticky mud felt good, and he wallowed in it with the same enjoyment as a mud hen would and done about as good a job plastering himself.

When he stood up he was all of a buckskin color with mud, not at all like the thoroughbred he was and the son of the great Montezuma. But that sure didn't worry him any right then, the mud plastering would keep the flies away, and now the raw and bleeding gash was also well covered and protected. It would still be when the mud dried and caked, as would most of his body.

He went further into the pool, took a few more swallows of clearer water and, now much refreshed, went up out of the hole to join little Charro, ready to travel on some more.

Into the Wind:
Wild Horses of North America

by Jay F. Kirkpatrick

Jay F. Kirkpatrick is a widely renowned authority on wild horses. He taught at Montana State University-Billings for 23 years. He is currently Director of Science and Conservation Biology and Curator of Animals at ZooMontana in Billings.

Put yourself in the hooves of a young Pryor Mountain stallion. Born into a band, you've lived your life among many other horses. At age three, although the harem stallion rudely runs you off from the band and separates you from the only companions you have ever known, you find comfort with other equine soul mates who have suffered the same fate. You join your new acquaintances in a bachelor band. While it is not as cohesive as the harem band, you enjoy the companionship of other horses. And later, when you are perhaps seven or eight and in the prime of life, you masterfully acquire a harem band of your own. Though guarding them is sometimes tedious, you are rewarded with the companionship of your mares and sons and daughters. And then one dark day, when you are fourteen or fifteen, you are challenged and defeated. Driven out by the victor, you find yourself not only alone but alone forever.

Horses are remarkably gregarious and social, and the horse alone is not a happy animal. Stress begets disease, opening the door to death. By our standards it sounds cruel, but it is nature's way of ensuring that only the fittest can pass on their genes. Such is the life of the wild stallion....

As seasons change, so do the lives of wild horses, although the degree of change will depend upon the particular location of the herd. Horses living far to the south—where temperatures change little and food and water are always available—change habits less than those living in mountain environments or in more northerly latitudes. But, regardless of the location, the same adaptability that characterizes every other aspect of the wild horse also guides them through yearly seasonal changes....

By mid-July the breeding season is over. Stallions relax and the bands return to a less hectic life. Everyone focuses on eating. The stallions begin to fatten up on the good grass and gain back some of the weight they lost during the "horse wars" of the breeding season. Although they still sleep and play a lot, the foals are old enough to follow the band, and they rapidly learn its rhythms and necessary social behaviors. As the sun warms the timbered slopes, many members of the band lie down for periods of up to an hour, guarded by the one member that remains standing and alert.

It is a time when communication skills are being honed. A mare nickers to her foal to get up off the ground. The foal nickers in response and whenever it returns to its mother. These are the same nickers that stallions use when courting a mare, and this form of communication probably represents quiet "talk" for wild horses. The foal also learns the meaning of the whinny. Enthusiastically exploring, foals often wander far from their mare. A robust whinny from the concerned mare brings the foal galloping back, or at the very least elicits a return whinny from the foal, betraying its location. The whinny, when used in this context, is therefore something of a mild, long-range distress call. Wild horses can clearly recognize an individual's whinnies, allowing them to communicate without actually seeing one another. The neigh is a special call that stallions use to call back a foal that has wandered too near another band. In addition, horses can also tell one another apart by sight. I have always been amazed when a wild horse identifies another horse by sight alone, even though the one being identified has no apparent markings....

Summer days pass lazily for Pryor wild horses. Only the daily trip for water interrupts rhythmic bouts of grazing and sleeping, and these trips are short because of the ample drinking water and lush grasses resulting from melting snow. The horses enjoy both the cool, high-elevation temperatures and the fact that this coolness keeps insects to a minimum.

The horses now find water in seeps, small springs, and even several old abandoned mines, until the coming of the first snows. These journeys take the horses to progressively lower elevations, where they encounter other bands. More time is spent testing the air before moving in to water, and any sign of other horses or potential predators results in loud blowing and wheezing snorts of alarm. Blowing seems infectious. Once the stallion has snorted his alarm, others in the band do the same, until all are snorting and blowing, making a tremendous racket.

As bands begin to cross paths in the fall, one of the most poorly understood stallion behaviors becomes apparent. Wherever there are wild horses, there are numerous large mounds of feces, better known as stud piles. No one knows exactly why a pile site is chosen, but once a stud pile has been built, no stallion will pass by without contributing to the heap. Mares rarely defecate on these piles, implying this is an evolutionary trait common only to the males. Some piles are impressive in their size, and it is apparent when a pile is "in use" and when it is old.

Voice of the Curlew:
J. K. Ralston's Story of His Life

as told to John A. Popovich

See page 31 for biographical information about **John A. Popovich.**

J. K. Ralston, one of Montana's most important artists, was born on a ranch near Choteau in 1896. He spent his early adult years working as a cowboy on some of the famous Montana cattle ranches. He drew artistic inspiration from the colorful but grueling day-to-day life of the cowboys, Indians, and pioneers of the changing western frontier. Driven off his family ranch by drought, grasshoppers, and economic depression in 1936, Ralston settled with his family in Billings, where he found patronage for his artistic efforts.

Well, I had two of these RL horses in my string. I'd heard plenty all my life about RL horses, how tough they were, I mean bucking horses. There used to be a saying in the country, "Any man who could ride the rough string from the RL didn't need to be afraid of anything else he'd ever see." I drew two of them and I know they were plenty tough for me, but I rode them. I came in mounted, not afoot. But I think I only rode one of them twice and the other one once, then this bunch were sold.

So after we were through, Wild Bill, Fred, Blondie and I rode in to Forsyth. The other man stayed in camp at our mess tent, everything was still up just a ways from the stock yards. When we got in, now the 79 was out of business for keeps, they paid off everybody except a few that were going back to the ranch, and I was one of them. The reason I went back to the ranch was that my saddle horse was there. I had hired out, at the ranch, so they carried me on the payroll. There was about six of us left. Benny Cox, the cook, was still with us, he was driving the mess wagon back. We still had the nighthawk, but the wrangler was paid off and gone. Fred Gibson was with us, of course, he wasn't drawing any money, actually he was the H Cross rep. Our bed wagon had gone to Powder River, but we didn't need it, we put all our stuff in the mess wagon. We were over on the Big Porcupine now on the way home. It was kind of a sad time when looking back on it now.

I don't think I knew exactly where my private horse was. I figured I'd just go back to the ranch and get a 79 horse and go after him. He was supposed to be somewhere on the Little Porcupine. We had to get rid of our horses as soon as we started the roundup. Jimmy McGraw was good enough to say, "Oh, hell, we've got a big pasture with horses in there now, but it's alright, you boys can take your horses there." I don't remember now if I knew where my horse was but when I got to the 79 ranch, he was over there. Somebody had brought him on over to the 79 ranch. Probably Matt Roake had some-body going by there and said, "Pick those horses up and take them to the ranch."

On the way back to the ranch I was riding this damn horse. The only reason I was riding him was that I knew him, but I hated him. He was the most miserable horse I ever rode. He was an old XU—that was the only name he ever had. That was the brand that was on him when they bought him. He was big, rough and tough. He weighed about 1250. He'd wear you out to ride him. I never saw a horse that could almost go from under you like he would be about half unloaded. All he'd have had to have done was just sneeze to unload you, but he'd turn around and look at you. I used to think, "God damn, if you only had brains enough, hell you could unload anybody," if he'd just throw that trick and go to bucking before you got set. But he never did, he would just look at you that way and snort, blow his nose at you, too.

We were on the Big Porcupine. I had just been talking to old Benny up there on the mess wagon, but he was pretty drunk, so I left and went back to visit for a while with Fred Gibson who was following behind. Fred had just bought a new wagon because he bought a ranch on Lodge Pole and was getting fixed up to quit the range and go to ranching.

Anyway, I got about half way between Fred and Benny when I heard this sack fall off the wagon and hit the ground. It was one of our white canvas bags to carry tent pins in. I hollered to old Benny, but he didn't hear me or else he waved to let Fred pick it up. I started to ride up to that white sack, hell, you couldn't get anywhere nearer than one hundred feet to it with this horse. So I got off of him and as I was standing there waiting for Fred to come up, I would get him a little closer and a little closer to it. Well, I final-ly got right up to the damn sack, I had got him that far. It never occurred to me that since I was up to it I'd have any more trouble with him. Just as Fred was driving up to me, I reached down and took hold of the sack. Damned that horse, I had my hand on the reins, and that s.o.b. spun me just like a top. I don't remember if I lost my feet or not, but anyway he sure upset me and then run. He just went out a little ways and spun around and stopped. I dropped everything, pins and all, to go after him, and I remember Fred's words at the time, of course, he was laughing at the same time. "Oh, Curlew, let the s.o.b. go, let the s.o.b. go. That's the one thing that s.o.b. knows, is to stand!" And that's all he was doing, he was standing there. He would just run as long as the reins were in the air, and just as soon as they hit the ground, he'd spin around and stop. That was the most worthless horse I ever saw. Fred had ridden him when he first worked for the 79. He said of all the goddamn horses he'd ever ridden in his life, that one was the worst. Like all those horses are, there was no use trying to put a heavy rider on him because he would wear you out instead of you wearing him out. He was tougher than wire, he was an ornery s.o.b. and he had that damn scariness. Every time after, you would think, "Maybe next time I'll know how to set him," but he always caught you and spun before you would know he'd started.

Placed and Dis-Placed in Montana: Finding Home in Memory and Locale
by Walter B. Gulick

Walter B. Gulick is professor of philosophy, humanities and religious studies at Montana State University-Billings. He has served on the Montana Committee for the Humanities, received two Fulbright grants to teach abroad, and currently serves on the board of the Institute for Peace Studies at Rocky Mountain College.

In this essay, I want to reflect with you on the many meanings of home....Our meandering inquiry will be centered about three questions:
1. Where are you from?
2. Is where you now live your home in the ideal sense?
3. If it isn't, what might make it home?

1. Where are you from?
...To have a home is to have a place upon which to stand. Such places have both a geographical location and a spiritual meaning. I use the term "spiritual" advisedly, not intending to conjure up any religious image or to suggest any dualism between bodily husk and true internal self. Rather the spiritual dimension of home indicates a felt place—a place where we feel comfortable being who we really are. When we are truly at home we know what is important in our life. Home grants us the power to sally forth to work and play with confidence.

Alas, for most of us most of the time home becomes confused with a domicile. My house can be awfully demanding: fix the porch, paint the hall, redo the tile in the bathroom. Indeed, houses do have a sort of personality. Just as in relating to people we cannot be slobs sponging off their good will and expect to build a friendship, so with a house: we cannot ignore the maintenance needs of a house and expect to build a home. Friendships require some care and personal sacrifice—some mutuality and maintenance. So do houses if they are to be homes in something approaching the ideal sense.

These reflections lead us to our second question.

2. Is where you now live your home in the ideal sense?

If you can answer this question with some clarity, you can probably understand much about your present state of happiness. As each of us ponders this question, I would like to turn to some Montana literature to see how others might respond. I'll include two poems by Gwendolen Haste, who wrote them while living in Billings prior to their publication in 1930. Listen first to see whether the ranch wife in the poem, "The Ranch in the Coulee," is at home in her ranch....

> He built the ranch house down a little draw,
> So that he should have wood and water near.
> The bluffs rose all around. She never saw
> The arching sky, the mountains lifting clear;
> But to the west the close hills fell away
> And she could glimpse a few feet of the road.
> The stage to Roundup went by every day,
> Sometimes a rancher town-bound with his load,
> An auto swirling dusty through the heat,
> Or children trudging home on tired feet.
>
> At first she watched it as she did her work,
> A horseman pounding by gave her a thrill,
> But then within her brain began to lurk
> The fear that if she lingered from the sill
> Someone might pass unseen. So she began
> To keep the highroad always within sight,
> And when she found it empty long she ran
> And beat upon the pane and cried with fright.
> The winter was the worst. When snow would fall
> He found it hard to quiet her at all.

The ranch wife finds her house to be a barrier separating her from the world of action and purpose. Her husband's practicality—having wood and water near—pulls her away from the loftiness of sky and mountain. House has become a prison, and she lives trapped in her emotions, which are severed from the engaged life she yearns for. She lives in a house in exile from home....

3. If where you live is not your home in the ideal sense, what might make it home?

Just living in a place for a long time does not make it home. We saw in Gwendolyn Haste's "The Ranch in the Coulee" that a house can come to seem a prison if it is not a place where one can be happily engaged in living.

...In Montana, the vistas are such that our sense of a locale can be on a vastly larger scale than in an area where flatness of topography and denseness of vegetation deprive one of distance. The geography I identify with includes the rolling prairies and piney outcroppings around Billings, but also the majestic Beartooths 60 miles to the southwest. They are one of the prominent skyline features visible from Billings—why not include them as part of the landscape that signifies home for me? Actually, this is not just an agreeable possibility; it is a spiritual necessity for me to include the Beartooths in my understanding of home. For it is during those relatively few days when I go hiking in the mountains that life takes on a memorable clarity and I am most liable to return home to myself. More and more my years seem marked by what new discoveries I have made during summer treks in the mountains rather than by significant events in town or journeys elsewhere. I will remember 1991 as the year I climbed Crazy Peak and Whitetail Peak. Somehow I live more fully when I am immersed in the lands, especially in the wilderness.

...Gwendolen Haste gets at the contrast between town and country I am interested in through another poem, "Horizons."

> I had to laugh,
> For when she said it we were sitting by the door,
> And straight down was the Fork,
> Twisting and turning and gleaming in the sun.
> And then your eyes carried across to the purple bench beyond the river
> With the Beartooth Mountains fairly screaming with light and blue
>   and snow,
> And fold and turn of rimrock and prairie as far as your eye could go.
>
> And she says: "Dear Laura, sometimes I feel so sorry for you,
> Shut away from everything—eating your heart out with loneliness.
> When I think of my own full life I wish that you could share it.
> Just pray for happier days to come and bear it."
>
> She goes back to Billings to her white stucco house,
> And looks through net curtains at another white stucco house,
> And a brick house,
> And a yellow frame house,
> And six trimmed poplar trees,
> And little squares of shaved grass.
>
> Oh dear, she stared at me like I was daft:
> I couldn't help it. I just laughed and laughed.

Haste's joyous pleasure in her house with a view is to be contrasted with the paranoia of Haste's rancher's wife in the coulee. When one has horizons, it's as if one's spirit can expand, whereas if one is isolated in claustrophobic surroundings, one's feelings turn in on oneself and one's spirit is starved. Haste also captures well the threat of the town, with its artificial order and lack of engagement with anything expansive....One need not choose between the town which stimulates one's spirit even while it cuts one off from the land, nor need one live on the land but yearn for cultural opportunities. If one defines one's locale broadly enough, one can be a citizen of both town and country; it all depends on where one draws one's horizon. Since I have learned to draw mine broadly enough to include the Beartooths, I have felt at home in Billings. Similarly, if isolation threatened Laura by the Clark's Fork, she could draw her horizons to include Billings....

How does one make a house a home? Place it in a physical context you care about; give it a locale. Then live and love in it fully, taking care to remember and report what this place means. Here is no recipe for success, but the challenge of life.

Home. It's that place from which we go but never really leave. It's where we are centered, where we have roots. Home is our castle, our place of security. May you be so fortunate as to have found home.

poetry by Gwendolen Haste

Born in Illinois in 1889, **Gwendolen Haste** was raised in Wisconsin and graduated from the University of Chicago. She lived in Billings from 1915-25, and subsequently published her collection of poems, *Young Land,* focused in part on the homesteading experiences of women. She later held a variety of jobs in New York City, where she lived until her death in 1979.

The Stoic

She guessed there wasn't any time for tears
Because her heart had held them all unshed
While one by one her little hopes had fled
Down through those racking, windy, drouth-filled years.
The frozen winter when the cattle died,
The year the hail bent flat the tender wheat,

The thirsty summers with their blazing heat—
She met them all with wordless, rigid pride.

But when, sometimes, the children in the spring
Searching through barren hill or ragged butte,
Would heap her lap with loco blooms, and bring
Clouds of blue larkspur and bright bitter-root,
Then would she run away to hide her pain
For memory of old gardens drenched with rain.

Antelope Stage Station

by Thelma Van Sky

Broadview in Review: 80 Years along the Buffalo Trail

Billings resident **Thelma Van Sky** was the only daughter and middle child born to Yellowstone County homesteaders, Ross and Essie Ballard. She was raised, educated, and lived in Yellowstone County all her life. A year out of high school, she married her high school sweetheart. They moved to his grandfather's place where the Antelope Stage Station was located and lived there for 54 years.

The Antelope Stage Station was constructed of hand-hewn logs circa 1883. It is significant for its historic association with the stage coach era and the vital role that that period played in the development of our great country. The people associated with Antelope Station and those that drove the stages were truly pioneers....

Antelope Station is located on the route from Billings to Lavina....Coming out of Billings the stations were Twenty-Mile, Antelope, Fairview, then Lavina. Actually freighting, mail carrying, and passenger service were very closely related.

Stage stations were placed along routes at various intervals, usually not over 20 miles apart. Some were only to provide a change of horses, others had meals and overnight accommodations. Twenty-Mile was so named for its distance from Billings; Antelope was about six miles from Twenty-Mile. In the book *Horizons O'er The Musselshell* on page 36, Florence Lindstrand Seifert wrote—"During 1896 and 1897 Dad and Mother worked for Bob Leavens at the Antelope Station. This place was about half way between Billings and Lavina and this was where the stage drivers changed horses and had meals. Dad had charge of the horses and Mother served the meals for the drivers and their passengers."

...A caption in the *Gazette* of July 24, 1932 read: "A view of Lavina stage station, an important point on the old Lavina stage line from Billings to Fort Benton. The stage route was established in 1882 with Walter Burke as superintendent. T. C. Power was interested in the enterprise. Several holdups took place on the route, particularly in the early nineties."

Broadview

Taken from the *Landowner News* January 20, 1912.

Broadview is situated on the Billings and Northern Railroad, about 35 miles northwest of Billings, Montana. It is ideally situated in the heart of the "Broadview District," completely surrounded with fertile lands, which reward the efforts of the good farmer with fields of golden grain. At Broadview may be witnessed a practical demonstration of what intensified farming of these lands may bring in crops and money.

Where one time roamed flocks of sheep and herds of cattle and horses, now may be found fields of winter wheat yielding from 15 to 40 bushels to the acre. It was in this section that 18 bushels of winter wheat was produced in 1910 which was a drouth year throughout the country.

The same land in many instances returned 40 bushels to the acre for the year just passed. The Broadview district is now covered with a blanket of snow of sufficient depth to be a guarantee that a remunerative crop will be produced the coming season. Exhibits of grains and products at county and State fairs, both in this and other States, [have] never failed to take down a prize. Its greatest winning was at the New York Land Show. The Broadview wheat district always makes good.

Broadview has a general store, dry goods store, bank, hotel, restaurant, harness shop, livery and feed stables, lumber yard, seed house, grain elevator, newspaper, and other business concerns. Its citizenship is among the best in the county, and the business men are wide awake and enterprising. Broadview offers many opportunities to the homeseeker and investor.

River Crossings: South Bridges

by Monica Weldon

Trails & Tales South of the Yellowstone

Monica Weldon is a ranch wife in the Blue Creek area. She, with several
volunteers, served as organizer, compiler, and writer of historical material and
family histories for this area history book.

The original South Bridge was built in 1894, by the Billings Business
Company (this company had been formed in January of that same year).
The simple wooden structure was a toll bridge and served as the only bridge
in the Billings area until the East Bridge was constructed in about 1905.

Before the bridges were built travelers would ford the Yellowstone River
at crossings during low water times. Several of these fords include the three
most frequently mentioned in recorded history of those traveling to the area
south of Billings. One was near the East Bridge (where Bitter Creek flows
into the Yellowstone). There were other fords near the James Cooper place
(above the present-day South Bridge) and in the vicinity of the old South
Bridge. For those crossing with wagons and farm implements, ferries also
operated in approximately the same locations.

Several prominent Billings business men served on the Board of
Directors of the Billings Bridge Company. These men formed the company
with $15,000 of capital stock. They had raised the money by selling shares
at $100 each. The Board of Directors decided to build the bridge at the
Cummings Ferry location, which was at the end of what is now known as
Washington Street (for years after, this street was called "the South Bridge
Road"). During the time of construction of the bridge many of the workers
boarded at the Ed Newman Ranch (located on the north side of the river
near where the bridge was being constructed). The cost of constructing the
bridge, dikes and approaches was estimated at $16,869.50.

The South Bridge was opened on December 6, 1894. The tolls were
decided by the Board of Directors: they ranged from one cent for each hog,
goat, and sheep to one dollar for a wagon pulled by four horses, mules, or
oxen. Each additional trail wagon or team and a single horse and buggy or
cart was twenty-five cents. Seventy-five cents was charged for a two horse
team and wagon and fifty cents for a two horse team pulling a buggy. A
saddle horse and rider cost fifteen cents and ten cents for any extra horses,
footmen, loose cattle, horses, or mules. Six days after the initial price setting,
the rates were cut in half for sheep, hogs and goats after the first one
thousand head and provisions were made so that loose stock could cross only
fifteen at a time.

The board voted to allow "any extra passenger known to belong to the same outfit to pass without charge." A half rate was set for Catholic priests from the Mission and the mail carrier—provided they used the bridge on every trip. Some years later, the Bridge Company agreed to give free passage "to all persons coming and going to the fair during four days thereof, and to all Indians during Fair week."

As time went on, Yellowstone County purchased the bridge, and it was opened as a non-toll structure. This move made the Billings businessmen very happy as they found the toll bridge costly to their businesses. The old South Bridge served all residents living south of the Yellowstone in the Billings area until the Duck Creek Bridge was built in 1915.

Several early day residents of Blue Creek recall the bridge being dangerous to cross during high water times. Some even remember bailing water out of the buggies or wagons in which they were riding. Center spans of the bridge gave way to flood waters and were washed downstream at various times during the duration of its use.

In 1949, the Yellowstone County Commissioners realized it was necessary for them to request the Montana Highway Commission to replace this original bridge with one more suitable to the changing conditions of traffic. During the early 1950s a steel bridge originally located near Huntley, Montana, was dismantled and relocated: one and one half miles upstream of the "Old" South Bridge. At this time, three miles of approaching road also replaced the "Old Blue Creek Road" to better serve the residents of the Blue Creek area. (Rain storms and spring run-off draining off the slope of the high blue shale bluff that bordered the road made travel difficult on the old road.)

To accommodate the increased traffic to and from the growing Blue Creek and Pryor Creek areas a new, larger concrete and steel bridge was completed in 1972. This present bridge was dedicated as the Thomas Dolan Bridge, but is still simply referred to as the South Bridge.

"Lest We Forget..."

compiled by the Shepherd Historical Book Committee:
Sharon Wolske, Nell Kinghorn, Marguerite Gerringa and Luella DeVries

The Shepherd Historical Book Committee members were long-time (some life-time) residents of Shepherd and all had a strong interest in getting Shepherd's history into print. It took over two years to contact families for their stories and then compile the writings for print.

Prologue

There is an area in southcentral Montana that encompasses many distinctive features. Part of it is bench land adjacent to the Yellowstone River; part of it is the rocky foothills of the pine covered Bull Mountains; part of it is sliced by several seemingly dormant creeks with soil ranging from sandy-loam to alkaline-gumbo.

Inhabitants of the past are interesting, too. In this area, an abundance of obsidian, chert, and agate chippings can be found on every prominent point of observation overlooking the Yellowstone River. For centuries, it is obvious that the area had much hunting activity in the river valley, as well as along the benchlands overlooking the buffalo trails that came from the north. Indian scouts with time on their hands fashioned spear and arrowheads while they watched for their next food supply or for their enemies.

Directly across the river is the mouth of the Pryor Creek that leads deep into the heart of Crow Country. The Crow Indians originally claimed all land south of the Musselshell River as theirs, and Pryor Creek valley was one of their main trails into and through Crow Country.

In 1806 Captain William Clark returned from his exploration of the Pacific via the Yellowstone River. He and his party floated by here in their cottonwood dugouts on their way to meet Lewis at the mouth of the Yellowstone, where it runs into the Missouri.

Along the extreme southeastern portion of the Shepherd area is a location originally known as the McGirl Landing, and trappers frequented the area in the hard winter time. These gatherings were often called the college of the Rocky Mountains, where much was learned in the cold days of the Montana winter. Jim Bridger was considered one of the "professors."

Then came the buffalo hunters and the military parties charged with protecting the railroad surveyors. Brevet Major General George A. Custer [was with] one military contingent through the area on the Yellowstone Expedition in 1873, and the "Custer Trail" he blazed is still evident along the river breaks. A wagon road, called the "Tongue River Trail," later wound its way down from the hills along the Yellowstone and crossed the benchlands to Coulson and Bozeman. With the military came the supply boats, such as the *Far West* and the *Josephine*. The *Josephine* passed here in 1875....

During this time, too, the Sioux and Cheyenne became frequent intruders into the area, with a battle taking place opposite the mouth of Pryor Creek. It was between a contingent of the military under Colonel Baker and a group of Sioux. Several Indians were killed in the battle.

In 1876 General John Gibbon from Fort Ellis came through on his way to meet Custer and General Alfred Terry at the Tongue River. Gibbon was part of a pincer plan to trap Sitting Bull and his camp, but the plan resulted in the loss of Custer and his command at the Battle of the Little Big Horn. Then in 1880 came the longhorn trail herds from Texas—driven by cowboys who were fearless, adventurous men. Some stayed in the Shepherd area and worked for and established cattle ranches. Names such as the Kirby, Dover, Tolliver, McGirl, O'Donnell and Reona were well known ranches utilizing the wide open spaces. The Reona Ranch was the location where the U.S. Cavalry camped when in the area, and it became known as Headquarters.

In 1883 the Northern Pacific Railroad was completed, thus ending the dominance of the Red Man over this part of the wild and wooly West. Shepherd lay dormant then until the Carey Land Act, passed in 1894, which set the stage for arid land development. This act provided that the government cede arid land to the states, with irrigation programs set up to make the land productive, and individual ownership the final result.

Under the plan, the control of these lands could be placed into the hands of developers, and in 1903 plans began to take shape toward this end. The Reona Ranch was designated as Headquarters for this operation, and the Billings Land and Irrigation Company based its selling operation and building program from there.

Mr. Leo Nobel, who came in April of 1906 at fifteen years of age, remembered going to a prominent outcropping not far from the Baker Battlefield. He remembered that the settlers called it "Bear Head Butte." After throwing his lariat up into a crevice, he climbed up to a ledge and beheld the skeleton of an Indian, in all likelihood the namesake of the picturesque natural monument.

Leo Nobel continued, "The whole bench was a flat desert plain. There were a few homes and farms down on the river bottom, but no homes or cultivated areas north of what is called Twelve Mile Creek—located about twelve miles north and east of Billings. The unimproved land was all owned by the Billings Land and Irrigation Company. Already water was being taken from the river above Billings, flowing through a tunnel that is through the rimrocks. Their canal flowed just east of broken hill country and west of the bench. Herds of cattle had the freedom of the whole bench north of Twelve Mile Creek."

Leo Nobel had horses available, and rode the countryside after his father's dairy cows. There were no homes, farms, fences, or improvements anywhere in the neighborhood. In fact, he did not know it at that time as Shepherd. It was called Headquarters. The BL&I Company had already set up Headquarters at the Reona Ranch. His father's venture there included an agreement with the BL&I to construct laterals from the big canal out to the various farms. He employed twelve men and had as many teams working for two or three summers. There was no bridge across the river at Huntley in those first years. Billings was the rail head, and source of all supplies, equipment, and manpower.

The settlers came. There were the Dutch who populated the area just south of Headquarters and on to the Yellowstone River. They built their church near the Headquarters, and some called the location Little Holland.

Then the Germans came, settling to the northeast of Headquarters—on Razor Creek with Reverend Robert Maurer as their leader; and the Scandinavians arrived, too, and inhabited the area to the west and northwest of Headquarters, adjacent to Crooked Creek and its upper reaches. Pastor Halvor S. Quanbeck led this group in their endeavors.

By 1908 over seventy-five families had contracted for land, with Headquarters as the hub. After the Dutch erected their church just southwest of the Headquarters, there followed a general merchandise store, a livery stable, a blacksmith shop, a creamery, and a bank.

Billings & Central Montana Railroad

Prior to 1913, a company was formed to plan, promote, and build a "farmers' line" railroad from Billings, Montana, to the Bull Mountains in Musselshell County. The road was to be twenty miles long, starting at the Burlington Railroad Depot in Billings at 28th Street, then traversing the Billings Bench to the northeast, and proceeding through the Holland Dutch settlement—to a terminus at the eastern end of Crooked Creek where coal and timber were plentiful. The diminutive railroad was to be used to carry passengers and freight, and also help promote the sugar beet, dairy, and ranching industries.

Russell E. Shepherd was elected President of the company, and held the position along with major holdings in the Billings Land and Irrigation Company. The B&CM Railroad was financed by eastern capital, and the farmers provided the right of way. The BL&I was a heavy contributor. Hayden S. Cole of St. Paul, Minnesota, was Vice-President, and an engineer by the name of Egan was hired to stake out the road.

The Dutch settlement known as Holland officially became the town of Shepherd in 1913, upon advice from the United States Post Office. It was also in 1913 that the B&CM Railroad reached Shepherd, but was never extended to the Bull Mountains as previously planned. The line, when completed, had sixteen miles of road bed. Construction was completed in time to take the 1913 sugar beet crop to Billings.

A typical train on the B&CM Railroad consisted of the engine, a coach, a freight car, and a caboose. It hauled hay, grain, beets, cattle, coal, and lumber, along with anything else needed by the early day residents. It was affectionately called "The Sagebrush Limited." Passenger arrival and departure time was scheduled to accommodate those who rode back and forth to Billings. They departed from Shepherd at eight o'clock in the morning, and returned at five o'clock in the afternoon. Mr. Ed Gallagher was the conductor.

Hard times finally caught up with the "Sagebrush Limited," and daily passenger runs were discontinued in 1925. Sugar beets became the mainstay product hauled, and the road was leased by the Great Western Sugar Company to haul beets to the company factory in Billings. However, since it became too expensive to lease the line, it was dismantled in 1968.

Those who remember the B&CM Railroad, remember the large beet loading dock at Shepherd, and the horse-drawn wagons used to load beets in the early days. They remember traveling on the B&CM to and from Shepherd, and the settlers and homesteaders who came on it. The little railroad holds a special place in the hearts of the early day residents who themselves first saw Shepherd from a coach window. Now it is no more, but warm memories still linger on.

Well, I Guess I Was Just Lucky!!

by Leland P. Cade

Born on a homestead in Golden Valley County in 1925, **Leland P. Cade** worked as a county extension agent for 16 years in Montana and Alaska and served as editor of *Montana Farmer-Stockman* for 21 years. The following passage comes from his book about his parents' homesteading experiences.

During the summer, the three small lakes north of the house were our backyard swimming pool. Even though the water was always muddy from livestock traffic and wind, we had fun getting wet. One of our pastimes there was to try to find a kildeer bird nest; we never did. Their eggs are laid on the surface of the ground and resemble rocks.

[One time] Dad said to me, "All the fences are out in Twin Coulee. We have to go find our horses." At the time, we had probably 40 or 50 horses in Twin Coulee and area, some under fence. The peak count sometime during the 1930s was 82. Dad and I saddled up. I rode Old Dime; he rode Tess. We never took drinking water or lunch. If we needed a drink, we drank from a spring in Twin Coulee or at Sibley Spring. There were two springs in Twin Coulee, on Pound land, maybe a hundred yards apart. Cattle would drink out of the south one, but not the north one. When we got hungry, we paid no attention. All day long we rode around east of Twin Coulee, up towards Sibley Spring, up and down the coulees, towards Emory, past Dunwalds', and we stopped in at Pete Jensen's. It was maybe 2:00 p.m. Pete had been to town the day previous, and he wanted to share with us the one lemon he had purchased. He went to town maybe three or four times a year, and each time he would buy possibly a dollar's worth of groceries, no more than two dollars' worth. This time he bought one lemon, possibly a loaf of bread and a can of fish.

He wanted to show his hospitality by serving us lemonade. To make lemonade, Pete needed a container that would hold water. The best place to look for a container was on the floor. He spotted a can, went to the door, held up the can and looked toward the sun. A hole. He threw it on the floor. He spotted another can, looked, another hole, and back to the floor. He picked up another container, same results. Then he looked toward the coal pile and spotted the coal pail. He spilled out the coal and held the pail towards the sun. No hole. "Red, would you go get some water?" he said to me. "Yuh, I will." I knew the details. His well was below the house at the edge of a coulee. The well was above the dam. The dam was full of water from the flood three days earlier. The dam was below his barnyard a couple hundred yards. The dam water and the well water were the same. I swished the pail back and forth to haze away the floating barnyard cooties, and then took Pete a gallon or so of water. We had lemonade in Pete's coal pail, enhanced with coal and barnyard flavors.

"Wilsons are having a sale Saturday, leaving the country," Pete told Dad. Slim Wilson and his family were starving, just like the others that had gone previously. When we got home Dad told Mother, "I think I better go to Wilson's sale." "What do you think you need this time?" she asked. Mother thought about the dollar or three he would spend that she could use for the house. She had heard that gasoline-powered washing machines were a big improvement over the hand-powered one she used. And she wanted a nice set of dishes to replace the bruised ones she was using, although she never said such out loud. It was the story of the homestead era: if a family was to survive, living standards had to be sacrificed. "Wull, I could use a few more collars, and a harness or two. And I might get a wagon cheap," Dad said. Mother responded, "Bring me some fruit jars." She always needed more fruit jars for canning beef.

We took a team and wagon to the sale. The wagon was the centerpiece of our farm equipment. We used it for fencing and hauling hay. We used it

We dressed up in nice new clothes when the Wonder Box came. From left: Dan, Don, Leland, Betty, Marian. We thought we looked pretty spiffy, even if the clothes didn't fit. Photo courtesy Leland Cade.

for transportation to everywhere. For quite a few years, we used the wagon to haul ice during the winter to the ice house to make ice cream in the summer. Coal from Alexander's mine was hauled in the wagon. Earlier, when Dad had grain to sell, it went to town in the wagon. At times we hauled posts and corral poles from the Snowies on the running gears (no box). Wheel bearings were iron on iron, exposed to a continuing shower of dust. Every time we went anywhere, the first chore was to grease the wagon axles, also the bolster.

At Wilson's, the items for sale included a few chickens, stove or two, crock, lamps, harness, wagon, plow, wire, lath, posts, three horses, two cows, cream separator, milk pails, copper boiler, galvanized tub, wooden clothes washer. "Rattatta tatt atta Rattat," the auctioneer droned. "50¢?" "How much for this pile of real good harness? Some of it looks new. 50?" "Two bits," Dad said. That was his top bid for a pile of junk, and most of the time he got it, a real bargain. "Sold to Joe Cade."

Two days later, Dad sent Dan, Don and I with a team and wagon to get his new purchases. We loaded up the harness and collars, a copper boiler, some fence wire, a few wagon parts, a fresno for moving dirt. He had spent probably $3 at the auction. Behind, we tied a wagon that he had bought for 50¢. West of Pete Jensen's place, we headed down a hill. Just then, Babe on the left bit Gumbo on the right. Gumbo's bridle fell off; he had no blinders. Both spooked and away they ran, down the hill as fast as they could go. With a bridle on only one horse, they were out of control, like an auto going 150 miles an hour without a steering wheel. They edged toward the fence on the north side of the road. We knew if a wheel hooked a post, wagon, riders and contents would be hurled into space. Don and I considered jumping, but we couldn't jump out the back end because we would jump right into the path of the wagon we were trailing. And it was nearly impossible to jump out the side because of the bouncing and lurching. We stayed on and hoped for the best. After a mile or so, fear disappeared and tired took over and the horses stopped. We fixed the broken bridle with fence wire and went on home.

…We got home from this expedition and unhooked the team. Mother had a meal waiting for us, including an angel food cake. She would never let Betty and I sit together at the table because we always had to fight a little. After supper Dad took Dan and Don to the shop and put them to work oiling harness. Oil preserved the leather and kept it pliable and strong. Dad fixed a single tree that had lost a clip on the end. When that chore was completed, they returned to the house. Dad sat down by the kerosene lamp to read the "Rip Snorter," Mother's name for the *Ryegate Weekly Reporter*. *The Lavina Independent* had been gone already for nine years.

Suddenly Betty burst into the living room. She was excited. "Goat! Goat!! in the outhouse! Goat!! Outhouse!" she screamed. Dad thought she was saying "ghost." "There aren't any ghosts in the outhouse," Dad assured her. "Goat!! in the outhouse!!! Goat!! Goat!!" Dad figured it out. She was saying "goat," not "ghost." At times we had a goat or two around. "What do you mean goat?" Dad asked. They went to the outhouse. Betty told him the story. "I opened the door and the goat was in there. It scared him. He jumped on top of the seat and fell down in the hole." Dad held the lantern down in the hole and there was the goat, looking for a way out. It took him a while to rescue the goat.

Parmly Billings 1884

by I. D. O'Donnell

Montana Monographs compiled by I. D. O'Donnell

Ignatius Daniel "Budd" O'Donnell is one of the seminal figures in Yellowstone County history. Canadian-born, he arrived in the Billings area in 1884 and soon became active in a series of crucial business ventures: the Billings Farm, the Minnesota-Montana Land and Improvement Company, the Billings Sugar Factory, and the Huntley Irrigation Project. In 1914 O'Donnell was appointed "Supervisor of Irrigation" for 17 western states by the Secretary of the Interior. He also promoted and contributed to the Parmly Billings Library, Billings Polytechnic Institute (now Rocky Mountain College), the Yellowstone County Fair, and the YMCA. O'Donnell collected many stories of the region in *Montana Monographs*.

One of the most interesting recollections I have of the late Parmly Billings is in connection with his taking up or filing on a preemption claim. Parmly had during the summer of 1884 filed on a 160 acre tract as his preemption right. For claims of this kind one made his filing, had thirty days to put up his cabin and start his residence and then he had to reside on it for six months. After paying $2.50 per acre you got your title.

Parmly had made his filing in regular form but was slow in building his cabin and making settlement, thus leaving an opening for the "Jumper." The jumper proved to be Frank Church, although he had not as yet made any settlement or put up his building.

As soon as Parmly got word of the jumping he was all excited. He hired a Max French, who was a carpenter, and a team to haul a load of lumber out to the claim, 12 miles west of Billings. Parmly invited me to come out as his guest and stay overnight.

We got to the claim and had the cabin (10x12) built by dark. For our supper we had bread, bacon and coffee cooked on a camp fire, Parmly in the meantime making all kinds of excuses for the poor service he was offering. He also said that it was the only home he had, and the best he could offer at the time.

That night we had only one small roll of bedding and bunked together as he had no bed. There was no mattress and the light bedding did not make a very comfortable bed for a young millionaire. We did not sleep very much as Parmly was all worked up over the jumping and we talked most of the night. The talk consisted of Parmly saying it was the only home he had and the first home he ever had. He complained many times of the meanness of a man who would try to steal his home. "It isn't much," he continued, "but it is all I have and at this particular time it is the only prospect I have for a home. Don't you agree with me?"

Neither of us had much sleep that night and our morning breakfast consisted of coffee and bread, with Parmly still complaining of the dirty deal the jumper was giving him.

After our breakfast we saddled up our horses, rolled up the bedding and put it on the back of our saddles and were about to mount when Parmly turned to me and said, "Budd, I'm through. I would not put in another night like that for all the land in the Valley. Frank Church can take the land and go straight to — with it. He can have the cabin to boot. Budd, when we get to Billings I will get you a good breakfast as my guest." And he did.

Needless to say, Parmly never went near the claim again and the jumper got away with it.

How Liver Eating Got His Name

by Judge J. R. Goss

Montana Monographs compiled by I. D. O'Donnell

James R. Goss arrived in Billings in 1882. He served as a pioneer judge, was elected to a term as mayor, and was very active in community affairs.

[The following is one of many stories of how "Liver Eating" got his name and is undoubtedly more accurate than most. According to his Civil War enlistment papers, his name was John Johnston. He was 5' 11½" tall.]

Liver Eating Johnston was a Civil War veteran and by reason of that he and I were drawn together as I too had been in the Civil War. Liver Eating Johnston was a trapper and a hunter and in that way made a living in those days by shooting game and trapping beaver, including buffalo and in fact— anything that had ready money value. His nature was such that his demands were very few so that while he accumulated no particular wealth, he lived conveniently upon what he managed to get. He was known far and wide as an Indian fighter.

He must have been a man six feet two and was very powerful, glorying in his strength and in his hardihood, ready to meet apparently anybody or anything.

The story that he told me of how he acquired the name of Liver Eating Johnston was this: The real early men who were here before the coming in of the rails and before there were any towns between Bismarck on the east and Bozeman on the west, rather resented the incoming of men from the far east. These eastern men always were called Pilgrims and designated as such, without the necessity of knowing what their real names were.

The word passed among these hunters and trappers who came to the Fort that there was an unusually fresh specimen of an easterner, who was out in the west, to be initiated into some of the mysteries of the Noble Redman. The trappers had it understood among themselves that they would undertake to teach them some of the comings and goings of both and traders and trappers with their dealing with this Noble Redman that the easterner had come to see.

On this particular occasion that I have in mind, there had been an Indian killed in the immediate vicinity of Liver Eating—that being what we called in the Civil War the Grape Vine Route. It traveled with the usual means of transmission that this chap was coming and to be on the look out for him and to give him something that he was not looking for. When this man appeared, Liver Eating gave him the usual salutation among trappers and hunters of "How! How!"—without any explanation. Liver Eating then pointed to the Indian and said to the young man, "Did you ever taste Indian liver?" and the young man fairly gasped his astonishment and in utter disgust said, "No!" Liver Eating said, "There is no better opportunity for you to be initiated into the wild ways of these western men, who are in constant danger from these Indians," and without the knowledge of the young man, Liver Eating managed in some way to smear his lips with the blood from the edge of his knife and said, "It's good!" That is as far as the program went toward giving him the name of Liver Eating Johnston.

Calamity Jane

by Katherine A. Shandera

Billings: The City and the People
by Roger Clawson and Katherine A. Shandera

Katherine A. Shandera grew up on a Wyoming ranch originally homesteaded by her grandfather in 1916. Shandera has worked as a free-lance writer and editorial consultant in Yellowstone County since 1987. She, her husband Steve, and their daughters have found Billings a hospitable home.

When it comes to romance beating the stuffing out of reality, there's hardly a better story than that of Calamity Jane. There are so many versions of Calamity Jane's life that finding even a portion of the truth is nearly impossible. Historians do agree on a few things. They're almost sure she was born as Martha Jane Canary in Princeton, Missouri, around 1852. And they know she lived the last years of her life in a cabin on Canyon Creek near Billings.

In between, things are pretty murky. It seems young Martha Jane came west with her family to Montana's gold mines around 1864. Sometime after they reached the gold camps, her parents either died or left. Martha Jane may have cared for her brothers and sisters for a time. Some people say she earned her nickname in the camps, because whenever an epidemic of miner's fever or other calamity occurred, Martha Jane would be there working hard to care for the sick.

At any rate, Martha Jane eventually emerged from the mining camps, without a family, but with a new name. From then on, Calamity Jane roamed the mountain territories and worked a variety of jobs. She claimed to have been an army scout for General George Custer, a stagecoach driver, and a bullwhacker with a freighting firm. Eastern newspaper reporters and novelists wrote stirring tales of Calamity Jane, the beautiful young spitfire who could ride and shoot better than any man, yet was a saintly nurse when illness or misfortune struck.

Calamity said she was once married to Wild Bill Hickok. Others doubt that story, but believe Calamity could have been married—some reports give her as many as 12 husbands. Still others say her involvement with men was more likely prostitution. Calamity did have at least one husband, a man named Clinton Burk (or Burke). There may have been others too. A 1901 article in *The Billings Gazette* refers to "Mrs. R. S. Dorsett, better known as Calamity Jane."

Calamity was very much a part of street life in early Billings. She is mentioned as living on a ranch near town in an 1886 *Billings Gazette* article. In 1895, she bought her Canyon Creek property, where she lived for the next eight years. Around Billings, Calamity is known to have made her living by driving a stagecoach, hauling wood, and cooking. Some people believed she earned extra cash by stealing horses.

In 1893, Buffalo Bill Cody hired her to tour with his Wild West Show. By this time, however, Calamity's hard life had taken a stiff toll on her appearance and abilities. There's speculation that the woman who appeared on posters and in the show was actually a stand-in. In Billings, old-timers defended Calamity Jane as a woman with a heart of gold who would indeed stand by any man down on his luck. But it was tough to recognize the legendary heroine in the foul-mouthed, tobacco-chewing, cigar-smoking, belligerent old drunk who was the real Calamity Jane.

Calamity's sprees frequently got her into trouble with the law. In 1901, a drunken Calamity was thrown in the Billings jail for trying to attack a couple of store clerks with a hatchet. In spite of her orneriness, residents seem to have regarded Calamity with tolerance and a measure of affection. When she boarded a 1903 train for South Dakota without a ticket, passengers took up a collection to pay her fare. Calamity knew she was dying and wanted to get back to Deadwood so she could be buried next to her old friend, Wild Bill. And she was.

After Calamity's death, a Billings woman, Jane Hickok McCormick, announced that she was the daughter of Calamity Jane and Wild Bill. McCormick said she had been brought up by a wealthy East Coast family because Calamity realized she couldn't properly raise her own child. To support these claims, McCormick produced a diary supposedly written by Calamity Jane. At the time, it all seemed plausible enough, but modern historians believe the diary was falsified. McCormick lived in Billings until her death in 1951.

Rustlers and Wrap-Up

Montana Territory of Treasures

by Bob and Kathryn Wright

Colorado-born **Robert Wright** came to Billings with his wife Kathryn in 1942 to work for the Aldrich Lumber Company. Following service in World War II, he returned to the lumber industry and became a company executive.

Born in Colorado in 1912, **Kathryn Wright** joined the staff of *The Billings Gazette* as a general reporter, photographer, feature writer and, on occasion, newspaper carrier. She trained many young reporters, established a scholarship fund for journalism students, and worked on many *Gazette* supplements and special sections. She also wrote books on Billings and Montana history.

Rustlers had a system of secret trails with hidden hangouts and corrals connecting with the Owlhoot Trail. Along the Owlhoot and its offshoots, mapped only in the mind of a man dodging the law, riders with stolen stock could hide and get themselves and animals fed until safe to complete business.

One such hideout was Horsethief Cache, a tableland on a bluff overlooking Canyon Creek where Nez Perce Joseph gave Sturgis the slip in '77. The rustlers using Horsethief Cache ate at Calamity Jane's homestead shack on Canyon Creek's bank. From Jane's place a one-way trail led to the bluff and its rich native grass. Two of Calamity's boarders were Charles (Rattlesnake Jake) Fallon and Edward (Long-hair) Owens. They were to take leading roles in Lewistown's most memorable Fourth of July celebration.

But before their riddled corpses were dragged off Lewistown's main street, two other rustlers kicked air at the end of ropes looped over cottonwood limbs by a secret group.

"Yellowstone Kelly":
The Memoirs of Luther S. Kelly
edited by M. M. Quaife

Luther Sage ("Yellowstone") Kelly was born in New York in 1849. He arrived in Montana at the age of nineteen and spent several years hunting and trapping in eastern Montana. General Nelson Miles considered Kelly's ability as a scout equal to that of Kit Carson and Daniel Boone. After a long and adventurous life, Kelly was buried next to Black Otter Trail in Billings.

One evening while we were at the camp in Cone Butte Pass a party of eight or ten Crow Indians suddenly made their appearance while we were eating. They were afoot for a wonder, and came in that noiseless way habitual to the moccasin wearer. They were friendly, and when we accosted them they cried out "Absaroke! Botsots!" which means Crows, or good friends. After shaking hands all around, the circle about the fire was extended and our visitors were given a cup of coffee each with bread and meat. On first acquaintance Indians do not have much to say until they have broken their fast and smoked the pipe.

They are very observant of everything about them, though without appearing to be so. As a rule the wild Indians of the mountains and plains are well-bred in company, and possess a natural politeness and decorum of manner well worth observing. Transport one of them suddenly to a crowded drawing-room, and though the change would be startling it is safe to say that he would rise to the occasion and in bearing, at least, would conduct himself with all the ease and nonchalance of a man of the world. Of course Indians differ as other peoples do, and there was a marked difference in the scale of intelligence, in early days, before the government established schools among them. The Crows differ from the Sioux in feature and dress, and very much in language. Within the border of Wyoming and Montana territories there were eight or more tribes of Indians, each with a language of its own, differing from the others as much as English differs from Russian. Of these the Sioux, of which there are several dialects, is perhaps the most musical, affording a copious flow of words.

The men of the Crow tribe dress their hair in two long braids, wrapped in strips of otter skin which hang on either side of the head in front halfway to the waist. Over the forehead and banged with an upward curve the hair is stiffened and kept in place by an application of white clay. Around the neck brass ornaments and pink shells are hung. Leggings and blankets, or buffalo robes, plain or garnished with bead work or painted characters, complete the costume, while fringed or feathered leather cases for gun or bow add to the picturesqueness of their attire.

...With one of these men I turned aside to hunt in the cedar hills on the north side of the valley, where we ran upon a very large cinnamon bear, which at once put up a ravine. My companion and I separated, he going to the left and I to the right, though I saw no justification in shooting a bear at that season of the year. Presently I saw Mr. Bear only a few yards off in a hollow, and I plugged him with a .40 caliber bullet. He lurched and fell, tried to get up again, and fell dead. While I stood near his head regarding him, my companion returned and dismounting, fired point-blank at the head of the already dead animal, saying, "You can never tell when a bear may revive and rush one." I suspected, however, that his chief desire was to be in at the killing. When we overhauled the cinnamon he proved to be very fat. We estimated that several hundred pounds of fat covered his back and sides and that he would weigh ten or twelve hundred pounds, or perhaps more. The fur was poor and thin and of little value. I contented myself with taking a generous slab of back fat, one of his big paws, and the remaining claws, and then I had a load that was disagreeable to both the pony and his rider.

...The ice had gone out of the Yellowstone, and a small party of non-commissioned officers and soldiers was about to start on some business down the river in a large boat, or mackinaw, so I made shift to secure passage and I make no doubt but I paid my way in steering that old tub through perilous rapids and around the rocks and snags. I have a letter before me, written a few years ago by one of the soldiers, Mr. L. Barker, now of Clay Center, Kansas. "I have always held you in grateful remembrance since we made that voyage down the Yellowstone," he writes. "That ride through the ice and uprooted treetops worried me more than all the Indian fighting I ever did."

Turning a bend near the mouth of the river, we came suddenly upon an ice jam extending high above the banks that blocked the channel from side to side and we made haste to reach the shore. In the night the ice gorge broke with much grinding and din, leaving a solid wall on each side of the channel, and next morning, after a survey to see if old Minnishushu was clear, we made our way through this forbidding avenue of thrashing water until the broad and swollen current of the Missouri received our battered craft and wafted us along a wooded bend for the space of a mile to a plain on the farther bank, where stood the military post of Fort Buford.

The Old Scout Returns: The Interment of Yellowstone Kelly on the Rims

by Jerry Keenan

Jerry Keenan worked as managing editor in book publishing for more than twenty years. He has written extensively in the fields of western history and the Civil War. His 1990 article on "Yellowstone" Kelly, published in *Montana The Magazine of Western History,* won a Western Heritage Award from the National Cowboy Hall of Fame. He is currently working on a full-length biography of Kelly.

The procession left the Commercial Club at 2:30 that afternoon [June, 1929], moving slowly on foot to the soulful dirge and steady thump of muffled drums from the Rotary Club's Boys Band. West, along Third Avenue the retinue proceeded, turning south at Broadway to First Avenue North, then east to Twenty-second Street, where autos were boarded for the final leg of the journey to the crest of the rimrock.

It was an impressive group, headed by color bearers, then city officials, Boy Scouts, the band, and a firing squad [Honor Guard]. These were followed by a solitary horse with boots reversed in the stirrups and a saber hanging from the saddle. Finally, came the casket itself resting atop a flower-bedecked wagon drawn by four horses, followed by pallbearers, and an honor guard of veterans old and recent.

Most evident were the younger veterans of World War I, but here and there could be seen a few old soldiers in blue, aging members of the G.A.R., the Spanish, and Indian Wars. Proud and straight they marched, these veterans from an era long since passed, but not forgotten in the minds of those remaining few who had known and tasted the times of which they had been a part.

The day itself was warm and pleasant, typical of late June here in the magnificent valley of the Yellowstone. It was a day he would have appreciated, he who now lay peacefully within the confines of his flag-draped casket.

Reaching the top of the Rims, the casket was removed from the wagon and placed next to the prepared repository that would soon claim it for eternity. This final resting place, overlooking the great sweep of valley below, was a grand spot indeed. Made a man's heart ache with the beauty of it all, not to mention the memories.

From here, a man could gaze out across as fine a view as God ever created. From here, he could look downstream, eyes squinted against the glare of bright sunlight coruscating off the rushing waters of the Yellowstone and recall the time he had come upriver on the old *Far West* with Grant Marsh and Sandy Forsyth back in '73.

Just to the east rose Pompeys Pillar, that towering chunk of sandstone that had served as a register of historic passage from Lewis and Clark to the present, and offering a view nearly as splendid as that currently spread out before a man's musing gaze.

Two days' ride to the south, allowing of course that a man had a good horse between his legs, stretched those tawny slopes where George Custer and his men found their immortality.

To the north lay the Judith Basin, the Big and Little Belt Mountains and a score of other places that hearkened back to a time when life was sweet and strong; when a man was seldom out of sight of the vast buffalo herds that swarmed over the land, and the aroma of ribs roasting over an open fire produced a contentment of the spirit now vanished along with the herds themselves. Ah yes, if a man had to settle on a final spot he would be hard pressed to improve on this.

Presently, Mr. Ben Harwood addressed the group, briefly recounting the life of this man to whom they had come to pay their last respects. When he had finished, David Hilger, secretary of the Montana Historical Society and official representative of the state of Montana, paid tribute to the deceased.

Then the firing squad assembled and at the command, fired a volley toward the azure sky, the report trailing off into the high lonesome distance of this waning, early summer afternoon. Finally, American Legion buglers stepped forward and in a moment, the plaintive melody of "Taps" rose above the gathered assembly like the far, thin cry of the wolf whose own presence in this country was now but a memory, like the remains of the man honored by the haunting refrain that bade him farewell.

And so now, finally, it was finished. After nearly four score years and a life that most little boys imagine somehow will be theirs and most old men reach back for wistfully, Luther Sage Kelly had come home at last to his beloved Yellowstone Valley.

Building the Zimmerman Trail

Along the Zimmerman Trail

by Charles Zimmerman

Michigan native **Charles Zimmerman** moved to Billings with his family in
1890. He was a member of the Pioneers of Eastern Montana and a life
member of the Yellowstone Historical Society. He loved to tell stories rich
with local history. *Along the Zimmerman Trail* collects many of these first-
hand accounts.

In the spring of 1890, my father, Frank Zimmerman, and a man by the
name of Thompson built the Zimmerman Trail over the sandstone rimrocks
about five miles west of Billings for my uncle, Joe Zimmerman.

Mr. Thompson was a miner by trade and there was a lot of rock to be
blasted out of the side of the cliff to make a grade wide enough to pull up

This untitled photograph was taken by noted Western photographer **Richard A. Throssel**
(1886-1933), a mixed-blood French-Canadian and Cree and an adopted Crow. He had a
studio in Billings and specialized in Indian and landscape photographs.

Dated 1919, the original, reproduced here, is part of the Western Heritage Center's
collection. A variant, however, appears misdated 1891, in *Along the Zimmerman Trail* from
which the excerpt "Building the Zimmerman Trail" is taken.

Speculation is that Throssel staged this photograph inasmuch as the three female passengers would not likely have ridden atop the coach and Alkali Creek, not Zimmerman Trail,
served as the stagecoach route.

out of the valley with a team and wagon. Mr. Thompson did the blasting and Frank Zimmerman did most of the team work using a team of mules called "Jim" and "Jack" to move the rocks and dirt. The trail started down a little coulee at the top and approximately half way down there was around a 20-foot drop-off they had to fill in. Then they graded along the side of the rim. It took the two men all summer to build the trail.

Uncle Joe had the trail built so he could take care of a band of about 2200 sheep that he ran in the summertime on top of the rims. Before the trail was built, he had to go east to Boot Hill Cemetery around the rims, distance of 8 miles there and 8 miles back [to the sheep camp], which was a distance of 16 miles or a round trip of 32 miles. It would take him two days to make the trip and he had to make the trip to the sheep camp every four days. He had to haul water in barrels for the sheepherder to drink and cook with. By going over the Zimmerman Trail, my father could go to the sheep camp in about 5 hours. That way he had more time to manage the ranch for my uncle. Uncle Joe had three or four extra men working for him at that time and my father had to see that all of the men were kept busy.

Sometime in the 1930s they widened and changed the grade of the trail to the way it is now. Later it was surfaced and is presently being used as a cut-off road from northern towns in Montana on Route No. 3 to bypass Billings to get to Laurel. This saves about ten miles by not going through the city of Billings.

James Webb Memorial Drinking Fountain

Pieces & Places of Billings History: Local Markers and Sites

by Joyce M. Jensen

Joyce M. Jensen was born and raised in Billings. She taught in Montana and Alaska. In the 1980s she became a docent at the Western Heritage Center and began specializing in Billings history. She and her husband, Larry (now deceased), developed a slide show *Pieces & Places of Billings History*. That presentation served as the basis for her book by the same title.

James T. Webb Sheriff of Yellowstone Co. sealed duty with his life, March 26, 1908. A community's Tribute to Faithfulness.

These are the words on the James Webb Memorial Drinking Fountain [on the corner of the courthouse lawn at North 27th Street and 2nd Avenue North]. Sheriff Webb was the third of eight law enforcement officers from this area to be killed in the line of duty. Jim Webb was a very popular and successful sheriff. He learned that a horse thief named William Bickford was on the Woolfolk & Richardson ranch near Roundup. So Webb headed out on his horse Baldy to make the arrest. (Later it was said that Bickford may also have been wanted for murder.) Webb arrived at the ranch. He and James Richardson went to the sheep wagon (or perhaps tent) where Bickford was sleeping. Webb went into the sheep wagon, picked up the revolver beside Bickford and told him he was under arrest. For some reason Webb left the wagon, stood outside talking to Richardson and allowed an unsupervised Bickford to get dressed. Then Bickford appeared in the door of the wagon holding a rifle that Webb had overlooked. "Throw up your hands," Bickford said, firing at Webb's feet. Webb grabbed for his own revolver, but it stuck in the holster. Bickford fired again with a shot to Webb's heart. Bickford said to Richardson, "I do not want to shoot you. Get going." The rancher ran to spread the alarm. Bickford escaped on foot. Posses were raised, riding here and there looking for Bickford. Some were over near Lavina, others north toward Roundup and some east. One of the posses cornered Bickford in a cabin. During a shoot-out Bickford was killed (or perhaps shot himself).

Webb was always regarded as a brave and efficient officer. The fact that Bickford got the drop on him was a surprise to all. Webb's was one of the largest funerals in Billings. James Webb was buried in Mountview Cemetery, where his tombstone still stands. Ironically, the same day Webb was buried on top of the hill with much pomp and grief, Bickford was buried in a pauper's grave at the base of that hill.

The people, especially the children, of Billings raised money for the drinking fountain on the corner of the courthouse lawn to honor Sheriff Webb. At one time there were cups chained there and the faucet worked. It was evidently decades ago when the James Webb Fountain last had water.

A One-Class Society

Up To Now

by Louis B. Lundborg

Louis B. Lundborg was born in Billings in 1907. He was educated at Stanford University and subsequently served as that institution's vice president for university development and as director and vice chairman of the Stanford Research Institute. He was also board chairman of the Bank of America, and a director of the American Indian Institute and the National Audubon Society.

Billings in the 1910s was as nearly a classless society as anyone could envision. There were families with more money and families with less; but no one could see any line between the two.

We all attended the same schools; and not only did we all play on the same football teams, act in the same school plays, and belong to the same debating societies—but after school we went to each other's homes with no thought of "crossing lines."

In fact, when I look over the broad spectrum of human existence, as I have seen it or read about it, I would take small-town (or farm) 1910 America as the ideal. There were some pitfalls and minuses and I shall describe a few; but they were far outweighed by the pluses.

Calvin Coolidge, who has never been regarded by his critics or by historians as having any poetic gift, once wrote some of the most beautifully poetic lines that I know. When his fifteen-year-old son Calvin, Jr., died of blood poisoning, President Coolidge said his son would have the privilege of remaining a boy throughout eternity. I sometimes feel that I have had the privilege of retaining some of the spirit of a Montana small-town boyhood.

Billings is a big city now. But its character and its people have changed so little that I suspect that its effect on me was a compound of its small size and the frontier spirit that still pervaded it. In any case, it was small enough—halfway between a really small town and a small city—that I could have the feeling of knowing everyone in town. If I did not know them personally, I knew who they were; and I knew who lived in virtually every house on most of the streets.

The feeling of belonging, of identifying with neighbors and with the community was, in part, I am sure, a reflection of my own temperament; but it was also quite typical of that kind of community in that period. The founders of some of our New England villages sensed the importance of that feeling, and showed their wisdom when they adopted the rule in some areas that a village could be no more than one mile square—hence the proliferation of new, separate villages like Newton, West Newton, Newton Center, etc.

The loss of that sense of community and that feeling of identifying with others on a level of complete acceptance is a complex process; while there are other contributing causes, the movement of our people away from the farms and small towns into the cities has to be the root reason: a complete reversal from being 85 percent rural and small-town a century ago to being nearly 95 percent urban today.

I would commend to the social scientists and welfare administrators who now wrestle with urban problems that they study the inland small town early in this century, for clues as to how they can transplant some of the sense of community to present-day urban neighborhoods.

I was blessed with more than just that environment, ideal as it was. I had parents who had standards and ideals, for themselves and for their children.

We never had any money so we just went along doing the best we could with what we had. We never owned a car, even after cars had come to be thought of as absolute necessities. There were many other things we did not have or things we could not do that other families had or did—trips to football or basketball games in distant cities, for example. Being perfectly normal, human, thoughtless kids, we would whine and wheedle and beg, "Why can't I go too?" The pressure on Mother and Dad must have been brutal.

But in retrospect, I am amazed at how high their box score was in picking and choosing between the important and the merely desirable. They made sure we had everything that was really important; I can think of very little we missed that I could put in that category.

What we had that was most important was our parents themselves. As I said above, they had standards and ideals, and those were always reflected in the decisions they had to make. Above all, they wanted to be sure that their children would grow up to be decent, well-educated citizens. My father particularly, who was entirely self-educated, had great reverence for education and encouraged all three of us to plan and prepare to go on to college. Even with all the sacrifices they were willing to make, their meager resources would never have stretched over twelve or more college years anyway; and by the time I came to college age, Eastern Montana had been hit by the hardest of hard times and there was no possibility of my parents being able to help me. That compelled me to work my own way if I wanted to go; but as I shall point out in a later chapter, that became a happy circumstance.

Perhaps the clearest evidence that ours was a classless society was the position my parents occupied in our community. In spite of the fact that we lived in the wrong end of town, and that my father's earnings were never above a laborer's level (and in 1915 even a skilled laborer had no such wage scale, absolute or relative, as does today's worker) my parents were highly respected in town. My father was elected, successively, to the school board, to the Billings City Council, and later to the water district board. He was made master of his Masonic Lodge, and my mother was elected head of her lodges. (Their one recreation—they were great joiners!)

My father had so many talents—not only great mechanical skill, but obvious administrative and leadership abilities that he displayed in his political and fraternal activities—that he could have handled vastly bigger jobs than he ever held. But he was utterly devoid of any sense of self-promotion; in fact, the very thought of it was apparently against his principles. Even his campaigns for election to the local boards were always conducted so that his own personality or ego was always played down and issues played up. While I never saw the inside of his lodges, I am quite sure that his elevation there was always the result of his getting things done that needed doing, so that he gravitated naturally toward leadership positions.

Our living in the socially wrong part of town had its compensations. The county courthouse with its half-block of grounds marked the eastern edge of the business district, and we lived across the alley from the courthouse. (The "better" part of town was west and north of the business district. A real-estate analyst once told me that cities tend to grow outward toward the prevailing breeze at night; and Billings did just that.)

That meant that we kids had the huge cast-iron cellar doors of the courthouse to slide down during all our youngest years; but above all, it meant that all day and all night we could hear the courthouse clock boom out the hours and the half hours. When I later wondered how people in the tenements of big cities could possibly sleep through the noise of the elevated trains, I would remind myself that we always felt lost when the clock was out of order and we could not hear its soothing tones.

Lucky Diamond

Billings: The Magic City and How It Grew

by Kathryn Wright

See page 71 for biographical information about **Kathryn Wright.**

Stretching east of the business center on Minnesota was a long line of gambling places and Houses of Joy. The most lavishly furnished was the Lucky Diamond. Prominent citizens, cowboys and tinhorn gamblers sat side by side in its luxurious parlors; drank elbow to elbow at its long, mahogany, mirror-backed bar; danced with its girls. This young and so some thought, beautiful coterie was reputed to be the best on the whole northwest circuit. It was a sad day for them and their admirers and clients of the evening when the Lucky Diamond and other similar places were closed to conform with more straight-laced ideas of entertainment and relaxation.

Some of the demimonde left for more open fields; others scattered over town, reestablishing bordellos in roominghouses, behind drab facades of hotel walkups and in dingy cribs of an open red light district on First Avenue South, east of Twenty-eighth Street.

Among those who remained was Ollie Warren, a high-spirited, black-haired beauty, educated in a Denver convent and subsequently matriculated from a Billings affair to become one of the city's famous madams.

For awhile after her arrival in Billings she clerked in Yegen Brothers' Store. But that was not for long. She caught the fancy of a young, heavily mustached attorney; and he launched her, quite handsomely, into the flock of soiled doves that flitted about after sundown.

The attorney was successful in his law business; and Ollie was successful in her endeavors. Through her sponsor she was established in the Lucky Diamond and showered with jewels, clothes and highstepping horses. She cut a flamboyant figure galloping down rutty streets, side saddle on a handsome black horse, green velvet riding habit and plumed hat streaming in the wind. Many a long-suffering, neglected wife angrily gnashed her molars as she glared at Ollie from behind lace curtains.

When the Lucky Diamond was closed Ollie and her girls moved to a walkup on the north side of Montana Avenue between Twenty-seventh and Twenty-eighth Streets. It was popular, especially after Ollie erected an alley stairway. She told the lumberman from whom she bought the material: "Got to have a private entry for these stuffed shirts who patronize their churches once a week and my business every night."

Ollie had a ribald sense of humor; and, as the end of her days drew near and she was confined to the sickbed, she amused herself by watching the passing parade on Montana Avenue. When a prominent pillar of upright-eous society appeared she'd raise the window, thrust her head over the sill and call loudly enough for all in the block to hear: "Hello, you old ——. When you coming up again?"

Ollie's death and death of open prostitution in Billings occurred about the same time—the early years of World War II. At her funeral, arranged by a mysterious, unidentified young man, who appeared in the city with money and plans for the service and burial, she lay in her coffin, gray hair hennaed.

The beauty, toast of earlier years, had fled, giving way to a severe, almost prim look about the high cheek-boned face with its aquiline nose and wide thin mouth. She was buried in a brown taffeta dress of gay ninety vintage, its only adornment a wooden brooch carved in the form of a cluster of acorns.

Her mourners included gamblers of the old days, several of whom still are around, and a few of the doves of previous times. The latter still manifest jealousy of Ollie's popularity and affluence of her heyday. One of them, a grimy, obese, beringed ex-femme de joie voiced her feelings. "Hell," she told the author after Ollie's funeral, "she was a dammed liar. Never did tell the truth about her age."

The end of open prostitution in Billings came as a result of the visit of an armed forces health officer. At a meeting in the city hall attended by the author, the officer told city officials: "If you don't close this line down, the military will do it for you, and will let it be known why."

City officials had fence-straddled the issue for some time; and at the meeting demurred over absolute obliteration of the line.

"The line keeps prostitution under control," they said.

The military officer stared coldly.

"Gentlemen," he replied from his seat at the mayor's desk, "our health tests have proven that if a potential recruit spends 12 hours in Billings he's unfit for military duty."

"Well," put in a law enforcement official, shifting uncomfortably in his chair in the semi-circle facing the desk, "well, if you're going to close down prostitution why don't you start at the top with the hotels?"

The military man gave him a long, piercing look.

"I am not talking," he said in an icy voice, "about hotels where you infer your citizens avail themselves of certain pleasures at fancy prices. I am talking about your line of cribs where naked women lean over window sills and entice young boys in for 50 cents or a dollar."

He let that sink in and then came out with the ultimatum:

"Close that south-side line in 24 hours or the military will move in and do it for you."

The line was closed, at least to an extent satisfying the military.

Becoming History:
Of Della Mae, nothing but good...

Commentary by Addison Bragg

Addison Bragg has long been one of the most famous newspaper reporters in eastern Montana and northern Wyoming. His column "Bragg about Billings" has proved a source of pride, chastisement, and comic relief for the region.

She was a part of our town's past.

The obituaries in Tuesday's paper held no surprises for me.

I had heard some time ago that Della Mae Logan was not well and the chances of her getting better were not good at all.

So when I saw her name and picture there was more a sense of loss than one of shock. I had thought of her often during these past months—we talked for the last time when I met her one afternoon at the hospital about a year ago and I had every intention of dropping by and leaving word for her that I had been there—but we all know what happens at times with the best of intentions.

My first impression was that another part of our town as it used to be had become history and my second thought was now that Della had gone, who would draw breath, though certainly not (as Hamlet would have had it) in pain, to tell her story.

I had been a *Gazette* reporter for all of a week or ten days when I first heard about Della Mae—whose last name, by the way, was never known to many of those who knew or claimed to know her—and it was possibly a month or two later when I met her. Memory could be playing tricks on me by now but I could almost swear she was a red head then. Maybe not, but it's my impression that she was.

In the years which followed, we became friends.

We had an occasional drink together and I remember dancing with her once in the Golden Belle on either her birthday or mine, exactly whose, I forget—but the memory is important. Later, her father, who once lived in Kansas, came out here to live and I remember visiting with him after I got off work at the paper—us *Gazette* people used to park south of the tracks— as he sat on the porch of his daughter's rooming house on cool evenings and we would talk about Kansas.

Della did some things—all of which she freely admitted—of which many of today's society would disapprove. But she did many other things of which today's society knew little or nothing and I'm thinking of youngsters she helped put through school and of the birthday and Christmas presents she saw to it that others would get and the glasses she paid for and the dental bills and the coats and shoes and even college money going to others. Della told me of none of these things. I heard it from those aware of some of these unselfish acts from an unselfish woman.

Della often spoke of men who would pass her in daytime on the street without a sign of recognition but had no difficulty in knowing her "once the sun went down and the street lights come on."

And, typically of Della, she didn't blame them for it. "They be what they be," she said once, "and I be what I am and that's the way things are."

As long as I worked at the paper, I cannot recall even one instance of Della's being in trouble with the law. I don't say she never was, I just never saw or heard of it. In fact, I was a witness when a blind man named Otto— who sold papers and sometimes pencils along Montana Avenue—was struck by a car in front of a house where Della was sweeping off the porch and, after stopping to see how badly the man was hurt, the driver started back to his car only to be met by Della in the street with her broom in the air. She grabbed the keys and kept him and his passengers in the car at the scene until police arrived.

Pat Connolly, ex-*Gazette* police reporter, never returned to Billings after he became an Associated Press byliner without our dropping by for small talk and a drink with Della. And I had no problem in letting my wife know where we were headed after work. Her reply was generally the same: "Just one drink, then," she'd say. "I don't want you bringing Pat here for a cold dinner."

My oldest daughter knew Della from having ushered ball games at Cobb Field where there was no greater a Mustang fan than was Della Mae Logan. And she was there many years ago at my wife's funeral in Little Flower Church where she was overheard later telling someone "I just knew him and his daughter but I know of the family and his wife who must have been a good woman and I wanted to be here."

Della and I never met without mentioning Minnesota Avenue as it was and what it had become—in her words—a real ghost town, and as I think of her now I feel she too has found a place among those tough but tender, rough but honest, bawdy but genuine shades who now walk the shadows of China Alley and I am reminded of the old Latin adage: *De mortuis nihil nisi bonum.*

And where Della Mae, my old friend, is concerned, I find myself singularly unable, indeed, to speak of anything but good. May she rest in peace.

Between the Wars

A Century of Politics on the Yellowstone

by Lawrence F. Small

Lawrence F. Small is one of the central educational figures in Yellowstone County history. After receiving his divinity degree from Bangor Theological Seminary and his Ph.D. in history from Harvard University, he served as history professor, dean, and president of Rocky Mountain College. He has also served as executive director of the Montana Association of Churches and founder and board chair of the Institute for Peace Studies at Rocky Mountain College. His publications include *A Century of Politics on the Yellowstone* and *Religion in Montana.*

The fall of 1918 was one of the most eventful ever in Yellowstone County, with the visit of a popular ex-president, a critical congressional election, and the ending of the Great War. Early in October Colonel Theodore

Roosevelt was on a rousing western tour that would take him through the "Magic City."

...The former president, accompanied by Chamber president Frank B. Connelly and other dignitaries, arrived in Billings on the Burlington for a very full day. Breakfast at 7 a.m. featured trout and the first of eight speeches. On the Polytechnic campus, as the valley basked in an Indian summer day, he gave his last address at a college gathering. "This is the kind of school," he affirmed, "that builds character and trains for the highest type of leadership. It is out from these vast open spaces of the northwest and from the valleys of these magnificent mountains yonder that the big, broad-minded, virile leaders of America must come."

It was like being back home, for it was to these mountains and plains that a young Roosevelt had come 34 years before, distraught over his wife's death and his mother's passing, to find healing for the spirit and a new grasp on life. There was no other part of the land, he told an overflow crowd at the fairgrounds, "to which I can come with as full a heart and as strong a sense of returning to my own as here in the northwest." The dozen years he had spent here, he recalled, had really shaped the rest of his career, and, had it not been for them, "I would have never been president of the United States." He had returned to Billings in 1900 during his campaign for the vice presidency and again on his tour of April, 1911.

Lunch brought renewal of old acquaintances and talk of earlier times. Paul McCormick was too ill to attend meetings, so the former president included a call on him. It was indeed a "bully day" that did not conclude until 7 p.m. when Roosevelt boarded the Northern Pacific for the long trip back home to Oyster Bay. Old friends agreed that the one-time Rough Rider was "as strenuous as ever," but time was running out for the incomparable Teddy. Within a year he would be dead. "Roosevelt Day" in Billings, however, would live in the memories of many as one of the best ever and a fitting tribute to a great American.

...Six days after the general election on November 5 came the confirmation of the signing of the Armistice. Banner headlines proclaimed: "War is ended. Germans quit. Curtain falls on world tragedy." "All Billings celebrates as never before" reported *The Gazette* on the 12th. "Billings went mad last night. In a giant, spontaneous, reckless eruption of enthusiasm it shrieked its joy until the rimrocks resounded the echo." An estimated 15,000 (which was the total population of the town) "surged and milled and churned and howled their happiness at the final defeat of Germany." Giant firecrackers were exploded with abandon, as city ordinances were forgotten. Torches everywhere and thousands of dollars worth of pyrotechnics "made vivid the night!" It was another unforgettable moment in the fall of 1918.

...Against the advice of physicians and friends, the frail but determined president [Woodrow Wilson]undertook a strenuous tour across the country.

In St. Louis on September 5, in the hall where he received his party's renomination, he branded his opponents as "quitters" if they "don't see this game through." His adversaries in Washington countered each speech with strong criticisms of Wilson's views which also made headlines. Billings was on his schedule, and for the second time in less than one year, the "Magic City" would have an opportunity to greet an occupant of the White House. *The Gazette* for Tuesday, September 11, spread the town's sentiments on its front page. "Welcome, Mr. President, to Billings and the Real West."

Area Montanans had been flooding into the city, filling every hotel space and occupying available beds in private homes. A crowd comparable to that for Teddy met the president's train when it rolled in at 8:55 a.m. Then came the parade to the fairgrounds, led by the Midland Empire band, through flag-draped streets packed with the curious and wellwishers. City and county offices, businesses, banks, and schools were closed for the half-day in honor of Wilson's visit. A crowd of 9,000, *The Gazette* reported the next day, jammed the auditorium, while thousands more waited outside.

It was here in the West that Wilson had found the voter strength to edge Charles Evans Hughes in the election of 1916, and it was here in Billings, and other towns like her, that he derived from his encounter with the people renewed hope and purpose to see the treaty and the League through to the finish. "It's the people's treaty," he assured the cheering throng, "It's this one or it's none." But two weeks later at Pueblo, Colorado, on his way home, the weakened Wilson collapsed from physical and emotional exhaustion. Several days later in Washington he suffered a paralytic stroke which affected one side of his body. In the ensuing months, the invalid president remained strong in his resolve not to compromise the League Covenant with reservations. Enough Democrats honored his wishes that an amended treaty failed twice of Senate approval. In the confines of the White House, Wilson nurtured his dream for world peace and waited for vindication by the people in the upcoming election of 1920.

Hemingway Treated at
Saint Vincent Hospital

The Call to Care 1898-1998: Saint Vincent Hospital and Health Center,
the First 100 Years of Service

by Sue Hart

Sue Hart teaches Montana literature and creative writing at Montana State
University-Billings. She is currently researching and writing a documentary
about Dorothy M. Johnson. Her short story "Star Pattern" received the PEN
Award for Syndicated Fiction in 1989. The following excerpt comes from her
book about St. Vincent Hospital, a topic she knows well because she is an
Associate of the Sisters of Charity and volunteers extensively at the hospital.

In the fall of 1930, a patient was delivered to the hospital by a couple
who had come upon the scene of a one-car accident. The patient (who had
been "roughing it" in the mountains and at Yellowstone Park) was believed
to be a cowboy or sheepherder because of his appearance, and he was
assigned to a bed in a ward.

When Dr. [Louis] Allard arrived at the hospital to examine the new
patient's broken right arm, he asked student nurse Bernadette Martin,
"Don't you know who he is? That's Ernest Hemingway, the novelist. I think
he'd better be moved to a private room."

Since mid-July of 1930, Hemingway had been working on *Death in the
Afternoon* at the L Bar T Ranch located on the Clarks Fork branch of the
Yellowstone about twelve miles east of Cooke City, Montana, within the
Wyoming border. When he wasn't writing, he spent his time entertaining
family and friends at the ranch.

The auto accident occurred about thirty miles west of Billings when
Hemingway, who was driving, was apparently blinded by on-coming headlights and turned his car into a ditch. He suffered a spiral fracture above the
elbow on his right arm.

Initially, Hemingway was expected to spend only a week or so in the
hospital, but the arm did not heal properly. Dr. Allard had to perform
surgery in order to set the break and stabilized the arm by making use of a
kangaroo tendon. As a result, Hemingway spent seven weeks in Saint
Vincent Hospital. He later wrote about his experience there in a short story
called "The Gambler, The Nun, and The Radio" (included in the collection
Winner Take Nothing, 1933).

This story, which Hemingway claimed was written just as it happened,
reflects one of the author's favorite themes: the testing of one's courage and
determination against what appear to be overwhelming odds. Every element
in the title contributes to this theme. The gambler has been shot and is not

expected to live. The nun, "Sister Cecilia," has hopes of becoming "a saint," a goal which Mr. Frazer (the thinly-disguised Hemingway character) says she has "three to one" odds on reaching. And the radio rented for Frazer's room as a way to fill the long hours of convalescence brings in the play-by-play of a national championship football game in which Notre Dame is a definite underdog.

Ernest Hemingway, photographed by Dr. Louis Allard in 1930, recovering at Saint Vincent Hospital from the automobile accident in which he fractured his arm. Photo courtesy the Allard Collection, the Western Heritage Center, Billings, Montana.

Courage and determination pay off for both the gambler, who lives, and the Notre Dame team, which wins. The reader must assume that Sister Cecilia's odds of becoming a Saint are very good, too.

The character Sister Cecilia is based on Sister Florence Cloonan, who spent a great deal of time with Hemingway during his stay at Saint Vincent. Sister Florence was working in the hospital office when Hemingway was admitted. She often delivered his mail, one of his few diversions, and stayed to visit with him about current events or sports.

Sister Florence was an avid baseball fan who prayed many of her favorite teams to victory. An associate of Sister Florence, Sister Dorothy Hanly, recalled that "Sister Florence would take sports teams into a chapel and tell them, 'This is where games are won.'"

Like Mr. Frazer in Hemingway's story, Sister Florence enjoyed listening to sports broadcasts on the radio. Sister Marian Berry, another associate of

Sister Florence, remembered that Sister Florence "had an old-fashioned radio. She'd sit with her ear almost glued to it to hear the games. There was a radio in the Community Room at the motherhouse, but it was only on at certain hours. Sister Florence kept her radio in the storeroom, where the sewing machine was also kept, and when a game was on, she'd go to the storeroom to 'sew.' "

In Hemingway's story, Sister Cecilia declares that she knows much more about baseball than football. When Notre Dame has a 14-0 lead at half-time, she asks Frazer what the score means: "I don't know anything about this game. That's a nice safe lead in baseball. But I don't know anything about football."

According to Sister Marian Berry, Sister Florence "knew all the baseball players by name. She would write to them and tell them she was praying for them. They sent her autographed baseballs, and for quite a while there was a glass-case display of her collection at the Saint Vincent Home for Boys in Denver."

Eventually Hemingway's medical treatment at the hands of Allard, whom he referred to in "The Gambler, The Nun, and The Radio" as "a most excellent Doctor," brought him to a stage in his recovery when he could leave the hospital. On December 21, 1930, he was discharged and left for Piggott, Arkansas, with his wife Pauline to complete his convalescence. After the first of the year, the Hemingways traveled to Key West, and Hemingway can be seen in pictures from that period still holding his arm as though it is in a sling. His friend and hunting guide, Chub Weaver, who drove Hemingway's car to Florida after it was repaired, told his son that Hemingway was, in fact, disregarding doctor's orders by not keeping the arm in a sling; Hemingway claimed that the sling interfered with his fishing.

Other, less prominent authors, also wrote of their time at Saint Vincent Hospital and of the interest there in Notre Dame football. In *Being Crippled Is a State of Mind*, Bruce Milne, Ph.D., recalled his days as a patient in the Hospital School program (1938 to 1942) in a series of poems, including one called "Dr. Bean" about a physician who would bet each hospitalized child five cents that Notre Dame would lose its next game. The doctor would come in the day after the game to settle his bets:

> *What fun we had as he gave each of us*
> *Our nickel and we all laughed as we sang*
> *The Notre Dame fight song*
> *Led by the Sisters of Charity.*

Fourteen Cents & Seven Green Apples: The Life and Times of Charles Bair

by Lee Rostad

Montana native **Lee Rostad** ranches with her husband near Martinsdale. The author of several books and articles, she studied as a Fulbright scholar at the University of London. She received the Governor's Award in the Humanities in 2001.

[Silent movie actor William S. "Bill"] Hart commented on the statue of himself which now stands above the Rimrocks in Billings. The statue had been originally planned for North Dakota, but [Charles] Bair got it for Billings.

The unveiling of the Bill Hart Monument took place during a Founder's Day Celebration, July 2-4 in 1927. Photos taken by Peter Billings of the event are revealing. The real-life Hart faces the life-sized bronze of the movie cowboy and his horse. Of the two, the bronze is the more dominant, the more heroic-looking. The cheekbones are more pronounced; the chin is more determined; the stance is more assured. The real-life Hart sports the beginnings of a pot belly. To the right of the bronze stands Bair, the man responsible for bringing the statue to Billings. By then, Bair is 62, and his figure is portly. With his hands he seems to orchestrate the details of the unveiling with an air of concern.

The Hart statue was done by Charles Christadoro. At the dedication ceremonies, Hart called the West, "The land of staunch comradeship, of kindly sympathy, of kindred intellect, where hearts beat high and hands grip firm, where poverty is no disgrace and where charity never grows cold..."

[Later he wrote to Bair] "...I love what you say of the old pinto and the bronze cowpuncher high up on the rimrock. It is good to know that they will always keep guard over the Valley of the Yellowstone. It gives me a warm glow to think of them."

Dick Logan, the airport manager at that time, said that Bair, "Martinsdale sheep rancher and intimate of Hart," had donated the money to add a brand to the statue horse. Bair stipulated that the horse bear the brand of an outfit headed by Russell when he was "farmhanding" in the Great Falls country. Hart agreed with the choice. Bair realized the long-continuing importance of brands in Montana since he had begun concentrating on the ranch at Martinsdale.

Bobby Brooks Kramer: One of a Rare Breed

by Wallace C. McLane

Wallace C. "Wally" McLane developed and administers a nonprofit organization whose focus is people who are marginally physically challenged. He is also active in the Billings Exchange Club.

As with any youngster raised on a ranch, [Bobby Brooks] Kramer was practically born on horseback—getting her own saddle at three years of age and being put in charge of the ranch's saddle stock at six.

Eastern Montanans grow up on a diet of grit and determination, seasoned with hot, dry summers and cold winters with blowing snow. The snow will blow until it disappears in the horizon or sticks to something— like you and your horse as you check on your livestock.

Kramer experienced all of this first hand before any of today's modern conveniences—things we now take for granted. So, while she may shake her head when she thinks of her "early days," those experiences are what made her the woman she is—a woman who has drive, determination, yet is patient with youth and livestock, and believes in strong family values.

While her name was still Brooks, Kramer experienced a piece of western life not many men have tried, much less women. She rode saddle broncs in rodeos. Her introduction to this "sport" was as the result of a bad choice and "divine" intervention.

Kramer was at one rodeo—with her two brothers, and gambled away the lunch and gas money. Later that day, the stock contractor offered her some money to ride a saddle bronc. Thinking the horses wouldn't be any worse than the rough stock at the ranch—not to mention what her brothers would do to her if they found out about their money—Kramer rode the bronc to the whistle and was paid.

In the more than four years she rode in rodeos, she was only injured once—when the pickup man dropped the bucking horse rein after Kramer finished her ride. There was a wreck with Kramer getting a broken arm....

Ranching and working with horses was…in her blood. When she started to think long term about her future, she studied and became a licensed beautician. The day she was to start her first job, a rancher stopped her on the street; and…asked her if she would be interested in training some horses for him. She turned right instead of left, and that has become her life, her heritage.

One of the many lessons Kramer learned from her father was when you have some money, buy land. Her father stressed it would never be that cheap again, so buy it when you can. This lesson was really stretched thin one time, shortly after marrying Bud Kramer. Bobby bid on 30,000 acres of land. As it turned out, she was the only bidder. The 30,000 acres cost her less than $65,000. But she only had $500 in the bank. Her new husband and her father, the former sheriff, were "concerned." Kramer managed to get a loan to cover the deal. By the time the Kramers decided to move on to something else, their empire consisted of 76,000 deeded acres and another 76,000 acres of leased land. They also had almost 10,000 head of horses—from broncs to registered stock.

Horses were relatively easy to acquire at the time, because when the ranchers went off to fight World War II they just turned their horses loose. When these ranchers returned to start up again, the ranges were over-run with horses. So the Kramers contracted to round them up—paying canner prices to the owners of the branded stock and claiming all of the unbranded stock. The unbranded stock were the result of all the horses running loose and breeding.

It was during this time Kramer decided if she had a plane some of the ranch work—like locating livestock—would be much easier. So she learned to fly—qualifying for both private and commercial licenses. When "Silver"—her 172 Cessna—wasn't airborne, it was tied to the hitching post in front of the house.

...The Kramer operation was [so big], it would take Bobby 45 minutes, in Silver, to go from the house to the front gate. Also, like any good "mount," Bobby's and Silver's relationship was not always "smooth." Bobby did, however, manage to walk away from those forced, spur of the moment landings.

During the Kramers' bucking stock hey-day, she spotted a young horse at an auction. Being able to read a horse like a book, she bought him for their herd. Her eye was right. This young horse became Descent. That's Descent, as in five times World Champion Bucking Horse.

In the 1960s [the Kramers began showing their registered horses]. Kramer and the ranch have accumulated a substantial number of awards—many of which are displayed in her home. Many people have said when she gets on her horse, the horse and rider become one—something all riders hope to attain.

Befitting Kramer's strong will she campaigned six horses for their AQHA Championships in 1994 and got them. She was only 81.

Kramer is a grand showman, but she is, first and foremost, a hand. Word has it there was a trail class in which Kramer was riding a young horse. The horse decided, to his regret, he had enough of this class and was going to deposit his rider on the ground and leave the arena. Being the hand Kramer is, she "educated" the horse right there, then apologized to the judge, and left the arena....

Through the years, Kramer has received many honors from her peers. A few of the highlights are:

•1990–She was Grand Marshal of the Miles City Bucking Horse Sale Parade and was one of the hands chosen to participate in the Montana Centennial Cattle Drive [1989].

•1993–She was Grand Marshal of the Billings Diamond Jubilee Parade and was featured in the documentary film on women bronc riders of Montana, *I'll Ride That Horse.*

•2000–She was nominated to the Cowgirl Hall of Fame in Fort Worth, Texas.

Golden Opportunities: A Biographical History of Montana's Jewish Communities
by Julie L. Coleman

Born and raised in Chicago, **Julie L. Coleman** taught social studies in Billings for many years before becoming a stockbroker. She has also served as a board member and president of the Montana League of Women Voters.

Congregation Beth Aaron remains a viable presence in the Billings community, and its members now participate widely in community affairs. The establishment of the Yellowstone Country Club after World War II provided an opportunity for golfers to belong to a country club, no matter their religion. Young Jewish matrons have been invited to join the Junior League, and a number of members of the Beth Aaron congregation have served on boards of philanthropic organizations and have been active politically. Rabbi [Paul] Ehrlich and Rabbi [Robert] Ratner taught classes at Eastern Montana College in Billings under the sponsorship of the Judaic Studies grants, and were well received.

The reappearance of the Ku Klux Klan in the 1990s in Billings has brought a different response than it did earlier in the century. A marked surge in hate activities occurred in 1993. At Rosh Hashanah, vandals turned over most of the headstones in the Jewish cemetery at that holy time and as a long-time member of the community was being buried. The threats are reminders of the Klan's hatred, but this time there has been widespread community support and outrage at the vandalism and threats against Jewish people. After *The Billings Gazette* printed the story and pictures and television news showed the damage, help was immediately offered to repair the damage. Shortly thereafter, when there was a bomb threat made to the congregation during the High Holy Day services, an armed guard had to be employed to guard the building as the congregation came in to worship. Again, there was community support.

Chanukah brought more outrages. Rocks were thrown into windows of two homes, barely missing small Jewish children, and hate messages accompanied the acts. Since then, there have been pamphlets circulated maligning Jewish members of the community as well as Jews in general. A strong Human Rights Commission in Billings and an enlightened newspaper spotlighted these terrible events, and community outrage resulted in a candlelight vigil by the general citizenry the night of Chanukah services. The paper printed full-page menorahs and asked readers to post them in their windows to show support for the ideas of peace and unity. Many churches and individuals joined in putting menorahs in their windows—and unfortunately found themselves targets of the same bigots who had been harassing the Jewish community. The First Methodist Church had several of its windows broken, and a number of cars were battered because of their owners' sympathies with Jews. The Beth Aaron congregation, meeting to discuss the above events, felt that the acts were those of a small group, and that the overwhelming friendship shown by the majority of the Billings community was indeed a welcome change from the cooler climate of earlier years.

Why a Book on High Plains

Gardening in the Northern High Plains

by Alice O. Hamilton

Alice O. Hamilton was born in Ohio in 1906. Her family settled in Fergus County in 1919. She graduated from Eastern Montana College and taught elementary and high school for 29 years. For many years she wrote the gardening column for *The Billings Gazette*. In 1985, the American Association of University Women, Billings Chapter, awarded her a named gift in the Educational Foundation Program for the value of her writings to the public.

All the people in the world everywhere are ultimately dependent on food, not imported oil. The Mayan civilization, their population outreaching their food supply, collapsed. It could happen again with uncontrolled population growth in much of the United States and the rest of the world.

The Gallup Organization recently computed that 38 million people who gardened raise ⅓ of all the vegetables eaten in our country. All the machinery and know-how of the professional farmer does not produce as much per square foot as the home gardener produces in the same area.

Gardening, either food or flower type, can add good years to your life with the fresh air and the exercise. The relief from tension, fears and worries may not be as noticeable but it is a bigger plus than the fresh lettuce. Look at your garden as a healing place, a retreat found without a car and without traveling miles on congested roads.

The chief problems on the High Plains are the short and dry seasons. Our average rainfall for May is 2.8 inches. In June it is 2.61 inches. July only has .87 inches and August records an even 1.00 inch. This does not come near the "inch a week" which is usually mentioned as necessary to do any food gardening. Supplemental watering is a must.

Powell, Wyoming, is 1000 feet higher than Billings. We are both in zone 3 of hardiness, but for each 250 feet of altitude temperatures average a degree less. Altitude is not the whole story, though. How is your wind? More trees are killed by drying out in summer and winter winds than from extreme cold. If trees are in a protected spot sheltered by nearby buildings they might survive where unprotected trees will not.

The average late frost in the Billings, Montana, area is May 18. The rest of the state varies from June 1 in Bozeman to May 10 in Corvallis. North to Lewistown and beyond finds May 20 as the average late spring frost date.

Our High Plains area is not the most kindly one for gardening, but it is what we have and most of us living here love it and would have it no other way—or not much different, anyway.

It's DRY. So this small book will try to answer some of the questions on most adaptable herbs and trees, as well as how to conserve on watering. Tricks which have worked to overcome our short season and cold nights will be shared for an ever wider circle than from whom they have been gathered.

Our soil is different. But many have found ways to improve it. You might find something new to you, or be reminded of half forgotten tactics.

Choosing the right plant varieties, increasing the water retentiveness of the soil, and learning how to water effectively at least cost is necessary to meet our problems. We hope this collection of experiences will be of help to you.

A food garden 20x30 feet, just 600 square feet, can produce vegetables worth $300.00 to $600.00 a year at 1980 prices. That would help a wee bit in taxes, wouldn't it? Why not try a small patch this year and find out.

And who can live without roses?

Billings, My City, My Home

by Ed Harris

Ed Harris was born and raised in Forsyth. He received degrees in music and music education. An oft-honored music educator, he has appeared in many musical and theatrical productions and has over one hundred compositions in print.

BILLINGS, MY CITY, MY HOME

Words and Music by
ED HARRIS

Additional verses:

3. It has cottonwoods, good neighborhoods, and chuckholes by the score,
   It has ditches, buses, freeways, parks, 'n that's not all, there's more.
   You're a swingin', singin', city
   And you're really rather pretty,
   Billings, My City, My Home. (Refrain)

4. But the best part of my city is the people who live there,
   They all greet you when they meet you 'cause those people really care.
   They say "Hi!" as they walk by you
   Breathing unpolluted air,
   Billings, My City, My Home. (Refrain)

The story behind the song

My composition was created and intended to be an easily singable song with the simplicity and sentiment of an old western folksong. In it are mentioned some of the things that are unique about our town, such as the Yellowstone River, the Rimrocks, and the warm and friendly people.

Local reaction was mixed. Bill Fox was city mayor at the time and was so taken by the song that he had the Council adopt it as the "official" city song. There was negative reaction from some quarters, because there had been no announcement or competition for a "juried" selection process. There were some complaints that the phrase "chuckholes by the score" was certainly not putting our city's "best foot forward." My response to those critics was that they could simply substitute the word "chuckles" at that spot if they so desired.

Western Meadowlark © Gary Leppart

See page 12 for biographical information about **Gary Leppart.**

Don Miller of Miller Photo recalls that his mother, Kathryn, always told him that the meadowlark sings, "Montana is a pretty little place."

Beginnings

Untitled
Will James
carbon pencil on paper (n.d.)
Courtesy Yellowstone Art Museum
Permanent Collection, gift of Virginia Snook
(Reprinted with permission of The Will James Art Co.)

Ethnographic material extracted from

Archaeology of the
Crow Indian Vision Quest

by Stuart W. Conner

Stuart W. Conner was reared and educated in Montana. He served in the U.S. Marine Corps in World War II. After four years in the FBI, he returned to Montana and practiced law in Billings for 31 years, during which he developed an intense avocational interest in Montana archaeology, ethnography and history.

A vision quest in the culture of the Crow Indians is a quest for personal supernatural power. Power is usually acquired by the visitation of a guardian spirit in a dream induced by fasting, praying, and formerly by self-mutilation. The guardian spirit can be anything in nature, but traditionally was often the moon or the morning star or an animal or bird invested with supernatural power. The power is passed to the faster by the guardian spirit, usually with instructions for making a medicine bundle, and with a medicine song and ceremonial procedures to be used to invoke the power when it is needed.

The acquisition of power sometimes does not involve a visitation by a guardian spirit, but is transferred in the form of a vision of a thing or event with which the faster will be involved, such as a specific horse he will capture or buffalo he will find at a particular place in a time of scarcity. This type of vision does not confer permanent power; it is like a self-fulfilling forecast of success to be accorded the quester at some time in the future.

More often, the experience takes place in solitude on a topographic eminence after a ceremonial sweat bath and smudge in the smoke of the leaves of a pungent plant to remove the human odor which the Without Fires, the spirits, find repugnant.

The fast can last as long as four days, if necessary. Often, a more experienced Crow instructs the vision seeker on proscriptions and taboos to be observed during the fast and interprets the faster's dream when he is fortunate and has one.

Formerly, younger teenage boys were culturally encouraged to seek power through a visitation by a guardian spirit in a dream. But adult men and women did and do seek the advantages of a supernatural helper at any of life's critical points.

Crow Indian vision quests still occur regularly. The principal changes are the discontinuance of self-mutilation, the appearance in visions of modern technological items as well as the traditional guardian spirits, and the discontinuance of war honors visions which were formerly common.

The powers secured during vision quests by recent Crow fasters reflect the constancy as well as changes in Crow lifeways. The power to heal illnesses continues to be a power commonly acquired on vision quests, as I think it always was. Wealth and prestige were and are sought and received in both old and contemporary vision quests.

One surviving early attitude is the strong feeling among modern Crow vision seekers that the more hazardous the quest site, and the more a faster is made to suffer by the spirits or by the elements while fasting, the more likely he is to have pity taken on him by the supernatural powers and the greater will be the power that he receives.

In the nomadic days, the vision quest was the most important of the Crow religious practices. The results of a vision could decide the course of a man's life. The vision quest is still significant in Crow Indian religion, but to a diminished degree.

I do not have an adequate current sampling to be completely confident that I understand the place of vision quests in contemporary Crow culture. For one thing, it is more than 10 years since I was deeply into this topic with certain Crows. From the indications I do have, however, it seems clear that, in the period following the time when the Crow men who grew up during the last of the Indian wars became middle aged, there has been a lessening of the rigors and discipline followed by those Crows who seek supernatural visitations.

I attribute this primarily to two aspects of acculturation. With the passing of the militaristic aspect of Crow culture when men attained high status principally through war deeds, there was also a relaxation of the importance of physical discomfort and physical bravery in the face of danger or pain. This carried over into the vision quest, minimizing the value of physical discomfort during a fast for power.

The other factor is the adoption of Christianity as another religion, not in lieu of the traditional religions of the Crows, but as an additional layer of beliefs. Many, but not all, of the modern Crow fasters are members of and adherents to the Roman Catholic Church or one of the Protestant denominations that have a church on the Crow Reservation and/or to the Native American Church which uses peyote in its ceremonies and fosters many Christian concepts and beliefs.

Although I have talked to a number of those who have fasted, I have not probed into the prayers and supplications for power that they have employed while fasting in quest of a supernatural visitation. That aspect has seemed too personal for my intrusion. Knowing something of how some of these same folks have welded certain Christian beliefs onto those of the Crow Sun Dance, I assume that the supplications of some modern vision questers incorporate some aspects of Christian beliefs which, of course, do not encourage individual war deeds as an acceptable means of attaining social status.

The powers sought by recent Crow fasters about whom I have knowledge usually includes "success," as the faster conceives "success." That notion not infrequently includes wealth, honor, and prestige. Some fasters I know have prayed for peace and good will among all people.

While fasting remains a Crow practice, substantial changes in the specific attainments that are sought are known. While the importance of the vision quest in Crow religion diminished with the termination of the militaristic character of Crow culture, I do not doubt but what the modern quest for a supernatural visitation is often still a profound experience.

Eagle Feather for a Crow
by Alice Ryniker

Alice Durland Ryniker was born and educated in Billings. She studied watercolor painting with Ben Steele and Rex Brandt, AWS. Her watercolors have been displayed in local and regional shows and galleries. She is Professor of Art Emeritus at Rocky Mountain College.

There is a wide and lonely pass in the Pryor Mountains of Montana which is called the Gap—Pryor Gap. On hot summer days the wind slides down in lazy ribbons from the pines of the foothills to the cottonwoods along the creek. This is Indian country, the land of the Crows. It was theirs in the old, free hunting days; it is part of their reservation now. The wind remembers, singing softly to itself. Listen to a story which the wind has to tell.

...The mountain air was cold at night even in the summer. Charley hugged himself so tightly, trying to keep warm, that his arms began to ache. He was staring into the darkness when the ledge of rocks across the coulee beyond him began to glow with a faint light. In its dimness he could make out a rough ridge ringed with buffalo skulls. Flickers of light played in and out of the dark pines behind. Gradually he began to realize that he was hearing the beat of tom-toms—or was it the yapping of the coyote? His mouth was so dry he found it hard to swallow, and his eyes felt as though they would pop out of his head in his effort to see.

As he became aware of movement inside the circle, the light seemed to brighten. Someone was dancing slowly around and around in a heel and toe shuffle. Charley could see that he was a pale warrior dressed only in a breech-cloth and moccasins. His face and body were fantastic with war paint, which made him look more ghostly than ever. On one arm he carried an ancient war shield, while his other arm brandished a long lance. Two feathers waved on his head. As his steps became faster, his dance became an intricate series of swoops and bends behind the circle of skulls.

Two other dancers appeared suddenly beside him. They were also dressed like warriors of old, painted, as Charley's grandfather had often told him, the way men did before the war parties started out. In the unreal, shifting light, the warriors seemed much smaller than ordinary men. A thought raced through the boy's mind. Could these be the Old Ones—the Little People? Charley shrank back against the rocks. The ghostly rhythm of the drums beat faster and faster. The dancers leaped and whirled, twisting and turning, now low to the ground, now high in the air. They seemed to be shouting their victory cries, yet not a sound came out of their mouths. Only the tom-tom was beating wildly—or was it his pounding heart that Charley heard?

How long this eerie dance went on the boy could not have told. It seemed like hours, but perhaps it was only minutes. The flickering light began to fade, and two of the dancers slipped away, dissolving in the shadows. The third one suddenly turned and jumped high into the air. His eyes shone red and his mouth was a huge gaping hole. "Who-o-ee-ahh!" The ancient war cry echoed down the mountainside. It could have been the owl again, but that thought did not occur to Charley. In frozen fascination he continued to stare at the ghostly figure. Suddenly the pale warrior drew back. Then with a violent lunge, he threw his feather-tipped lance straight across the coulee and into the bank above the frightened boy.

Pretty Eagle's Story

Blankets and Moccasins: Plenty Coups and His People the Crows
by Glendolin Damon Wagner and Dr. William Allen

See page 34 for biographical information about **Glendolin Damon Wagner.**
William Allen arrived in the Billings area in 1877 and remained until his
death in 1944. He tried his hand at blacksmithing, Pony Express riding, stock
raising and flour milling. He also became a pioneering dentist in the region.

"So today Pretty Eagle will tell to White Eagle [Dr. Allen], the brother of
the Crows, the secret history of our tribe. He will write it…so that Crow
boys may read and remember."

…"The Crows love their land," Pretty Eagle stated, gravely. "That valley
of the Echeta Casha (Yellowstone River) which the White Father in
Washington has given them to be theirs as long as there is one Crow left to
claim it belonged to them many hundreds of snows ago—before moccasin
of white man ever pressed the plains. White Eagle knows I do not speak with
crooked tongue?"

I nodded. He went on:

"Nowhere else is to be found such beauty of mountain and valley. There
sparkling streams of cold water never dry nor does tall, rich buffalo grass ever
wither. The Crows have never feared winter cold nor summer heat for they
have had many buffalo and elk to give them food and to clothe them, to
shelter them from falling snows and sun's rays. They have had wild geese and
ducks and sage hens, deer and antelope. The Great Spirit placed along the
streams for His children plum thickets, service bushes, chokecherry and bull-
berry bushes. The mouths of our papooses are red in spring with strawberries. Everything man needs for his health and happiness is to be found in the
valley of the Echeta Casha—the land of the Crows.

"All this White Eagle, friend of the Crow people, already knows. This our
enemy, Sioux and Blackfeet and Pawnees, also knew. And though the Crows
said nothing when enemy came to hunt our buffalo, yet the enemy were not
satisfied. They wished to possess our beautiful land for their own.

"It is said by our fathers, who were told by their fathers' fathers, that once
the Absarokees, known to the palefaces as 'The Crows,' were part of the Gros
Ventre tribe, speaking the same language, and that we all came from the
Dakotas. We know now only that for many long snows we have lived in this
valley extending from the Big Horn Mountains and the Pryors down to the
Echeta Casha which the palefaces call the 'Yellowstone River.'

…In the valley south of Pryor Pass, near Pryor Creek, even today, are
mounds covered with stones and overgrown with greasewood, two very

high mounds and many smaller ones. Some say they are to mark an old trail, but that is not so. No paleface knows their history. All Indians riding by, even to this day, add a stone to the pile, though few understand why. They do not know they are erecting a monument to Crow warriors killed in the fiercest battle ever fought by Indian tribes.

…"You palefaces know that valley. Your cattle graze there. You go to build camp fires on Pryor Creek and make coffee and then lie down to sleep where all is peace and stillness, without thought of fear. None of you knows of that day three hundred and fifty years ago when hearts beat fast with fear, when the air was loud with shrieks of warriors, when the long grass was stained red with blood of Crow and Sioux and Pawnee and Cheyenne, when the pure waters of the creek were dammed by heaped-up bodies of the dying, staggering there, mad with thirst.

…Some few of Rolling Thunder's braves fell that day under shower of enemy arrows. When he thought that most of the arrows had been spent, he, with those of his men who were left, dashed back across Pryor Creek and past the mouth of the canyon. On he went with his small band, the enemy close at heel, yelling, ready to spring on them with war clubs and scalping knives, riding into the trap set for them.

Suddenly the thick forest of little trees fell as though before a strong wind and from out the canyon, closing in upon the surprised enemy, poured all the hidden Crow warriors. They were still outnumbered three to one, but their horses were fresh and their arrows many and they were fighting for that which was nearest their hearts—home and children.

All through the long day they fought until the air was filled with the whine of flying arrows and shrieks of wounded horses and moans of dying men. Men pulled arrows out of dead bodies to use them over again. They fought hand-to-hand with war clubs and knives. They fought until, as the sun sank down behind the mountains, those of the enemy who were spared went crawling back through the Pass to their camps on Wind River, leaving dead and dying.

Then the victorious Crows killed dying warriors and dying horses, to end their suffering. And they placed bodies in piles—both the enemy and their own people—one at the foot of Red Rock Peak, another farther north along the trail and still others as they fell, here and there across the valley. They placed beside them strips of dried meat to last them on the journey across the Slippery Log, and war clubs, and the bodies of their horses. Then they covered all with mounds of earth and stones. That was over three hundred years ago but the mounds are still there.…

"I, Pretty Eagle, Chief of the Mountain Crows, have told this to my white brother, White Eagle. It is the story of the fiercest battle ever fought between Indian tribes. He will put it into a book for palefaces to read so they may understand why the Absarokees whom you speak of as 'Crows' love their land, the valley of the Echeta Casha Asha, with such a deep love. It was purchased with the blood of brave men. I have spoken."

Foreword

by Arthur H. DeRosier, Jr.

Pioneer Trails West, Don Worcester, editor

Arthur H. DeRosier, Jr. has served as president of Rocky Mountain College since 1987 and is credited with revitalizing the college. He has published an important study of the removal of the Choctaw Indians. He previously served as president of East Tennessee State University and The College of Idaho.

After all other routes are studied and given places of honor in our history and our hearts, there will always remain the Oregon Trail, standing before us with a majesty rivaled only by the mighty Mississippi itself. I know some may disagree and cast their own vote for "most significant trail" to the various Indian Trails of Tears from Georgia and elsewhere to Indian Territory. Or, in the arena where suffering reigns supreme, many nod knowingly and appreciatively when they contemplate the conquest of adversity by Latter-day Saints, who were unwelcome in Illinois and on the bloody trail westward to the Great Salt Lake. I know that the trails followed by Missouri Fur Company trappers were important threads of commerce, bringing forth entrepreneurs and great wealth rivaled only, in enterprise and audacity, by trails bringing miners to California and then inland to Colorado, Idaho, and anywhere else rumors of gold and silver moved adventurers to gamble all on the harsh odds against finding that one great strike. Cowboys and Indians, miners and Mormons, missionaries seeking lost souls and soldiers seeking recalcitrant Indians preferring freedom to reservation life—all, yes all, moved by overland trails waiting to be rediscovered so they can share secrets with those of us eager to learn.

Still, above all the rest, there is the Oregon Trail. I admit partiality to this trail because I can drive less than fifty miles from my home [in Caldwell, Idaho] and touch the deep rutted seams that continue to defy change. I can stand on this southern Idaho ground and hear the sound of wind carrying the laughter of men and women nearing The Dalles in Oregon and the sobs of those burying their own on the prairie or in the side of some mountain through which the Oregon Trail wound. It was a magnificent curved thread from the flatlands around Independence, Missouri, to the awesome beauty of America's most majestic sight—Mt. Hood, Oregon. And it was a long 2,000-mile thread that took all who challenged it through the heat and wind of the Great Plains to the Continental Divide and beyond, offering for relief along the way only a handful of forts where one could refresh and start again or give up.

The wind suggests more than the sound of laughter and crying. It offers, too, the realization that those who laugh and cry, all of whom have a tale to tell about why they left the relative security of a rich but small Indiana farm, or what it's like to get pregnant or give birth along a route that tested the bravest and the strongest, or how adventure and the need to see beyond the next mountain motivates many to taunt danger and to die seeking answers. It's not that the folks on the Oregon Trail were better or braver than others going elsewhere on overland routes (for myriad reasons—even to deliver the mail); rather, it is the majesty of the enterprise and the odds facing all those who gambled that they could court so much potential danger and still reach an unseen goal 2,000 miles away. There were easier things to do than make one's way through Indian country and live to tell about it! How many steps are there in 2,000 miles? How many horses and oxen are needed to make the trip? And what about water, food, clothing, weapons?

Ellen Gordon Fletcher
Diary and Letters, 1866

Journeys to the Land of Gold: Emigrant Diaries from the Bozeman Trail, 1863-1866 Volume Two

edited by Susan Badger Doyle

Susan Badger Doyle is an independent scholar in ethnohistory living in Pendleton, Oregon. She wrote her dissertation on intercultural dynamics in the Bozeman Trail era, 1863-1868. As a writer and consultant she focuses on 19th century American western expansion and U.S.-Indian relations.

Nellie Gordon, a neighbor of the Fletchers, became acquainted with Billy Fletcher and their friendship soon grew into love. In January and February 1866, Billy was seriously ill with typhoid fever for four weeks. During these weeks while Nellie nursed him, he proposed. Nellie had misgivings at first and wrote in her diary on January 22: "He asked me how long it would take me to get ready to go back to the mountains with him. I could not help a sort of shrinking when I thought of going but I love him dearly & know that he loves me too."...Billy and Nellie were married in late March and soon afterward they left New York for Montana....They traveled by railroad and steamboat to Bellevue, Nebraska, Billy Fletcher's home before he had gone to Montana in 1863....

Fletcher's diary and letters are the only known detailed accounts written by a woman while she traveled the Bozeman Trail.

...July 4, Wednesday. The musketoes were very thick last night & troublesome. Waked very early. Started at half-past five, glad to leave that place of sage brush & alkali water. One of the wagons broke an axle but it was soon fixed. Had a good many bad pieces to go over. Steep hills, traveled until about twelve & camped for noon just across a dry creek. There are a few trees & an Eagles nest in the top of a large one. Mr. Reed sent over a nice box of lemonade or rather sugar of lemons prepared for lemonade. Townie brought it to me with Mr. Reed's compliments. Mr. Mills a man who is with Mr. Reed brought us a large piece of cheese & another a nice piece of antilope. The men are all very kind & generous. This is the 4th of July! how little to remind one of this great national anniversary. Passed a long range of rocks which looked like walls which had been built. They extended from 5 to 10 miles. [Note:...sandstone rock-wall feature near East Fork Pryor Creek.] There was a regular gateway & one could easily fancy that some olden city might appear beyond were we to enter the gateway. Camped in a cozy place near a cool spring of water which was very refreshing to us all. I could hardly drink enough.

July 5, Thursday. Started at half-past five. Had bad roads most of the way, though a little way we had nice green grass. Crossed a clear stream of water [Pryor Creek] when some of the men took their gold pans & washed to see what they could find. About two miles beyond this an axle to one of the wagons broke & we had to stay there the remainder of the day. It is a dull dreary looking place, nothing to be seen but bleak looking hills covered with sage brush. The water is very poor, & we all feel tired being warm & some musketoes. Had a shower just at night. Chell found enough gooseberries for tea.

July 6, Friday. Had to wait a while in the morning for the men to finish fixing the wagon, which made it late starting. We came to a very steep place about noon. The road had been over hills but we then came to some of the roughest wildest looking hills we have had to pass over. [They were in the rugged hills on the south side of the Yellowstone, opposite present Billings...] I had been sleeping & Billy waked me to get out & walk. Will & I started out & went over a long ridge of sandy looking rough.

July 8, Sunday. […On this day, they came to the Yellowstone River, went two miles up the bottom, turned south and went ten miles over the bluffs, and came back to the Yellowstone at the mouth of Duck Creek.] It was a lovely morning. Started at half-past six after traveling a couple of miles the road again went up over the bluffs. Found it quite level and pleasant. On the right was a steep bank which overlooked Clark's Fork & Yellowstone rivers. C's Fork [Clarks Fork] empties into the Yellowstone near here. Had a fine view of the snow capped mountains this morning. We could see them for a long distance. Traveled 8 or ten miles & found upon reaching the river [Clarks Fork] that we should be obliged to cross by boats as at the Big Horn. [They were at the Clarks Fork upper crossing, three miles above its mouth.] Some one from the train ahead of us have built some boats & stopped to ferry trains across. We laid over after reaching the river [Clarks Fork]. It is very warm & the musketoes are plenty. Billy has built a smudge all around the tent & the wagons. I tried to find a cool place in the shade but the musketoes drove me away. Mr. Welch went hunting. Killed two antilopes. Townie has been playing cards & everybody seems to have forgotten that it was Gods holy day.

July 9, Monday. Very warm. The men have been at work down at the river [Clarks Fork] all day. I have done quite a large washing & Chell made a large batch of bread. Billy told us that we must be through all by noon in order to cross but we did'nt have to go. Billy made some dumplings for breakfast. They were nice & light. I washed Ella's & my dress & they were dry in a few moments. In the afternoon we had a nice quiet time to sew. I had plenty of mending for Ella & myself & the day passed swiftly away. Several of the wagons have crossed, but we are yet on the wrong side of the river.

July 10, Tuesday. Billy was sick with a terrible toothache, nearly all night. The night was warm & today the heat is oppressive. Our wagons were the first to cross. The boats are not as large nor as good as those at the Big Horn. We couldn't ride across in the wagon box but sat on some boxes in the boats. Had no difficulty in crossing before we crossed the Cooper train came up. The most of them came down to see us. Mrs. C.[ooper], Mrs. Mandeville & [Mrs.] Todd. They seemed very much pleased to see us & had a sad story to tell. Mr. M.[andeville] lost part of his wagon, all of his fruit, tea, coffee, all of his provisions except the flour & bacon. Mrs. M.[andeville] said that two or three hundred D[olla]rs [were lost].

We Pointed Them North:
Recollections of a Cowpuncher

by E. C. "Teddy Blue" Abbott and Helena Huntington Smith

E. C. "Teddy Blue" Abbott embodied the cowboy life of the open range. After migrating to Montana with the cowherds in the 1880s, he settled down on a ranch outside Lewistown with his wife, Mary, a daughter of Granville Stuart. *We Pointed Them North* is the classic account of early ranching culture in the state.

The rest of the cowpunchers couldn't understand why I would quit a good string of horses on the roundup to go with a trail herd. But I wanted to do it because they was going three hundred miles further up north, and that was what appealed to me. It was all new country up there and I wanted to see it, and anyway this other, in Wyoming and southern Montana, was getting settled up. There was ranches every few miles.

I met them at the crossing of Powder River, like I told you, and went on up with them. Ten days later we got to the Yellowstone, which has drowned more cattle and men than any other river on the Texas trail. The Yellowstone doesn't look like much of a river because it is narrow, but it is fast and awful cold, and it has an undercurrent. When we got to the bank, we stopped to loosen our cinches, getting ready to cross, and I took my clothes off. The other men with the outfit said: "What are you taking your clothes off for? Hell, it's nothing but a crick." One man wouldn't even take off his boots. He said: "I'm not agoing to take my boots off to cross no crick." I told them: "You'll think it's the Atlantic Ocean before you've got to the other side."

We crossed at Fort Keogh, which is right next to Miles City, sending the wagons over on the ferry. The danger of swimming rivers is that the cattle will get to milling, and the first thing you know they will start to jump up and ride one another, trying to climb out, and down they will go and you will lose a lot of them. You have to keep them pointed for the opposite bank, which means that in the water each man has to hold his place alongside the herd, just like on the trail.

It was cold, and there was a lot of new ice along the banks, what we call mush ice. When we took the water, I was all right, because I was riding a big Oregon horse named Jesse, that kept his tail right up and wouldn't let the water run over the saddle. But the other men had a tough time. I can see those little Texas horses, with their heads in the air and all the rest of them under the water—because the damn little stinkers will keep reaching for the bottom with their hind feet, so it's all you can do to keep from being drowned off their backs. One man, as soon as that cold water struck his belly, gave a yell and dove off over his horse's head, and he was near drowning. Somebody yelled: "Grab a steer by the tail," and he did, and he never let go until the steer dragged him halfway up the bank, and it took all the skin off his knees.

When we got to the other side they were all sitting on their horses, shivering, with the water running off them, and a fellow said: "That's colder than any ice water I ever drank in Texas." He was a south Texas brush popper who had never been north before. All the way up, after I struck them, he kept asking: "How far is it up no'th?"—as though "up no'th" was a place on the map. I asked him how far he'd ever been up north. He said: "I been no'th clear to San Antone." Then he wanted to know: "Is it cold up no'th?" and I told him: "Colder than you've ever seen it." He said: "Oh, I've seen ice half an inch thick." He was like a lot of those Texas fellows—put him afoot and he didn't know a thing. But he held the right point of that herd all the way from the Guadaloupe River to the mouth of the Musselshell. He was Cow—one of the best cowhands I ever saw.

After we got across the Yellowstone they furnished us a Frenchman named Nado, an old American Fur Company man, to pilot us in. He was supposed to show us where water was and save us a lot of riding. But we'd have been better off without him. He thought water for four horses was water enough for us, with our 150 head of horses and two full herds of better than 2,000 head in each. He'd been over the country with a couple of pack horses, and that was the limit to his ideas. The year before, when I was with the F U F herd, we had another of those old fellows for a pilot, an old army bullwhacker and mule skinner by the name of Buckskin Joe, who had been in that country for years before the cowmen ever got there. We was curious about "up no'th" ourselves, so we was asking him all kinds of questions. "What kind of a climate is it in Montana?" we asked him, and he give the best answer I ever heard. "I'll tell you what kind of a climate it is. You want a buffalo overcoat, a linen duster, and a slicker with you all the time."

The Drive

by Ben Steele

Montana-born **Ben Steele** portrays his native state in a variety of media from oil painting to lithography to pen-and-ink drawings. He has illustrated a number of histories of the Yellowstone area, including *Tracking Billings' Past*. A Professor of Art Emeritus at Montana State University-Billings, he has served as president of the Billings Arts Association, the Montana Institute of the Arts, and the Yellowstone Art Center Board. He and his wife, Shirley, were awarded the 1992 Montana Governor's Award for Distinguished Achievement in the Arts.

The Drive
Ben Steele
pen and ink drawing (1992)
Courtesy of the artist

On Flatwillow Creek: The Story of Montana's N Bar Ranch

by Linda Grosskopf with Rick Newby

Linda Grosskopf grew up on a ranch outside Billings, riding horses, working cows, raking hay and feeding custom combiners, and otherwise learning to work. She currently edits *Agri-News*. The following excerpt comes from her history of Montana's famous N Bar Ranch.

The story of the N Bar begins in 1878 when cattlemen E. S. ("Zeke") and Henry (H. L.) Newman settled in the Nebraska sandhills next to a deep canyon of the Niobrara River near the present-day town of Gordon. Originally from Texas, the Newman brothers, with their N Bar brand, were among the first ranchers to establish a spread in northwestern Nebraska, an area that had belonged to the Sioux Indians until their removal—in 1877-1878—to the Rosebud and Pine Ridge reservations in Dakota Territory. And the Newman brothers were among the first entrepreneurs, as Robert H. Burns has written, "to see the vast potential of the great, grassy plains" for raising cattle.

In 1878, the Newman brothers obtained a government contract to supply the Rosebud and Pine Ridge reservations with fresh beef. To meet the terms of their contract, they ran 10,000 to 15,000 head of cattle on their new Nebraska spread. By 1882, the Newmans' Niobrara Cattle Company was ready to expand northward, and that summer its trailhands drove 12,000 cattle—purchased in the Grande Ronde country of Oregon and branded with the N Bar—into Montana's Powder River Valley. On September 6, 1883, *The Breeder's Gazette* of Chicago reported on the Niobrara Cattle Company's extensive holdings:

"The firm's ranges are now scattered from Montana to Texas. They have two in Wyoming, one on the Powder River and the other on the Tongue River, reaching into Montana; one in Nebraska on the Niobrara; one in the Indian Territory extending down into the Texas Panhandle; and one upon the uplands in far western Texas....The Powder and Tongue ranges will alone support 30,000 head of cattle."

The headquarters for the Newman brothers' Montana range lay south of Miles City, at the juncture of the Little Powder and Big Powder rivers, about eight miles from the present town of Broadus. In 1883, Zeke Newman helped found the Eastern Montana Stockgrowers' Association at Miles City, and in 1884, the Niobrara Cattle Company drove 4,000 head of cattle to the mouth of the Musselshell River, establishing yet another Montana outpost for the N Bar brand. Then, in 1885, disaster struck in Nebraska: a giant prairie fire raced across the Newman brothers' range, scorching it beyond recognition. Left without sufficient grass to winter their Nebraska herds, the Newmans turned northward, moving the rest of the N Bar cattle onto their three Montana ranges.

Barely a year later, the combination of drought, low cattle prices, and one of the worst winters in Montana history would once again spell disaster for the Niobrara Cattle Company. Extraordinarily dry summers in 1885 and 1886 had left the range in poor condition, and there simply was not enough forage for the hundreds of thousands of cattle that crowded Montana's vast prairies. One rancher noted, "There is so much stock now on the public land that we can't cut hay or rather, find any to cut," and in September 1886, the *Rocky Mountain Husbandman* warned, "Beef is low, very low, and prices are tending downward. But for all that, it would be better to sell at a low figure than to endanger the whole herd by having the range overstocked."

Most Montana cattlemen, however, ignored that sage advice, holding on to their herds in hopes that the next year would bring an upsurge in prices. And so, when the winter storms of 1886-1887 unleashed their howling winds, driving snow, and temperatures that plunged to minus 63 degrees Fahrenheit, the range was indeed overstocked, the ordinarily rich prairie grasses were stunted from lack of rain, and there was no hay to be found. "We have had a perfect smashup all through the cattle country," wrote future U.S. president Teddy Roosevelt, and, in Montana alone, some 60 percent of the territory's range cattle—over 360,000 head—lost their lives in the winter's brutal blizzards. Of the 220 separate cattle operations in Montana Territory in 1886, only 120 managed to escape bankruptcy the following year. A typical casualty was the Newman brothers' outfit. In the fall of 1886, the Niobrara Cattle Company had listed assets of over $1 million. By the spring of 1887, the Newmans were worth less than $250,000.

While Zeke and H. L. Newman were losing their cattle to a legendary winter, a legendary Montanan was busy buying up the spread that would soon be known as the N Bar. In the fall of 1885, Helena millionaire Thomas Cruse, who had made his fortune in mining and banking, expanded his portfolio with the purchase of the Montana Sheep Company, which included 2,842 acres on Flatwillow Creek near Grass Range and six bands of sheep totaling 13,779 head. Always a savvy businessman, Cruse took advantage of the low cattle prices following the hard winter of 1886-1887 and, in 1888, bought up the remnants of the Newman brothers' Musselshell herd and the right to use the N Bar brand. No record of the sale has survived, but according to Newman brothers' hand John Sherman McCumsey, the Niobrara Cattle Company branded some 7,000 calves in 1886 and owned another 6,000 miscellaneous heifers and steers. Probably somewhere between 2,000 to 4,000 head of the original N Bar cattle survived the 1886-1887 blizzards and found home on Tommy Cruse's growing spread along Flatwillow Creek.

poetry by Loujincy Polk

Colorado-born **Loujincy Polk,** née Lula Cobb Jones, moved to Forsyth with her family in 1905. She worked for the *Yellowstone News,* organized the Montana Presswomen's Association, and published many poems before her death in 1976.

The Devil on Barnett Creek

Windy Bill had rode the range
Since the summer of '83;
He worked for the XIT one year
An' stood night guard with me;

I give him the name of Windy Bill
From a yarn he told one night,
When we had the cattle all bedded down
An' the stars was shinin' bright.

An' the moon looked jist like a silver ball
Hangin' in the sky,
When all at once, Bill grabbed his gun
An' I asked him to tell me why

He had to act like a locoed fool
When ever'thing was quiet;
Bill said: "Yes, Pard, I'll tell you why,
I saw the devil one night.

"A bunch of us fellers was settin' up
With a corpse one pitch black night,
On Barnett Creek, when down the road
We saw a dim blue light.

"We thought some neighbor was comin' up
To join the vigilance,
When Tom McClair said, 'Boys, I'll swear
That feller stepped over the fence.'

"That fence was four wires high, my friend,
An' tight as a fiddle string;
We thought Tom lied, an' some of the boys
Began to snicker and grin.

"Tom turned around with a frightened stare
We'd never seen before.
Jest then the Devil with his little blue light
Walked in at the cabin door.

"He stepped right up to the wooden bench
Where the dead man's body lay,
An' lifted it up under one arm
An' turned an' walked away.

"Us guys was paralyzed for sure,
Brave fellers—every one,
Jest set like dummies on our seats
An' never teched a gun.

"They say the feller that died that day
Was wicked as he could be;
They say he cussed Almighty God
Ever' time he went on a spree;

"An' when he was sober he cussed his friend,
He cussed the wind an' the sun;
He cussed his faithful saddle-hoss
An' beat him with his gun;

"I guess he belonged to the Devil all right,
But I ain't forgot that night;
An' the reason I grabbed my gun jest now,
Was - - - I thought I saw - - - a dim blue light."

The *Josephine*—War Horse and River Queen, Freight Hauler and Servant to the Military

by John Willard

John Willard was born in a ranch house on the Rocky Mountain Front near Augusta. He worked as a political reporter for several Montana newspapers and provided outdoor writing for several western journals. For the last thirty years he has edited *Hoofprints from the Yellowstone,* devoted to the history of the Yellowstone Valley.

Don Powers was an authority on steamboats in our region. He built the model of the *Josephine* and donated it to Parmly Billings Library.

From the start the majestic *Josephine* was a military symbol. Built in 1873 at Freedom, Pennsylvania, it was named for the daughter of Colonel David S. Stanley, who that same year commanded the expedition up the Yellowstone River to guard surveyors for the westward-advancing Northern Pacific Railroad. It had a length of 178 feet, was 31 feet wide and had a four-

Scale model of the *Josephine*
Don Powers
Parmly Billings Library Montana Room
photo courtesy Don Miller

foot, six-inch depth of hold. Power came from two boilers fueled by river-side cottonwood.

Stanley also commanded his 22nd infantry on the 1873 expedition, and General George Armstrong Custer commanded the 7th cavalry.

Apparently the *Josephine*, part of the Coulson fleet of river boats, was the exception to Coulson's naming its boats with seven letter titles—*Rosebud, Far West, Key West, Western, Montana, Wyoming, Dakotah* as examples. Its maiden voyage was a military duty, carrying supplies for the 1873 expedi-tion, its principal destination being Stanley's Stockade, just above the pres-ent site of Glendive, Montana. Its captain was John Todd, who navigated it safely to the stockade in June of that year....

In 1874 the *Josephine* made its first visit to Fort Benton on the Missouri, goal of all river traffic. During its 34 years of service the *Josephine* made 40 trips to this head of navigation on the Missouri in central Montana, served the U. S. Corps of Engineers, and even ran several western Canadian rivers.

In 1875 the *Josephine* was back in military service. It left Yankton, South Dakota, May 19 with the noted Grant Marsh as captain, and with other officers and a crew of 37. Its first stop was at Fort Abraham Lincoln to pick up famed scout Lonesome Charlie Reynolds, then across the river to Bismarck to board Lieutenant Colonels James W. Forsyth and F. D. Grant. Orders were to cut for a general reconnaissance of the Yellowstone, which the *Josephine* entered May 26. To be examined thoroughly for possible military use were any streams flowing from the Black Hills, Tongue River, Big Horn and the Rosebud. Also along for scientific observation were scientists from the Smithsonian Institution.

The *Josephine* experienced good navigation until about 27 miles above the mouth of the Big Horn where it struck a maze of islands and rough water. About two miles west of present Billings, Forsyth decided there was no point in going further and the officers then concluded the Big Horn mouth was a practical head of navigation on the Yellowstone. Establishment later of Terry's Landing at that point confirmed their judgment.

En route the expedition stopped at Pompeys Pillar to look at Captain William Clark's signature carved June 25, 1806, on the big sandstone. Not to be outdone, Captain Grant Marsh inscribed "*Josephine*, June 3, 1875" on the rock. He then returned to the boat, selected an American flag given to the *Josephine* at her launching, and planted it on the Pillar. He kept on the boat a second flag given to him by Colonel Stanley in honor of his daugh-ter. The *Josephine* thus set a record for navigation above Billings on the Yellowstone. In 1876 the *Josephine* again was called for military duty, this time to resupply and patrol for the army in the Sioux-Cheyenne campaign in which Custer was defeated on the Little Big Horn. She had served her country well and continued to do so until she struck an ice gorge and sank in 1907, the end of a gracious lady.

Junction City—
Haven of Bullwhackers, Trappers and
Soldiers, Witnessed Many Dramatic Episodes
by W. H. Banfill

William Banfill was born in Illinois in 1887. He came to Montana as a homesteader and taught school in Stillwater County and Lodge Grass. Transforming his love of literature into a journalism career, he worked as a reporter at *The Billings Gazette* until his death in 1933.

Hunters, Trappers Stay. Fort Pease Passes

After the abandonment of Fort Pease some of the trappers and hunters stayed on in the vicinity. The first permanent settler in Pease bottom was John C. Guy of Bozeman, an early sheriff of Gallatin county, who took up a ranch of 160 acres in the fall of 1876 or early 1877. About the same time a trapper for Durfee and Peck, Missouri River fur traders, had a cabin near the present Custer, Mr. Guy established a steamboat landing and woodyard on the river near the ranch. He also had a general mercantile store, a stage station, saloon and postoffice called Eschetah, the Crow word for horse. As late as 1882 the steamboat *F. I. Bachellor* took on wood there, according to Mrs. M. I. Draper of Fort Pease ranch, whose first husband was Capt. C. P. Woolfolk, the boat's captain.

How Junction City stole the postoffice bodily from Eschetah and then was forced to bring it back is an incident of early day history which Mrs. Draper relates. The enterprising citizens of Junction City secured the appointment of Joe Allen as postmaster, but he did not have the necessary supplies and furniture for a postoffice. With the aid of T. Wiley King, the stage driver, the Eschetah postoffice was loaded on the stage while Guy was away, and it was taken into Junction.

When Guy discovered the loss of his postoffice, he went to Junction City and laid before his enterprising competitors the likely consequences of the theft of a United States postoffice. He told them that there was a deputy marshal across the river at Custer station and that he intended to report the matter to him. The Junction citizens, impressed with his version of their offense, loaded up the postoffice again and returned it to him.

...A ledger and daybook of the Paul McCormick & Co., kept in 1878 and 1879, was in the possession of Charles Spear of this city until his death a few years ago. Mr. Spear, who was related by marriage to Mr. McCormick, was in the store for several years and in the later days of Junction the firm of Donovan & Spear, of Billings, bought the business.

Accounts in the book contain many names well known in frontier history: "Yellowstone" Kelly; George Herendeen, scout with Reno; Tom Irvine and "Jack" Johnson, early Custer sheriffs; Major Logan; Lucius J. Whitney, first postmaster at Billings; Hoskins & McGirl, of Huntley; Scout John Smith, who ran a saloon at Junction and later at Billings; P.W. McAdow & Bros., of Coulson; George W. Miles; W.A. Burleigh & Co., at Miles City; and Broadwater, Hubbell & Co., the famous Diamond R freighting outfit.

Some of the names of customers reflected the pioneer custom of not inquiring too closely as to a man's name. There was Antelope Charley, Jeff Davis, Red Siwash, Flick, California Rogers, Miss Nellie, Montana Jim, Missouri Jim, Bismarck, Cayuse George, Gros Ventre Johnny, and Wipple, hunter; Andy, driver; Van, drum major, Fifth infantry; Frank, barkeeper; and Jessup, wolfer.

Prices listed are interesting. Thus six pounds of sugar cost $2; a gallon of coal oil, $2; can of fresh oysters, $1.50; pound of tea, $2; collar button, $1; box of figs, $1; half sack of flour, $5; three pounds of onions, 90 cents; 22 pounds of potatoes, $3.30; four pounds of butter, $2; box of yeast powder, 50 cents; plug of Cable Twist, 75 cents; package of Lone Jack, 25 cents; bottle of Jamaica ginger, 75 cents; quart of port or sherry, $1.50; four bottles of champagne, $5; pair of boots, $8; pair of overalls, $2; eight yards of denim, $2.80; suit of underclothes, $2.50; shawl, $14.50.

There were about 20 permanent families in Junction, according to Mrs. Frank McCormick who came there as a bride about 50 years ago. Mr. McCormick, who was a brother of Paul McCormick, was engaged in the stock business and in other projects at Junction and on the Crow reservation where he had important contracts at Fort Custer. He was for some time deputy sheriff at the Junction.

Coulson

Shallow Diggin's: Tales from Montana's Ghost Towns

by Jean Davis

Jean Davis, born in Fargo, North Dakota, in 1909, homesteaded with her family in Saskatchewan. She served as librarian at the University of Montana-Missoula and Eastern Montana College (now Montana State University-Billings) before her retirement in 1972.

As the railroad moved west, it, too, spawned towns across the state that were to live and die with the coming and going of men working on the rails.

Bud McAdow stood on the banks of the Yellowstone (in the early fall of 1877) and, gazing for miles across the Clarke's Fork bottom, saw, like Jacob of old, that it was good. And like Jacob, he had a vision; the railroad, then at Bismarck, Dakota, would bring to the spot a city; hundreds of farmers would be drawn thither, now that the Sioux no longer menaced the settler; it would become a cattle center; the hub of a vast area potentially rich. Perry W. McAdow was not an illusionist nor a dreamer; he was a practical Missourian who had good horse sense. He at once acquired a large tract of land at the lower end of the bottom and built a store, stocking it with goods hauled by team from Bozeman or the nearest landing place of the river steamers; for boats, before the advent of the railroad, came up as far as Junction City, at the mouth of the Rosebud, one, the *Josephine*, reaching a point nearly opposite to where Billings now stands.

The trading point was named Coulson, presumably in honor of one of the steamboat captains, and by 1881, had become a place of some importance, being provided with a postoffice, an eating station for the overland stage, a saloon, a gambling hall, a livery stable, a blacksmith shop and was the center of railroad grading operations. Coulson was about to occupy a place on the map.

The winter of 1881 brought the adventurous pioneer by all manner of means, stage coach, wagon train, on horseback and on foot. It became apparent that at this point must arise one of the great centers, a "Denver of the North." The winter was cold, bitterly cold, for those who had to abide in the hastily built shacks, floored and covered with dirt. Those there were who were privileged to sleep in McAdow's store. Not infrequently a Crow Indian, high in his council, became an occupant of these quarters, announcing the duration of his stay by the height in which he hung his headgear on the wall....

In this pleasant company, partaking of Bud's open hospitality, provided he furnish his own blankets, was Muggins Taylor, a soldier of fortune, who, but a short time previously had been in the employ of the government as a 'Trailer' or scout. It was he who took the message of Custer's Massacre to the wires and gave the *New York Herald* readers an account of this memorable tragedy....

"Liver Eating" Johnston was another member of Coulson society. For a time he held the office of deputy sheriff, and while he had no jail in which to incarcerate his prisoners, this was not necessary. For when 'Liver Eating' finally came to the conclusion that it was time to act, he acted so thoroughly and so effectively that the wrong-doer was more in need of a hospital than a lockup.... [A.K. Yerkes in the *Hardin Tribune,* April 16, 1920]

Next to McAdow, John Alderson was considered Coulson's leading citizen. With his wife and child he had arrived in Coulson and staked out his acres on a beautiful bend of the Yellowstone. Unfortunately another pioneer, Dave Currier, chose the same land and a bitter feud developed.

Currier, seeking to get the law on his side, boarded the stage for Bozeman, the nearest recording office; Alderson, getting wind of this, saddled his fastest horse and made a record-breaking trip to Bozeman beating his opponent's time by several hours.

Currier, still unwilling to cede the land, took justice into his own hands, and a few days later, while Alderson was perched atop the ridge pole of his ice house, Currier, gun in hand, sought to slip up on him. However, Mrs. Alderson saw the little drama, hurriedly passed a rifle up to her husband, who from his superior position, settled the dispute once and for all.

After establishing himself, Alderson made far-sighted plans for the growth of his city. He erected a dance hall and imported seductive ladies from the East. He promoted saloons and other business to attract the miners, freighters, and cowboys. Soon wolfers and buffalo hunters were making Coulson their headquarters. In 1880 one fur dealer shipped 32,000 buffalo hides and 12,000 robes worth $164,000 down the Yellowstone.

Coulson was on the path of the growing cattle industry, and cowboys, horse thieves, and speculators crowded her busy streets.

> Coulson...had a main street of creditable length, and log houses for the families were on every hand. It had a newspaper, lawyers, doctors, real estate agents, and all that go to make up a city. The leading citizens, voicing the sentiments of the principal land owners, McAdow and Alderson, were unalterably of the opinion that no power on earth could cheat Coulson of its ultimate greatness. [A.K. Yerkes in the *Hardin Tribune,* April 16, 1920]

The *Coulson Post* shared the optimism:

> With every prospect of the early building by the Northern Pacific of a principal feeder to Fort Benton from this point, the commencement of the track laying season and the opening of the boating season, the presence of a vast amount of lumber, Coulson can truthfully be said to have the most glorious future of any Yellowstone City.

> But almost within sight of this hustle and bustle, men set to work to lay out another city and what they did to Coulson was a-plenty. When June came and the railroad had left Miles City on its way to the coast, Heman Clark, a townsite boomer, appeared and at once and forever stilled the pulsating hope and life of Coulson. He had builded better than the backers of Coulson knew. For he had gone to headquarters, secured the sanction and land of the railroad and by modern means of advertising and boosting stirred the whole western country with its promises and predictions. Lots were sold in Chicago, Duluth, St. Paul and Minneapolis, from the map, and then began the trek to the land of promise. People came from every direction and by all manner of conveyance, some even walking from the end of the track miles away. When the townsite was opened to sale at the town of Billings, then but the headquarters of the railroad engineers, people stood in line to get their first payment accepted. [A.K. Yerkes in the *Hardin Tribune*, April 16, 1920]

> …After the establishment of Billings, activity was sporadic in Coulson. Its days were extended somewhat by the establishment there of a brewery by William Boots and George Ash of Billings. As part of Billings' promotional scheme a streetcar service had been established between the new town and Coulson. This service was conducted by two gaily painted streetcars shipped in from Minneapolis and pulled over their rails by a team of lively cayuses.

> …If the car derailed, the passengers helped get it back on the track or if this was too much of a task, teams were brought out to hoist it back while the passengers, if they were in a hurry, continued on foot, as the entire length of the line from Minnesota avenue to McAdow's store at Coulson was scarcely two miles. [W.H. Banfill in the *Hardin Tribune*, July 19, 1929]

Since the streetcar ride to Coulson was a popular pastime and since water had to be hauled to Billings but not to Coulson, Boots and Ash decided to locate their brewery (Boots Billings Beer) in Coulson.

> A beer garden was conducted in connection with the brewery and the owners and the street-car proprietors struck upon a happy idea for bolstering up the diminishing travel to Coulson. A round

trip ticket from Billings to Coulson was provided which bore a stub good for one schooner of beer when presented at the brewery. As the brewers correctly reasoned, one schooner on a hot day would not be enough for the average man and many more purchases would follow.

During the days of the brewery, Coulson also provided drilling grounds for Webbs' guards, an organization of the state militia that flourished for a few years. The brewery was usually visited after the drill period. There was also an early day sportsmen's association which had its target range near Coulson. A keg of beer from the brewery was an important part of the day's program. [W.H. Banfill in the *Hardin Tribune*, July 19, 1929]

Laurel and Coulson
by Louis Allard, M.D.

Laurel's Story: A Montana Heritage
by Elsie P. Johnston

Louis Allard, son of a pioneer ranchman and stockman, was born between Laurel and Park City in 1887. He received his medical degree from Rush Medical College in Chicago. He became a pioneer orthopedic surgeon in Billings and was active in many professional and civic organizations in the region.

Elsie P. Johnston was born on a Fromberg homestead in 1902. After receiving her teaching certificates, she taught in a one-room schoolhouse and in Wyola. Upon marrying Paul Johnston, she settled in Laurel, where she raised her family, participated actively in the community, and composed her history of that town.

Laurel

Old Laurel was situated on the south side of the railroad track, about one half mile west of the limits of present day Laurel. It began when the post office was established in the railroad depot. In its heyday, old Laurel boasted of two saloons, a general store built by Mr. Rose, and shortly afterward sold to Mr. J. W. Gardner, who was referred to as "Shoestring Gardner," because the business was started with very little money. There was also a log blacksmith shop run by Phil Hohmann, who also had a two room log cabin to house his wife and four children. The Fentons had a small frame store building not far from Mrs. Malcolm's Hotel, and the Malcolm Hall was where the community dances were held. Jim Bundy established a livery stable after he abandoned his ferry which was immediately west of the railroad bridge of the Red Lodge branch. The only house north of the tracks was a small rooming house, run by a Mrs. Miles, which had been converted from a general store and residence following the death of Mr. Miles. In 1902, the railroad moved its depot to the present location, and the new Laurel was started. Several of the frame buildings such as the Malcolm Hotel, and the Malcolm Hall were moved to new Laurel. I can well remember old Mrs. Malcolm sitting in her rocking chair on the front porch knitting during the moving process. The hotel had been jacked up on heavy timbers and pulled by rolling these timbers over round logs, traction being furnished by a winch and a team of horses.

When the Northern Pacific Railroad went through, numerous section houses and depots conveniently distanced from each other were established and named. Most of the small towns were formed from this nucleus, and in many instances the original names were changed. For instance, Columbus was first called Stillwater, and later changed to Columbus, because of the confusion in the mail between Stillwater, Montana, and Stillwater, Minnesota. Park City was first known as Rimrock, the name being changed to Park City soon after a colony of settlers from Beloit, Wisconsin, colonized the Park City area. They planted trees in the town and established a small tree park. For a time the little town flourished, reaching a population of two hundred. It then stabilized; in fact, it has grown very little since. Park City like all the other small towns along the railroad had its usual component of small general stores, a meeting hall, and an abundance of saloons.

My father arrived at the old town of Coulson in the spring of 1880, along with a freight outfit that had left the rail head somewhere between Fargo and Terry, working his way for the privilege of being within the security of numbers. I do not know if they forded the Yellowstone or whether there was a ferry to accommodate the western flow of traffic. Apparently the outfit carried essential supplies to Coulson, Bozeman, and Virginia City. Father had come west for the definite purpose of establishing a home in what he considered a land of opportunity. He intended to take his time finding a suitable location as a means of conserving his meager financial resources in a land where prices for everything were necessarily high. He secured a job with McAdow's, a local mercantile trader, who had a vegetable plot irrigated from a private ditch just above the bend of the river south of Laurel. He later worked for the Newmans, who raised grain crops and hay on the river bank south of the present Newman School. Newman also supplied wild meat brought in by the wagon load as a result of short hunting excursions into nearby territory.

Coulson

Coulson, a town considered as a source of supply, was a rip-roaring community of tents and log houses with saloons aplenty! Being the only settlement of permanence on the Yellowstone Trail between Mandan on the east and Bozeman on the west, Coulson was the rendezvous for trappers, prospectors going west, and migrating cow outfits seeking suitable locations. Also there were freighters who stopped off to deliver their goods, rest their teams, and make repairs. Deprived by their occupation of communication with their fellow men, they were inclined to celebrate. Whisky of a sort commonly referred to as "Rot Gut," "P'ison," or "Fire Water," was plentiful. Gamblers took advantage of a natural desire innate in the human animal to risk his all in the hope of quick wealth, particularly under the stimulation of a few alcoholic drinks. Drunken brawls naturally accompanied this continuous process of riotous celebration. People were killed and little was done about it on this "Fringe" of civilization. Short trials in accordance with frontier procedure, without legal direction, always resulted in acquittal on the basis of self defense. Few were ever hanged for murder though several left the vicinity in a hurry. The victim was buried as he was, without benefit of clergy or undertaker. In a few short years, some thirty victims of violent death died with their boots on. They were laid away and soon forgotten. Boot Hill Cemetery will forever remain as the only permanent memento of old Coulson town.

Incidentally, with the coming of the railroad, a new town site called Billings was established. In an effort to postpone the demise of Coulson, a horse-drawn street-car line was established. Passengers to Coulson received a free drink of beer along with their purchase of a street car fare.

Newman School

Cornerstones of Knowledge

by J. Brock Lee

A Wyoming native, **Joyce Brock Lee** has lived in the Billings area for the past 35 years. From an early age, Joyce exhibited interest in drawing and painting. She has been a professional artist for nearly 20 years. Lee lives with her husband, Charles, and two children on the family farm/ranch south of Billings.

[In the year 1878] a small colony of ranchers settled along the river above Coulson; this area became known as the Newman settlement. The group consisted of the family of O. N. Newman and several other settlers, some of whom had come to the area with the Newmans. They all agreed it was best to stay together due to the Indians that roamed the valley and nearby hills. The settlement seems to have had a good relationship with the Indians as the Newman ranch often became their camping ground. However, one can imagine what went through the minds of the men and women when the Indians were near. Stories of the Custer battle [1876] and other recent raids along the river which resulted in death must have been fresh in their memories.

Even the cabin that was to become the first school for the settlers' children had been vacated due to its occupant's conflict with the Indians. An early-day trapper had built the cabin along the river but was "escorted" by the Indians from the area after some misdealings with them. The cabin was situated on the land adjacent to the Newman settlement. When it was decided to start a school, this structure was the likely choice since buildings were hard to come by at that time.

Capable teachers were even more scarce. A man by the name of N. B. Givens, who had a ranch in the area, volunteered to be the teacher since he claimed to have received some education in the East. Thus, the first attempts at education in the area began in the spring of 1879. Mr. Givens' position as a teacher lasted only a few months; his duties on his ranch forced him to resign. A new teacher was needed.

Several entries [in Mr. Newman's diary] refer to fixing the school and attending school meetings at Coulson. On October 2, 1879, Mr. Newman writes, "Went to Young's Point listing school children." Young's Point was a small settlement above present-day Park City and also the area where a family named Alling had settled. It is not known how Mr. Newman learned about Miss Flora Amna Alling who had had some previous teaching experience in Kansas, but on November 2 his diary tells us, "Miss Alling came to commence school." Thus, she became the first hired teacher, receiving $35 a month.

Over fifty years later, in *The Billings Gazette*, February 18, 1934, the former teacher told about this first school:

> I had 15 pupils to start with. The room was rather dark and there was a fireplace in the corner which was poorly ventilated and filled the room with smoke. . .I used to have to open the door at intervals to let the smoke out even on the coldest days in winter.
>
> The benches were made of cottonwood logs with sticks for legs and there were no desks. We sent to Bozeman for all the books and

there were no blackboards, every pupil using a slate and sponge. Each child was required to buy his own books....

Most of the children rode horseback to school and in the winter would leave the horses in the barns on the ranch. Occasionally, the boys would see a flock of mountain sheep across the river and would play "hookey" to go hunting after them....

The year 1883 was eventful, including several important beginnings: Yellowstone County was formed from the larger Custer County; new school districts were established, making the area encompassing the Newman land into School District #3; and Miss Alling married Ed Newman, one of Mr. Newman's sons. In the same year Ed Newman bought the land where the first log school was located and built a cabin nearby. This is where Ed and Flora raised their family.

Ghost Towns of the Montana Prairie
by Don Baker

Don Baker, a well-known area historian, has written three books describing eastern Montana and a pamphlet-sized celebration of Montana's centennial, *Montana Trivia.*

Railroads: The Northern Pacific

The Northern Pacific had a tortured beginning. Raising money for its construction was difficult beyond description because of factors outside the control of the original investors. A scandal centered around the Credit Mobilier involving the construction of the Union Pacific Railroad, creating a distrust of railroad promoters in general, as well as the political figures who benefited from involvement with railroads. Even the Jay Cooke organization, which succeeded in raising money on behalf of the Union during the Civil War, failed, and the construction of the Northern Pacific terminated at Bismarck, North Dakota, in 1873. Frederick Billings then assumed the construction from Mandan (across the Missouri River from Bismarck) west, completing the Northern Pacific line through Montana in 1883.

The Northern Pacific followed as closely as it could a water level route through Montana, laying track along the Missouri and Yellowstone until it crossed the Continental Divide west of Helena, where it then followed the Clark Fork of the Columbia River into Idaho.

This development benefited the few livestock interests who were already grazing sheep, horses and beef cattle on the knee high grasses of eastern Montana. Squatters took up homesteads on the creek and river bottoms because of the availability of water. Many of these settlers arrived with the longhorn cattle drives that originated in Texas during the previous ten years. The presence of a railroad allowed the livestock industry to graze their animals year around.

The winter of 1886-1887 reduced the census of beef cattle, with losses measuring up to ninety percent in some locations. Montana was no longer considered prime beef cattle country by British and east coast investors and syndicates.

Despite that setback, the Northern Pacific continued to expand settlement promotions and built numerous branch lines. One such line was built from Glendive, a division point, to Brockway via Circle. In time it became known as the CB&Q: Circle, Brockway and Quit. The original plan called for this branch to include the town of Jordan. However, several factors, including competition for services, negated the possibility of this expansion.

Another branch line was built to the rich coal fields south of Forsyth, another division point. Colstrip was a company town, where hundreds of equipment operators stripped coal for the railroads' own use, and for sale. A branch was also built from Laurel to Red Lodge. Coal was abundant in the foothills of Carbon County and a growing population produced a short line passenger service. Livingston, another division point, was also the transfer point for the branch that terminated in Gardner at the north entrance to Yellowstone Park. The resulting tourism traffic was a boost to the Northern Pacific because profits also came from the various coal fields at Aldridge and several coal camps between Bozeman and Livingston.

Junction (and the Musselshell Trail)

Close to the confluence of the Big Horn and Yellowstone Rivers, approximately across the Yellowstone from present-day Custer, a community appropriately named Junction thrived during the brief period of river commerce from about 1820 to 1880.

Manuel Lisa first established a trading post called Fort Manuel Lisa at this location where trappers exchanged the product of their efforts for cash, liquor, tobacco or clothing.

Junction succeeded Fort Manuel Lisa when river boat commerce began during the 1820s and it managed to survive for a brief period after river traffic ended with the construction of the Northern Pacific Railroad.

During that period though, Junction was the port of embarkation for goods that were freighted to Fort Maginnis, and during 1907 and 1908 it played a role in the delivery of supplies for the construction of the Milwaukee Railway.

The mission of Fort Maginnis was two fold: to protect the miners at Maiden and Gilt Edge, and to provide manpower for the growing livestock industry to points east of Grass Range and south of the Missouri River. Livestock rustling was endemic at the time and there seemed to be no end to authors of running brands.

The trail ran through the hills north of the Yellowstone River to Musselshell, a growing community. It then proceeded north following creek beds, including Flatwillow Creek, to Grass Range and thence to Fort Maginnis.

Nothing remains of Junction, though two photographs of the town at the Billings Public Library provide some sense of what the town looked like.

Coulson, the river town that preceded Billings, suffered the same fate but for a different reason. The Northern Pacific Railroad built about a mile north of Coulson, creating Billings, destined to become "the Magic City" because of its rapid growth.

Coulson was the furthest point west on the Yellowstone and both the *Yellowstone* and the *Josephine* were steamers that terminated there. The steel rails, completed in 1883, finished Coulson.

Reminiscences of a Home Missionary
1882-1883

by the Rev. Benjamin Shuart, compiled in the 1930s

First Congregational United Church of Christ: Our First Hundred Years 1882-1982

> Born circa 1850, **Benjamin Shuart** arrived in the new town of Billings in 1882, a few months before the railroad. He organized the first church in town. He also owned Hesper Farm, which he later sold to pioneering agriculturalist, I. D. O'Donnell.
>
> **The First Congregational U.C.C.,** the first church in Billings and still on the same corner of North 27th Street and 3rd Avenue North, was organized by Benjamin Shuart in 1882. It is one of two entities from earliest Billings remaining in the same location, with the same product and pretty much the same name.

On the 9th of April, 1882, I took the train on the Northern Pacific Railroad at Minneapolis, Minnesota, bearing a commission from the American Missionary Association of New York City to proceed to Billings Territory of Montana, there to establish a Congregational Church. As the terminus of the Northern Pacific Railroad, at that time under construction, was at Miles City, about one hundred and sixty miles east of my destination, it was necessary that I should provide myself with a conveyance with which to complete my journey from that place to Billings.

I therefore arranged for the transportation of my horse and buggy to Miles City by rail. I was required to ride in the car with my pony. A car was assigned to me, one end of which was loaded with machinery. Into the vacant end of this car I loaded my pony, buggy, a bale or two of hay, a box containing some books and wearing apparel, and a small box of provisions. For a bed, I suspended a hammock diagonally across the car above the machinery. For five days and five nights, we were trundled along over the ill-ballasted rails before reaching Miles City. We were now in the famous Yellowstone Valley—having left the Missouri River far to the eastward.

On the morning following my arrival at Miles City, I resumed my journey but now with my horse and buggy. I had anticipated an easy drive up the valley of the Yellowstone, assuming that the road lay along the river. It proved, however, that for a large part of the way to Billings the river skirt-ed the bluffs so close that the road was forced to the highlands; where, at intervals, it was intersected at right angles by small canyons which broke through the bluffs to the river.

The crossing of these canyons was difficult and at times somewhat dangerous. The road seemed to be a very old one and to have been travelled but little; and where it was very rocky the builders had undertaken merely to render it passable apparently with little regard to safety. In crossing one of these canyons I thought I was about to be "held-up." I had, with difficulty, made the diagonal descent along one of its sides into the bottom of the canyon, and had started on the ascent up the opposite side, when I was startled by a voice behind me. Checking my pony and looking back, I saw a man running after me and calling me to stop. When he came up, he angri-ly inquired if I had not seen a little sign, away back, notifying me that the road over which I had come was a toll road. I assured him that I had not. He then explained that the road by which I descended into the canyon had been practically impassable to vehicles until he, at the cost of much time and hard labor, had rendered it passable; and that being true, he thought he had the right to collect toll of those who reaped the benefit of his labor. I agreed with him, and ungrudgingly paid him the one dollar which he charged notwith-standing the fact that, in making the descent, I had escaped by a hair's breadth being overturned and spilled onto the rocks.

My faithful pony proved equal to the task of surmounting all the diffi-culties encountered on the journey and on the afternoon of the fourth day from Miles City, as we were travelling westward across a low tableland bordering the Yellowstone River, my eyes were gladdened by the sight in the distance of a large group of tents glistening in the beautiful May sunlight, situated in the valley below, which I knew must be Billings. A little further on, the tableland came to an abrupt terminus and broke down, steeply, to the level of the valley. At this point the road turned sharply to the left and continued on to a group of log buildings beside the river about a half mile distant which, from descriptions I had received, I recognized as the old trading post known as Coulson. Following the road into Coulson, I drew up before a small log building which bore the sign "Hotel" to make an inquiry. A man of about fifty years of age, having but one arm, and in his shirt sleeves, appeared promptly at the door and saluting me cheerfully, said, "Howdy, stranger, you are just in time, Sir; get right down and come in— dinner is all ready. Here, John, take the gentleman's horse and give it a good feed of oats. Get right down, Sir, and come in—dinner is all ready." I replied, "No, I thank you; I have not yet reached my destination. I have stopped merely to inquire the most direct road to Billings." "Billings," he exclaimed derisively, "Billings ain't no place for you to go to; here's where the town is goin' to be. Get right down and come in, Sir. Dinner is all ready." I said, "No, I do not wish to stop until I shall have reached my destination, which is Billings." During this brief colloquy he had evidently been subconsciously speculating as to what my business in that country might be. A conspicuous white tarpaulin which I had stretched over the box of books and clothing in the back part of my buggy to protect it from the sun and rain probably suggested the clue. Seeing that, he could not persuade me to stop for dinner, as I was about to proceed, he inquired with a confident air, "When you going to show?"

"Show what?" I asked.

"Why, when you going to show?"

"Show what?" I repeated.

"Why, ain't you got a show?"

"No, I am not a showman."

"What then, an engineer?"

"No, I am not an engineer."

"A doctor?"

"No, I am not a doctor."

"A lawyer?"

"No, I am not a lawyer."

"Well, then, what might ye be?"

With as much gravity as I could summon, I replied, "I am a home missionary, and have been sent out here by the American Missionary Society of New York City to start a Congregational Church in Billings." His countenance darkened. Pausing for a moment, he descended from the little porch on which he was standing, and with his gaze fixed upon the ground as though he was trying to think what he could say that would adequately express his sentiments respecting churches, he slowly walked around the rear of my buggy, and continued on until he had also walked around in front of my pony and was facing me; when he suddenly raised his head, and looking me straight in the eyes, he extended his arm and shaking his index finger at me, he said sternly, "Young man, you'll starve to death there—they won't give you anything to eat." Pointing to a range of snow-clad mountains on the western horizon, he said: "D'ye see them mountains yonder?" "Yes, I see them." "Well, now, Sir, you take my advice as a friend, and move on, and keep movin' till you've crossed them mountains and on the other side you will find a little valley called the Bitter Root Valley [Bozeman Valley]. It is settled with young married folks from Missouri; and they're your sort; and they'll probably take you in and give you somethin' to eat. But Sir, you'll S-T-A-R-V-E to D-E-A-T-H here!"

At the time of my arrival at Billings the only completed wooden building in sight was the "Headquarters" of the engineering force engaged in construction of the road bed of the Northern Pacific Railroad. Besides this, there were a few very small unfinished buildings, constructed entirely of rough lumber apparently to meet present necessities. The fact was that, until the N. P. Railroad was completed to Billings, so that lumber could be shipped from the east, the town was very seriously handicapped by lack of lumber with which to build; the only supply available being the product of a small portable sawmill located in the mountains about forty miles distant; the quality of which was very poor. Aside from the occupants of this headquarters building, the population already on the ground apparently was housed entirely in tents.

Not having brought any tent with me, my first problem was to provide for my personal bed and board. This problem was speedily solved as to meals by Col. Clough, head of the engineering department, who kindly extended to me the hospitality of the Headquarters cuisine until I should get settled; and in respect to bed, by one of the engineers, who offered to share his bed with me. His bed proved to be in a little shack which he had built on the open prairie, two miles from the town, to enable him to "hold down" a homestead filing which he had placed on the land. As it turned out, this little shack was to be my abode until the following month of August, when I returned to Minneapolis for my family.

I will stop at this point long enough to state that the only furniture which this shack contained, besides the bed, was one inverted empty nail keg and that I wrote more than one sermon with this keg for my revolving armchair and my knees for a desk, to the inspiring accompaniment of the larks as they disported themselves in the bright June-day sunlight, on the roof over my head, and headed forth their sweet notes as though their little hearts would burst with the very joy of being alive.

As for myself, I found a farmer about a mile distant, who could supply me with milk; to which I added such other food, as I could purchase, that did not require cooking and boarded myself.

Now, let not the reader get the impression that I regard this trifling experience of temporary inconvenience, which at the time I thoroughly enjoyed because of its novelty, as entitling me to a place on the Honor Roll of that noble and to be envied company of Home Missionaries, who, in the past were, and today are called upon to endure real hardships for Christ's sake.

At this early stage in the growth of Billings the gambler, the dispensers of strong drink and women of the "red light" were numerously represented in Billings and plied their several occupations, brazenly and without [shame]. And at times they rendered the nights hideous, to unaccustomed ears, by the revelries and drunken brawls in progress in the tents. This state of things, however, did not last long, for when the railroad was completed to within twenty-five or thirty miles of Billings, the greater number of these characters moved on to a new location, farther west. But a sufficient number of each sex remained behind safely to insure Billings against being cartooned as a "Saint's Rest."

At this time, aside from the ladies at the Engineers Headquarters, so far as I could ascertain, but one respectable woman had yet arrived in Billings. But there were already on the ground a considerable number of good citizens, and more were among those arriving daily, who were heads of families and who had come on in advance to prepare homes for their families before sending for them. The dearth of women was therefore but temporary.

I was the first missionary to arrive in Billings. I met with a warm welcome, and everybody I met seemed to be pleased with the prospect of having a church in Billings. Even a gambler who was standing at the door of his tent, as I was praying, accorded me pleasantly and during the conversation which ensued, he expressed an interest in our enterprise and said, "Of course we gamblers know that churches are death to our business—but who would want to live in a town without a church in it."

I had no trouble in finding Christian men who were willing and ready to cooperate with me and in a comparatively short time the Congregational church of Billings had been duly organized and was functioning as a church.

I was unable to hold a service the first Sunday after my arrival in Billings because of a lack of a place in which to hold it. The second Sunday I secured the privilege of holding a service in a small building designed for a saloon.

The third Sunday I secured a similar building intended for a bakery. In fact for the first two months after my arrival, I was dependent from week to week on finding an unfinished building which by reason of its location and stage of completion was available for religious services—which I was not always successful in doing.

By that time, however, we had been able to raise a sufficient fund by subscriptions to enable us to erect a little building of rough lumber, of sufficient seating capacity to meet our prospective needs, until we should be able to secure a better building. The lumber of this building was hauled by wagons from the mountains forty miles distant, and by the combined efforts of the carpenters of the town, assisted by some of the citizens, was erected in a single day. This labor was all donated. Through the agency of an alert reporter this little incident promptly appeared in the Eastern papers duly paragraphed as illustrative of the enterprise of the "Magic City," Billings. This building served our purpose of a house of worship until our new church was dedicated. In due time we had a Sunday School, a strong and efficient Ladies Society and an excellent quartet choir, composed of young men. The services were well attended from the beginning, both morning and evening, thus proving that Billings contained a goodly element of church going people.

The rumor was afloat when I arrived at Billings that the Hon. Frederick Billings of New York City and former President of the Northern Pacific Railroad contemplated giving the sum of ten thousand dollars towards the erection of a Congregational Church in Billings. A few months after my arrival at Billings, having first ascertained that the rumor was authentic, I wrote to Mr. Billings on the subject. He promptly replied that his wife wished to donate ten thousand dollars toward the erection of a Congregational Church when she should have assurance that the church already organized in Billings was prepared to handle the enterprise. And shortly afterward, Mr. Billings came on to Billings, in person, to look over the situation. Finding everything satisfactory, he authorized the Trustees of the Church to proceed to build. The foundation for the new church was begun October 24, 1882, but as all the material used in its construction, aside from the foundation items and the brick, had to be ordered from Minneapolis, the building was subjected to so many unavoidable delays that it was not dedicated until November 18, 1883. This church was attractive architecturally, and up to date in its internal arrangements. It was built of wood, but lined on the outside with brick, to give it the appearance of being constructed entirely of brick.

Before this church was completed, I was compelled by inveterate insomnia to resign my pastorate and to retire permanently from the ministry. I continued, however, to supply the pulpit, to the best of my ability until the church was dedicated and my successor, the Rev. Mr. Wallace, had arrived to relieve me.

Nearly a half century has elapsed since the occurrence of the events which I have now related. But some of the scenes which I witnessed and of the experiences which I passed, during my brief ministry at Billings, were too indelibly impressed upon my memory ever to be forgotten.

Billings

Montana in the Making

by Newton Carl Abbott

> Born in Wisconsin in 1879, **Newton Carl Abbott** taught in rural
> Montana, served as a superintendent at Havre, and became one of the origi-
> nal faculty at Eastern Montana State Normal School (now Montana State
> University-Billings) in 1927. His *Montana in the Making* is one of the foun-
> dational histories of the state.

Billings in its early days was called the "Magic City." The original nucleus of settlement that fixed its location was the little frontier hamlet of Coulson, founded in 1877, at the ford over the Yellowstone, just east of where Billings now stands. The Billings town-site was laid out on land that was a part of the Northern Pacific's land grant from the national government. The main line of the Northern Pacific Railroad crossed this site in August, 1882.

The growth of Billings dates from this event, and is due to its favorable location as a distributing point for a large region. In the great days of the range cattle industry it was much used as a shipping point. A stage line ran from there to Great Falls, until the line of the Great Northern was built to connect these cities. During the 1880's and well into the 1890's it was a great shipping point for wool. A large part of the Clark's Fork bottom on which Billings is located was put under irrigation, beginning in 1883, and since that date the irrigated area has been enlarged. Specialized farming in sugar beets, beans and other crops has meant prosperity for Billings.

Billings was incorporated as a city on March 10, 1885. At that time its population was estimated at 2,000. Probably the estimate was too optimistic as the census of 1890 showed 836.

Capitalism on the Frontier: Billings and the Yellowstone Valley in the Nineteenth Century

by Carroll Van West

Carroll Van West has written three books of Montana history, as well as numerous articles and book chapters. Presently he is preparing a companion volume to his *Capitalism on the Frontier* that will explore the history of Billings and Yellowstone County from the creation of the sugar beet company to the oil boom of the 1950s.

Perhaps [Frederick Billings'] description of his relationship with the town [in the piece following] was meant as some kind of inside joke, but it puzzled rather than humored local residents. Frederick Billings had been among the founders of the land company; he had agreed to Heman Clark's request that the town be named in his honor. Then after his October 1882 visit he had donated money for the local church and school, and his investments in local property totaling in the thousands of acres were widely known. Frederick Billings was far more than "an accessory after the fact" in the development of the town of Billings and the Clark's Fork Bottom. Why he characterized himself in this manner remains a mystery.

The Speeches

Verbatim Report of What Was Said by Billings, Evarts, Grant and Villard at Billings

Frederick Billings, a native of Vermont, was a philanthropist, lawyer, and conservationist who served as president of the Northern Pacific Railroad from 1879-81. As the following excerpts from the September 15, 1883, *Billings Herald* show, the city of Billings was named after him.

We published on the day following the visit of the Villard excursionists to this town, quite a lengthy account of their reception here, giving to our readers a brief sketch of speeches made by some of the distinguished guests. Now, through the courtesy of Mr. Kilner, secretary to Mr. Billings, we are enabled to publish in full the speeches of Messrs. Billings, Villard, Evarts and Gen. Grant.

The following is the speech delivered by the Hon. Frederick Billings, from the balcony of the Headquarters hotel:

"Ladies and Gentlemen: I suppose you consider me the father of this town, but the father is supposed to know something of the child before it is born, and I knew nothing of this town before its birth. So I can't be its father.

Nor am I its Godfather for a Godfather is supposed to be present at the christening and I had nothing to do with the naming of this town; and moreover, far from being its owner, I have unluckily never possessed a lot in the place. Being neither father, godfather, nor owner, I suppose I am what the lawyers would call an accessory after the fact; and as this is the great town of this great valley called Clarke's Fork Bottom, I suppose this town may be looked upon as the bottom fact of this region. And why should it not be. Here is a valley 30 or 40 miles long and four or five miles wide, of astonishing richness, needing only irrigation to produce everything that man needs in most marvelous quantities, and the ditch is nearly done which is to irrigate this valley and make it so productive, that really the water should have been let in to this city to-day. Then again right over yonder a few miles distant are the Bull mountains, (It was Sitting Bull yesterday at Bismarck, to-day it is the Bull mountains). There is the richest deposit of coal in the interior of the continent, from which the Northern Pacific Railroad and all this region are to draw their fuel supply. And there is not only [that], but there are deposits of the finest minerals to the north and to the south, and I am told that there is a train just coming in yonder, of bullion from the mines to the north near Fort Maginnis.

"With the immense grazing regions all round, from which the cattle for shipment must come to this point; the agricultural resources, the rich mineral deposits, and the probability of the Fort Benton road as well as the coal road starting from here, the place has unquestionably all the elements for great material prosperity.

"I feel honored by having my name given to it, and proud of its prosperity. The people of the Northern Pacific, now that their road is completed, are engaging in some other things. Yesterday for instance we laid the cornerstone of the capitol of Dakota, at Bismarck. I am in hopes when we come out a year or two later we may lay the cornerstone of the capitol of this great territory right here at Billings. I know of no spot so central and with so many elements in its favor, and so deserving to be the capitol of Montana as this very town.

"Whether it is to be the capitol or not this town will always have my friendship and I shall be glad to do anything in my power for its prosperity.

"Should it happen to be the capitol my friend, Mr. Evarts, of New York, has promised to come out and deliver the address at the corner stone...."

As the train was about to start, Mr. Billings addressed the citizens from the platform of his car as follows:

"When I said a few words to you from the balcony, I was not aware what an impression this town and the exhibits had made upon the gentlemen traveling on this train. Since then I have had the pleasure of going through the cars, and I desire before we leave to say that there is but one impression—that of unqualified admiration of the location of Billings, and the preparations which the citizens have made to show what can be raised here; and everyone expresses a sincere hope that your highest expectations with reference to your improvement and prosperity will all be realized.

"For myself, honored by having the town named after me, you can be sure that I shall always be its friend in the future as I have been in the past. I fully expect that this season the road will be commenced from Billings to the Bull mountain coal region, and I am in hopes that that will be the beginning in time of the road to Fort Benton on the Missouri. As a business man, I can see no reason why this town, taking all the circumstances into consideration, is not really destined to be the centre of great interests; and if you all here will keep pace in your moral and intellectual growth with the growth in material prosperity, you will gratify the man after whom the place is named and every man who is a lover of good things.

"And now as our train goes, I can only say that I am glad to have been here and glad to have had an opportunity of kissing the first baby born in the town. I hope to come back here very often, and shall continue to be the friend of all the babies and all the grown-up people too."

Three cheers having been given for Frederick Billings, he introduced his wife, saying the best part of Billings was Mrs. Billings. Cheers were then given for Mrs. Billings and "Mrs. Billings' baby," and the baby, Frederick Billings, Jr., a promising young fellow of seventeen years, bowed his acknowledgements.

This 1887 portrait of the Frederick Billings family is probably the last photo of the entire family. Left to right: Back row: Laura, Elizabeth; middle: Frederick Sr., Ehrick, Julia, Parmly; front: Mary, Richard, Frederick Jr. "Fritz." Courtesy the Billings Family Archives, Woodstock Foundation.

Letter from Parmly Billings
to his father, Frederick Billings

Oldest son of Frederick, **Parmly Billings** was the only member of the
family to live in the city named for his father. He moved to Billings in 1885
to oversee his father's interests, but he died of kidney failure in 1888 while
traveling home to Vermont. The family later donated money for a public
library named in Parmly's honor.

Billings, Montana.
Dec. 4th. 1886.

My dear Father:

Your welcome letter of the 29th. came to hand this morning.

Young Butler has a place here in a store in town. He gets his board and
fifteen dollars a month. The job is likely to last till the holidays are over. He
will then have a chance to put his powers as a rustler to a crucial test, and I
shall have an opportunity to go as surety for his meal tickets. When I get to
New York I shall call on the young man's father, and tell him that the prodigal is mighty near corn husks, and advise him to call the wanderer home. I
saw the boy this morning, and told him that he reminded me of a line in a
beautiful hymn, "Come ye disconsolate why do ye languish." He said he
thought that hit the mark. His ideas of the great glorious West have experienced a change, one of those sad, sad changes which destroy the fond hopes
and happy visions of youth. The rose tint that covers this country in the
minds of Eastern youths, the storied cowboys and Indians, together with the
fortunes picked up like pebbles on the shores of Old Ocean, fade away when
the youth is transplanted from his native heath to the prairies of everlasting
bunch grass and sage brush. As Bill Nye says, "Men in the West spend their
days in obtaining experience, and pass the nights in applying arnica to the
experience gathered in during the day." Such is life in the country pointed
out by Horace Greeley as the place to grow up with.

From what little experience I have had in this country, I should advise a
young man who was in search of some place where he could be thoroughly
lonesome, have no friends, that is of course intimate ones, where vice in its
worst types was omnipresent, where board was high, and grub proportion-
ately poor, to go direct to the town of Billings. It would come so near to filling the bill that he would have little cause for dissatisfaction. And yet after
all I don't dislike the country, and doubt if I should be willing to migrate for
good. There is a freedom and non-restraint which I have always wished for,

and now when I have it I feel no inclination to take advantage of it, and before I always was on all sorts of occasions, as you can probably testify.

Everything here is moving on in the old rut. I hope to get out of it for a month or two in the course of a few days.

The Man of Dover's Island

by Mildred Dover DeCosse

Mildred Dover DeCosse was born and raised on a ranch near Billings. A local historian, she wrote articles for *The Billings Gazette* and other regional publications.

On the early maps of Yellowstone County, Montana, in the twisting curves of the Yellowstone River and several miles downstream from the town of Billings, there is a large island marked Dover's Island. It was named after the man who homesteaded it in 1882 and who eventually established a home there for himself and his bride.

This is the true story of that man's first twenty-eight years—his boyhood in Illinois, his adventures in southern Idaho from 1879 to 1881, his entry into Montana to hunt buffalo, his decision to homestead, and his unceasing efforts to persuade his sweetheart in Illinois to leave her comfortable home, marry him, and share pioneer life with him in Montana. This is also an authentic history of the areas he traversed, and of the way of life of John H. Dover from 1862 to 1890.

The capricious October wind lifted dust from the bare ground and swirled it around the new green-log house. The year was 1889 and the chill air told of coming winter. The house wasn't a thing of beauty, but to twenty-eight year old John Henry Dover it was a partial fulfillment of a constant desire for a home for himself and Mary, the girl in Illinois he would soon claim for his bride.

The log house stood in a cove that sloped up from the cobblestone shoreline of the north channel of the Yellowstone River, about seven miles down river from the town of Billings, Montana. The cabin's hand-hewn pine logs were placed in an upright position, perpendicular to the gray sandstone foundation. The chinking between the logs was white mortar. It gave the house a startling, striped effect. Heavy black tarpaper covered the gabled ends, held firmly in place by thin strips of unpainted wood placed in a large, bricklike pattern. That would have to last until a better covering could be had. The roof was covered with bright new wood shingles. There were two tall windows on each side of the house and one on the north end. An off-center door opened to the front yard and another door was in the south end of the building. Inside, the twenty-two by twenty-seven-foot structure was divided into two rooms of equal size. The north room would be the kitchen and dining area, the south room would be the bedroom and parlor. Overall, the house looked sturdy and neat. John, pausing to admire it from the front yard, was mighty proud of his handiwork and hoped his bride-to-be, Mary Fidelia Moffitt, would like it, too.

It had taken hard labor to cut, trim and haul the logs by four-horse team and lumber wagon from Lost Canyon in the Bull Mountains, twenty miles to the north. He had hewed them accurately with a broadax into nine-inch widths and sawed them into ten-foot lengths. To erect them he had solicited the help of a friend. Now the house was completed except for a woman's homey touch. He still had to build a privy, split enough wood to feed the warming winter fires, and find someone to care for his horses, cattle and a few chickens while he made the trip from Montana to Illinois to claim his bride-to-be, Mary Moffitt. At long last she'd said she'd marry him.

As Shadows on the Hills

by Dorothy Weston Larson

A resident of Billings, **Dorothy Weston Larson** has used her painting to document the quickly disappearing reminders of Montana's heritage. When words serve her better than a paintbrush, she writes poetry. Her historical novel, *As Shadows on the Hills*, is based on the real-life stories of four women who lived during the early days of Billings.

Foreword

Defying the doleful predictions of its survival, Billings emerged from a wretched chrysalis of treeless, alkali-crusted gumbo flats and after only six weeks of existence had a vigorous population of 800. On the evening of August 17, 1882, the day tracklayers reached the banks of the Yellowstone, a crowd gathered at the riverbank to celebrate, shooting off fireworks.

A mile to the east, betrayed and by-passed by the railroad, Coulson, raucous little tent town strung out along the river bank, died prematurely and hard like some of its denizens planted in Boothill's unyielding gravel. Even the elixir of free beer at the end of the twelve-minute mule-drawn streetcar ride between them could not prolong its life. Billings' articulate progress drowned out its death rattle.

Days were filled with the sounds of hammers, saws, and sandstone quarry chisels. Streets, like the imprint of a great waffle iron in the dust, sprouted houses, stores, tents, barns and privies. At night yelping coyotes paced nervously along the edge of the surrounding rimrocks whose great stony faces were illuminated by the red-hot kilns of the two brickyards working full-force the clock around. Soon handsome falsefront business houses stood shoulder to shoulder along Montana and Minnesota Avenues exchanging reflections from opposite sides of the tracks. On Fourth Avenue the city's first school, the Lincoln, settled uneasily into the ooze of a slough. Eighty-five feet above the bustling scene, atop the Congregational church steeple, a new zinc weathervane's arrow swiveled and pointed into the west wind sweeping down the Yellowstone Valley.

Its cultural refinements of two daily newspapers, an opera house, a roller-skating rink, various literary and secret societies all attested to Billings' status as a city, but the vulgar odors of rancid ammonia in the stockyards, raw garbage and dust detracted. The smell of oven-fresh bread emanating from the several bakeries was welcome perfume.

The most-feared odor was smoke. Fire was an extravagance no one could afford. River water cost fifty cents a barrel. Every building wore a firebreak of bare soil. A hoped-for artesian well which would have eased the city's water supply proved fruitless when solid rock repeatedly bent tools and equipment, endangering men's lives. Water was negligible. The 900-foot-deep shaft was filled in and abandoned.

Lightning was indiscriminate. Storm-struck prairie fires bared their teeth, raced across the grassy hills, lighting up the night sky, leaving raw black wounds. Smoke, blue as soapy dishwater, sagged in the valleys until drained by the wind.

In many ways Billings, like its sisters along the country's railroads, was ugly but its location had unique beauty—the sloping valley floor between 400-foot-high layered and fractured sandstone cliffs on the north and the undulating clay foothills of the Pryors to the south. Across the western horizon, sixty miles away, the jagged Beartooth Mountains overlapped in a collage of blues.

Patriarchal cottonwoods and saffron-tinged willows shaded the river and creek banks. Sage, greasewood, chokecherry, currant, rose, cactus and grasses cast lesser shadows. Pines, like protruding arrow points, silhouetted against the sky.

The sky!

The absolute, immense, magnificent, immutable sky! miniaturizing everything beneath it, sweeping over the land in unpredictable moods, changing with the hour, season and wind.

In the near distance, on the periphery of man's noisy, smelly intrusion, the animals and birds gradually retreated, helpless to hold their established boundaries, but continuing their instinctive rhythm of giving, taking and sharing life.

With boundaries and new ways determined by the expansive reservation, the Crows acquiesced grudgingly, bowed in broken pride.

But some things continued, incapable of change—fish, breaking water in the deep pools; hawks, gliding on invisible spirals; the silent scarves of the Aurora Borealis, pulsating in the northern sky.

As the earth wobbled its way around the sun, Billings' initial surge of growth lost momentum and by 1885 its population leveled off at fifteen hundred.

Thus, the scene is set for the story of four women, gentle protagonists, each of their lives transient "As Shadows on the Hills."

For we are but of yesterday— our days upon Earth are as shadows on the hills." Job 8:9

Progressive Cookbook of the Methodist Episcopal Church of Billings, Montana, 1893

In 1882, a group of Methodists formed a church in Billings that is the forerunner of today's **First United Methodist Church.** In 1893, a Sunday school class raised money by selling copies of the first cookbook compiled in Billings.

How to Cook Husbands so as to Make Them Tender and Good

A good many husbands are spoiled in the cooking. Some women go about it as if their husbands were bladders and blow them up; others keep them constantly in hot water; others let them freeze by their carelessness and indifference. Some keep them in a stew by irritating ways and words; others roast them. Some keep them in a pickle all their lives. It cannot be supposed that any husband will be tender and good, managed in this way, but they are really delicious when properly treated. In selecting your husband you should not be guided by the silvery appearance, as in buying mackerel, nor by the golden tint, as if you wanted salmon. Be sure to select him yourself, as tastes differ. Do not go to market for him, as the best are always brought to your door. It is always best to have none unless you will patiently learn how to cook him. A preserving kettle of finest porcelain is best, but if you have nothing better than an earthenware pipkin, it will do, with care. See that the linen you wrap him in is nicely washed and mended, with the required number of buttons and strings nicely sewed on. Tie him in the kettle by a strong silk cord called Comfort, as the one called Duty is apt to be weak. They are apt to fly out of the kettle and be burned and crusty on the edges, since, like crabs and lobsters, you have to cook them alive. Make a clear, steady fire out of love, neatness and cheerfulness. Set him as near this as seems to agree with him. If he sputters and frizzes, do not be anxious; some husbands do this until they are quite done. Add a little sugar in the form of what confectioners call kisses, but no vinegar or pepper on any account. A little spice improves them, but it must be used with judgment. Do not stick any sharp instruments into him to see if he is becoming tender. Stir him gently; watch the while lest he lie too flat and close to the kettle and so become useless. You cannot fail to know when he is done. If thus treated, you will find him very digestible, agreeing nicely with you and the children, and he will keep as long as you want, unless you become careless and set him in too cold a place.

Miscellaneous

- Kerosene will remove bloodstains.
- Egg stains can be removed from silver with damp salt.
- Eggs covered when frying will cook much more evenly.
- If you heat your knife, you can cut hot bread as smoothly as cold.
- A cup of water set in the oven will keep anything from burning.
- Two apples in a cake box will keep cake fresh a long time. When apples wither, change them.
- To keep glass from breaking when anything hot is poured into it, wrap a damp cloth around it.
- A large slice of potato in the fat while frying doughnuts will prevent the black specks from appearing on their surface.
- To extract paint from silk or woolen goods, saturate the spots with turpentine and let it remain several hours, then rub between the hands.
- To remove fruit, coffee or tea stains, hold the spot over a pail and pour boiling water from a considerable height through it. Soap sets the stains and should never be allowed to touch them.

•To wash flannels so they will not shrink, wash them in warm, soapy water, but never rub soap on; rinse in warm blue water, and hang in house to dry, never outdoors. Have room of same temperature as water in which flannels were washed.

•To change feathers from one bed to another or from a bed to pillows, open the feather bed as far as the pillow is open, first having pushed the feathers into one corner, away from the opening. Then baste the two open places together; push the feathers into the pillow. Baste again, then rip first basting, and the work is done with no feathers flying around. This work can be done in the house.

Mathilda

by Catherine Feldman

Catherine Feldman, a graduate of Eastern Montana College, is a retired schoolteacher in Billings. She has been a life-long member of the Montana Education Association and active in many volunteer organizations, including Habitat for Humanity.

[Mathilda stops her neighbors from stealing a house off an abandoned homestead.]

Alex tried raising his voice. "Broncs can't be trusted. You know that, Mathilda. I'd hate to hurt a fine woman, and a neighbor at that, but I'm not sure about Joe's handlin' of them if we get any more flies around here."

The warning came too late. The greenest bronc of the group had kicked too high at a belly fly and his hoof caught on the tongue of one of the wagons on which the house was resting. With a squeal, he started bucking. As if at a signal, the mules backed into their doubletree and kicked backward viciously, hitting two of the broncs behind them. With horses' hooves flying, front legs pawing, and frightened animals squealing, Joe, Johnny, and Alex jumped as they saw their rig, with the house tipping sideways, barely miss Mathilda.

With ever so slight a flip of her hand, as if to brush a fly out of her line of vision, Mathilda settled back into the buggy seat just a bit more, slapped Topsy on the back with her buggy whip, and moseyed down the trail. Without a trace of emotion, she watched three frantic young men tearing after six wild-eyed animals and remnants of their harnesses and the load they were pulling.

Sod 'n Seed 'n Tumbleweed:
A History of the Huntley Project

written and compiled by the Huntley Project History Committee

> In 1976 a committee of seven local citizens gathered to collect the history and first-hand memories of Huntley Project. Committee members were L. Christine Seamans, James M. Stout, Alene Bowen, Ethel Fleming, Lois Hackney, William H. Hancock, and Edna Leonard, most of whom were sons or daughters of original homesteaders.

Foreword

The year 1977 is significant to us who live on the Huntley Project. Just seventy years ago the Huntley Irrigation Project was opened to settlers. The Reclamation Act of June 1902, seventy-five years ago, coupled with the Homestead Act forty years before that, which was signed by President Lincoln in May 1862, made possible the development of the irrigation project. This year, in February 1977, the Homestead Act was killed by the 94th Congress; the remaining wide open spaces are no longer to be settled and domesticated but to be preserved. An era of the American frontier is officially closed.

Homesteading was a great experiment. Never before in history had a Government practically given away to its citizens millions of acres with the provision that they tame the land and make it home. It was a challenge and a not unmixed blessing. Homesteading was once described as a system by which the Government "bets" so many acres against the entry fee that the settler cannot live on the land for five years without starving to death. Some could not, but many did.

Enticed by Government promises, railroad inducements, land office assurances, and chance word-of-mouth and lured by high hopes for a good life on land of their own, they came from all walks of life and from all over the United States, some of them recent immigrants from European countries and from South America. They came to a twenty-seven-mile-long valley, tapering at each end but expanding to four miles in width, nestled between smooth foothills on the south and the cottonwood-banked Yellowstone River and bluffs on the north. It promised hard work, heartbreak, independence, crop failures, new friends, unforeseen problems, mortgages, an excellent location, caring neighbors, rail transportation, tumbleweeds, the sound of train whistles, and hope. To many it became home. Some stayed because they were too hard up to move on; others left only their footprints here.

After seventy years the Huntley Project has become a rich valley of lush, level fields of alfalfa, corn, sugarbeets, and grain, bounded frequently by concrete-lined irrigation ditches. Fences once piled high with tumbleweeds have largely disappeared as tractors have replaced horses. Modern farm homes are surrounded by shops, machine sheds, well kept lawns, trees, flowers and gardens. Our school system, our churches, our organizations, and our progressive development are a tribute to the foresight, the faith, and the endurance of the early settlers. Their vision in working for a unified community—a meld of neighbors and nationalities and generations—has been our gain....

1901

Tent Town to City: a Chronological History of Billings, Montana 1882-1935

by Myrtle E. Cooper

Myrtle E. Cooper was born, raised, and educated on the West Coast. She was employed by the Parmly Billings Memorial Library from 1953 to 1976, where she became head of the Reference Department. Cooper was responsible for expanding the Montana Collection to one of the largest in the state, and upon her retirement, she was honored by the Library Board as Montana Room Librarian Emeritus.

January

City Hall and the Fire Department moved to the northwest corner of North 27th Street.

The Billings Gazette purchased the town's first linotype machine.

February

Billings' schools were placed on the accredited list for the first time, attaining this recognition over other larger cities of the state whose schools had not yet been accredited.

March

On a return trip to the Billings Opera House, Maude Adams played in *L'Aiglon* to an appreciative audience.

New interest in northern Wyoming for Billings' wholesale jobbers prompted a 128-mile branch line to be built from Toluca Junction through Pryor Gap and south into Cody.... This line was built by the B&M Railroad.

May

The U.S. Court of Appeals upheld Judge Knowles' decision that the

M&MLI Co. must pay $10,000 in delinquent taxes on land they owned within city, or the land would be sold.

August

Another school site was purchased in Block No. 2, Yegen Addition. This was to become the location of the new South School, later the Garfield School.

September

Manual training was first introduced into the Billings schools. The school board and H. M. Brayton organized a four-year high school.

October

Dedication ceremonies were held for the Parmly Billings Memorial Library. The library, which cost between $25,000 and $30,000, was presented to the city by Frederick Billings, Jr. [on behalf of the family] as a memorial to his brother, Parmly. It was built on the corner of 29th and Montana Avenue, on land leased from the NPRR for a dollar a year. Frederick Billings, Jr. attended with friends from New York, and Wilbur Fiske Sanders, a leader in the vigilantes of Virginia City days, was the principal speaker. Schools were let out for the occasion. Mabel Collins became the city's first librarian.

November

The Board of Trustees of the Parmly Billings Memorial Library met and adopted rules for the government of library patrons. The library was open for 85 hours per week, and fines were 5¢ a day. Its first trustees were: Reverend Father Van Clarenbeck, Reverend W. D. Clark, J. D. Matheson, J. R. Goss, I. D. O'Donnell, and A. L. Babcock. The library was supported by a levy of one mill.

December

Violence broke out in the "tenderloin" district at the "Hub" between a "boarder" and her lover. The jealous woman shot her man at point blank. The bullet was removed by the Drs. Chapple and Henry Armstrong, and the man was expected to recover. The woman was arrested but posted bond of $500.

Rocky Mountain Bell Telephone Co. opened an exchange with a long distance line to Big Timber, Livingston, Bozeman, and Butte. Originally there were 218 subscribers; by 1910, the number had risen to 784. Women manually operated the boards until 1931.

Images of Billings:
A Photographic History

by Carroll Van West

See page 142 for biographical information about **Carroll Van West**.

Original Parmly Billings Library, 1901. (Present-day Western Heritage Center, 2822 Montana Avenue.) Photo courtesy Parmly Billings Library.

Billings at the turn of the century stood at a crossroads between its legacy as a developing frontier town and its promising future as a transportation center for the northern plains. Two new buildings perfectly symbolized this turning point: the Parmly Billings Library and the Preston Moss mansion.

In 1901, the city of Billings turned out en masse for the dedication of the Parmly Billings Memorial Library, a striking stone building of Richardsonian Romanesque style, designed by the town's best architect, Charles S. Haire. Donated in honor of his brother by Frederick Billings, Jr., the library remained here until the late 1960s when it moved to its new location on North Broadway.

When constructed at the turn of the century, the library's commanding location on Montana Avenue, and its permanent masonry construction, symbolized that earlier era of the town's history when the Billings family had nurtured the town through the difficult years of the mid-1880s. Now the torch had been passed to a new generation of businessmen and entrepreneurs.

Looking Back—Moving Forward: The History of the Billings YWCA 1907-1988

by Margaret Ping

Margaret Ping moved to the Hardin area at the age of four. After receiving degrees from Oberlin College and Columbia University Teachers College, she started a 34 year career with the YWCA, which included serving internationally and as Executive Director of the Billings YWCA from 1960-64. She later began the continuing education program at Rocky Mountain College. Ping continues to volunteer actively for organizations such as Habitat for Humanity.

It was on November 3, 1905, that Mrs. H. H. Griffith, chair of the Bible Circle Department of the State Committee of Young Women's Christian Associations of Montana, met with the ladies of Billings and organized an affiliated Bible Circle with a membership of 37. This Bible Circle continued under the needed encouragement of Mrs. Griffith until on September 27, 1907, the "Pioneer City YWCA of the State of Montana" was chartered in order to foster expanded outreach to the community. The organizational meeting took place in the basement of the original Parmly Billings Library, at 29th and Montana Avenue, and Mrs. Dudley Jones was elected the first President. There were 50 charter members.

An editorial in the January 5, 1908, *Billings Gazette* said, "It is the intention of the Association to open a rest home where girls and young women, who would have to live in dingy rooms and eat unnourishing food, are enabled on the small wages paid to women to procure in a rest home excellent board and good rooms and be surrounded with a homelike and Christian atmosphere." The next month the *Gazette* reported that "a nine-room house, 17 North 30th," had been rented by the YW; "all of the rooms in the home are filled and there is a long waiting list. Between 25-30 girls take lunch at the home each day, and at dinner as many as can be accommodated." And soon after, an editorial in the *Gazette* stated: "One of the most important organizations in Billings today, one which should be fostered, encouraged and assisted by all citizens, is the YWCA which is making a most commendable endeavor to assist the young women and girls of the community along many lines, all of which, if persevered in, cannot fail to benefit them physically, morally, and spiritually, to render their lives more useful to themselves and to mankind in general." At the end of the year, the *Gazette* reported the first life member, Mrs. Charles M. Bair, whose husband paid $100 for the membership.

In the second year of operation, the YW found a new and more ample home at 107 North 29th Street. The Cafeteria—the major source of funds for the organization—featured this menu in September, 1908:

Cream of tomato soup	5 cents
Cold boiled tongue	5 cents
Creamed potatoes	5 cents
Stewed peas	5 cents
Blackberry cobbler	5 cents
Chocolate pudding	5 cents
Bread and butter	5 cents
Tea, coffee, milk	5 cents

There were 15-30 regular boarders for the three meals, but the regulations said that any women who came would be served. Non-members were asked to pay 5 cents extra for each meal. The four bedrooms were rented at $10.00 a month, with two girls in each room to share the cost. They were served three meals a day at reduced cost. As one report says, "This house and the women supporting it are a real boon to the tired shoppers and poor working girls." Billings, in this first decade of the century, was luring from small communities many young women looking for work. But wages for the untrained ran from $3.00 a week to not more than $10.00. So, as in many other cities and towns across America, the Billings YWCA made it possible for young women to live on inadequate salaries. In those early years it had not yet occurred to the leaders of the organization that they had another obligation to such young women: to improve the conditions under which they worked.

Five years of settling into a routine of service to young women passed, with the recognition that other needs existed besides the traditional ones of residence and food service. Thus, different kinds of program activities began to appear in reports. Travelers Aid work was begun early, with a framed notice in the depot inviting women to rest at the YWCA between trains. About fifty responded to this invitation the first year, and by 1914, 2025 people had been helped by this "department." A free Employment Service was established in 1913 and continued for many years to help women find "day" work. "Settlement work" was started in the form of emergency help with food, caring for the sick, and helping others cope with death and burial Headlines in *The Gazette* mentioned some of these programs: "YWCA offers Employment Bureau free for use of Newcomers" and "YWCA asks city for fund to aid nurses."

"Educational classes" had started as early as 1909, and had included Current Events, Arts and Crafts, and Fancy Work. In 1914, Helen Keller lectured in Billings, sponsored by the YWCA. During the war years, there was growing interest in physical activities for women, and gym classes were held at the YMCA. There were also club groups, some of which would be important to the YW for many years. In 1917 the first Business Women's Club was organized, and in 1918 the first club for teens, called Girl Reserves, was organized with a membership of 225. About this same time, the first YWCA work on an American Indian reservation began, with a circulating library established on the Crow Reservation.

From 1914 to 1921, Mrs. W. B. Cummings was the President of the Association, and during this time, the YW became more aware of its international connections. (Historically, the first international staff member from the USA had been sent to India in 1897, but during the war years and thereafter, many YWCAs were begun in other countries and local U.S. Associations were urged to help in their support.) The first observance of World Fellowship Week by the Billings YWCA was held in November, 1917, and for many years it continued to be observed.

The next "home" of the Association, beginning in 1918, was on the fourth floor of the Stapleton Building. This was a better location for the Cafeteria and Employment Service, but housing was unavailable, so this part of the original program had to be suspended until the YW had outgrown its facilities and moved again, in 1923. Interest was expressed in finding a home for 70 or 80 girls—an ambitious project, but as the ladies said: "Girls come to Billings and walk the streets looking for rooms, then pay such high prices and endure such pitiful loneliness."

Tunnels

Billings A to Z

by Karen D. Stevens and Dee Ann Redman

Karen D. Stevens and **Dee Ann Redman** are reference librarians at Parmly Billings Library. As part of the Library's centennial celebration, they wrote an informal, entertaining, thoroughly researched account of the "hidden history" of the city, *Billings A to Z,* from which this excerpt is taken.

Nearly everyone has heard of the dark, eerie "steam" tunnels which once connected many of the older buildings in downtown Billings. Legend has it that during Prohibition, bootleggers used the underground tunnels to move kegs of beer from one hiding place to another. There is no evidence to support either that tale or the story that a murder was committed somewhere in the tunnels. Nor was there ever a subway station in the tunnels! The truth is far less glamorous.

In late 1907, the Billings Mutual Heating Company began to pipe hot water, not steam, through an underground network of pipes which connected many of the downtown businesses between N. 29th and N. 27th Streets. The heating plant, owned by C. O. Myers and P. B. Moss, was located at 504 N. 29th. By 1909, they claimed to be the largest hot water heating system west of the Missouri River, with more than three miles of water mains heating over fifty businesses. *The Billings Gazette* of November 29, 1907, stated that hot water was chosen instead of steam because "the heat thus furnished is far more equable and certain than a steam plant can provide."

In 1914, Moss bought the plant and it became known as Billings Utility Company. The company went out of business in 1937 due to continual problems with leaking pipes. The building became the 5-0-4 Garage Company until it was demolished a few years later. Since then the tunnels through which the pipes ran have collapsed or have been backfilled. Only remnants remain beneath the old Babcock Theater and the Lincoln Center, now headquarters for School District 2.

A portion of one of the tunnels beneath School District 2 was used as a teachers' lounge when the building was still used as a school. The larger tunnels range from about five feet to seven feet high and are simply damp corridors no longer leading anywhere. Old pipes still run along the concrete walls. Most of the tunnels were much smaller, little more than concrete-lined trenches eighteen inches below ground with manholes to provide access to the pipes. Billings resident and historian Don Warfield, who once lived in an apartment above the heating plant, recalls the awful vibration that made it difficult to sleep. The vibration may have contributed to the recurring leaks, which eventually caused the company to go out of business.

A *Billings Gazette* article of April 7, 1977, describes the tunnel system and the subterranean shopping mall that once existed beneath the Babcock Theater. There was even a bowling alley on a lower level. The entrance to the bowling alley has been lost, concealed by a maze of storerooms and plywood walls, and the shops are long gone. Only legends are left, legends which tell of bootleggers and ladies of the night and kids playing hooky from school.

Up on the Rim
by Dale Eunson

Born in Wisconsin in 1904, **Dale Eunson** came west with his family to homestead "up on the rim" in 1910. He became a short story writer, novelist, and screenwriter. He now lives in Woodland Hills, California.

Papa and Mamma must have done their talking where I could not overhear them. Papa never mentioned it, and Mamma kept mum after that too. Then one Sunday night—it was April 14—I was informed that I was going to Billings the next day with Mamma. The doctor had made her promise to return for a checkup around the middle of April. Mamma said she would let the doctor check her up if it would make him feel any better, but personally she thought it was a waste of time and money. She was in Science now, and God's perfect child did not need checkups.

I should have been suspicious, Monday being a school day and all, but I did not question my luck because we were going to travel from Acton by train and would stay at the Commercial Hotel that night. I would get to see Genevieve and eat chop suey at the Chinese restaurant up the marble stairs and look in windows at the shiny new automobiles.

We arrived a little before noon and registered at the hotel so we could get rid of our grips. Then we walked up Montana Avenue, but we ran into a thousand sheep being driven to the stockyards for shipment to Chicago and we had to climb the library steps to get out of their way.

But finally we made it to Twenty-eighth Street and turned north toward Hart-Albin's where Genevieve worked. Mamma needed a new shirtwaist and a skirt and Genevieve could get 20 percent discounts.

It made me proud to watch my sister doing her job. She was no longer a clerk but had a very important position making change for all the baskets that zoomed at her from every corner of the bargain basement. It did not seem to fluster her at all. Mamma and I stood there quite a while before she even had time to look up. When she finally spotted us, she did not smile. That was odd, because Genevieve was always happy to see us—even Mamma. It took her a few minutes to remember that she and Mamma didn't get along.

As soon as she could she got another girl to take her place. Then she stepped down out of the cage and kissed us both and asked after Papa. Mamma asked her if she could come out for a bite to eat with us somewhere, and Genevieve said she simply did not feel like eating.

Mamma said she hoped she wasn't coming down with the grippe that was going around, and Genevieve said no, it wasn't that, it was the thought of all those poor souls.

"What poor souls?" Mamma asked.

"You mean you haven't heard about the *Titanic?*" Genevieve gasped.

"No," Mamma said. "What about the *Titanic?*"

"It hit an iceberg and sank. Nobody knows yet whether anybody at all was saved."

Mamma turned white and had to sit down. Genevieve got her a glass of water and I said if I had a paper I would fan her. But there was no newspaper today. It was Monday and *The Gazette* did not publish on Mondays. That was the reason we had been able to walk all the way from the Northern Pacific station to Hart-Albin's without hearing newsboys crying "Extra." But as the Associated Press dispatches on the disaster were received over the Morse circuit, they were pasted on the bulletin board outside *The Gazette* office.

Even a boy not quite eight years old living on a homestead in Montana knew all about the *Titanic*. There had been stories about her in the *Milwaukee Sentinel* that Uncle Charlie mailed to us every once in a while. She was the biggest thing afloat, probably the biggest ship that ever would be built, certainly the most luxurious, and claims had been made that she was unsinkable. And here, on her maiden voyage, laden with celebrities, she had gone to the bottom. If any of the twenty-four hundred aboard had been saved it would be a miracle.

After a little while Mamma managed to pull herself together. She felt in no mood for shopping, but "Life must go on," she said, and bought herself a new corset as well as the skirt and shirtwaist. I could hardly pull myself away from a pair of tan oxfords with brass toe-snubbers. Genevieve wanted to buy them for me, but Mamma wouldn't let her. They were dangerous, she said; a boy needed high-toppers when he lived in rattlesnake country. So Genevieve gave us a leather pillow with a picture of Teddy Roosevelt staring out across the ocean burned on it. Under it the caption read, WHAT ARE

THE WILD WAVES SAYING? THIRD TERM. Hart-Albins had stocked
the pillows because Teddy Roosevelt was stumping through town soon in his
campaign against President Taft for the Republican nomination.

The shopping had made everybody feel better, so Genevieve decided to
come out and have something to eat after all, especially since she could not
have supper with us; she had a previous engagement.

We all ordered clubhouse sandwiches, even though they cost thirty-five
cents apiece. Genevieve said it was her treat. She was sorry she could not
spend the evening with us but she had had this previous engagement for two
weeks and could not very well cancel it at this late date. If she had only
known we were coming to Billings...

Mamma said that did not matter at all. She and I would think of something exciting to do by ourselves. What was playing at the Babcock?

"Uncle Tom's Cabin," Genevieve said.

Mamma had seen that in Milwaukee years ago, but she thought I ought
to be exposed to it if it wasn't too dear. It was like an American history
lesson.

Genevieve said the third balcony usually cost seventy-five cents; that is,
if Mamma was up to the climb after her operation. Mamma said she would-
n't even tell the doctor about it when she saw him. It was none of his
business. We would go if we could get tickets.

We were having a good time. Nobody was mad at anybody, and then
Genevieve put her foot in it. She had gone to the Babcock only last
Thursday, she said. She and a new beau who was a real swell sat in the
orchestra and they had seen Mrs. Leslie Carter in *Two Women.*

"Mrs. Leslie Carter was right here in Billings and you didn't let me
know?" Mamma cut in.

"I didn't know she was a friend of yours," Genevieve said, tightening up.

She was not a friend, Mamma said, but she had seen her in Chicago
when she was playing in *The Heart of Maryland* and she would never forget
it. Mrs. Carter had clung to the clapper of a big bell and swung right out
over the audience.

"Why?" Genevieve said, flat. It seemed to me a reasonable question.

"Because if the bell rang," Mamma said, and turned to me as if I had
asked, "that was to be the signal that her sweetheart was to be executed. I'll
never forget it," she repeated.

I could easily understand that. It was something one would not easily
forget. Then Mamma turned back to Genevieve and said sadly, "And so Mrs.
Leslie Carter was here last Thursday, and you didn't tell me. We could have
made this trip then just as well as today."

Genevieve said she was sorry. If she had known how Mamma felt about Mrs. Carter she would have gone out of her way to tell her. But, she went on, *Two Women* was hardly appropriate fare for a seven-year-old-boy, and besides, Mrs. Carter did not swing out over the audience on any bell last Thursday. "We sat in the fourth row and I would certainly have noticed a thing like that," she said.

A long silence followed, and then Genevieve asked for the check. There was an embarrassing moment while she looked in her coin purse and discovered she did not have enough cash to pay the tab, but Mamma came to the rescue by lending her fifty cents. "I'll leave the money at the hotel tomorrow morning on my way to work," Genevieve said grimly.

"No need," Mamma said.

"Oh, yes, there is," Genevieve persisted. "I said it was my treat, and it is my treat!"

So far that day we had suffered two disasters: the *Titanic* and Mrs. Leslie Carter.

Diary of a Homesteader's Wife, 1913-1916

by Mrs. William Spencer

North of the Yellowstone, South of the Bulls

compiled by Marjorie (Jim) Barnard, John and Willora Brown,
Rosella Johanson, Ida Sherrodd

Mary Boyer Spencer was born in Colorado in 1885 and moved to Montana at the age of five. She and her husband William Spencer settled on a homestead on Hibbard Creek with four small children. A friend remembers of her, she was "hardworking, fiercely independent, and loved by all."

1913

January 13: Last evening's snow was only a squall. Soon quit. Twenty-six below zero this morning but nice and warm this afternoon. Will was down to Grandpa's this A.M. The new teacher came last night. Too much snow and too cold for Ernest and Clem to go.

Tuesday January 14:...Three wolves were here last night. Heard one howling in the night. Two howled this P.M.

February 16: Nice again. Water still running everywhere. Alvis Belless was here a few minutes. Just like spring. Will and Mr. Miller have gone to Grandpa's for the windlass. Never got home til dark. Worked on the well. Very lonesome.

March 3: Nice and warm this morning. Sprinkled rain some. Mr. Miller came down. Helped finish the well and they took the dirt off the roof and put on galvanite roofing. Opal is quite sick and very cross and everything is so **dirty.**

April 7: Nice warm day. Set out some onions. Planted some radish and onion seed. Am planting more little tomatoes, wonderberries, etc. Worked on a hat all afternoon. Will went to Grandma's. She sent me some horserad-ish root.

May 20: Nice today. Didn't do much this forenoon. Didn't feel well. Spaded the ground, carried manure and planted my flowers. Old Phoebe held up her milk this A.M.

May 27: Very hot. Helped pile [sage] brush this forenoon. Scalded the walls and beds with stock dip. Found a bedbug last night.

August 27: Quite hot again. I never saw it so hot for so long. Got five watermelons this A.M. They were quite good. Saw a band of sheep go past. Mrs. Miller, Orpha and Chas came down this afternoon. Had a nice visit. Ate muskmelons and watermelons. Charlie killed a rattlesnake in our garden today.

October 17: Killed and cooked two chickens. Made two lemon pies and two cakes—a chocolate and a cream cake. Just got ready when Mrs. Miller and the kids came. Went with them to the dance. The worst crowd I ever saw—mostly women—and what men there were didn't have enough life to move. We women danced some together.

November 27 (Thanksgiving): Thanksgiving and a beautiful day. They all went to Pineview and I have to stay home and Will is going back right after dinner so I don't feel very thankful. I am ashamed of myself. I have lots to be thankful for.

December 22: The boys went to school this morning. Had an awful time getting Clem started. He is so trying at times. He just wears me out....

1914

Sunday February 15: We went to the traps. Saw a coyote but it was a long way off. Gee! we have live neighbors here. Never see a soul week in and week out. Thawing.

Sunday March 8: Got home about 7 o'clock this morning. We all walked up. Left there about 5:30 o'clock. Had a fine time at the dance. A fellow got my basket and Will traded with him. He got Mary Haynie's basket. Left real early. Would have stayed longer if the children had been with us. Young Lane fell out of the wagon coming home. We sure laughed....

Sunday April 12: Easter! The calf drank his milk fine. Mr. Loomis finished plowing the garden last night. We planted peas, beets, carrots, onion sets and onion seed and Will sowed turnip seed…

June 23: Cloudy again and cool. Mended socks and stockings most all day. Just finished supper and Mr. & Mrs. Wallace came and said there would be a meeting at 8 o'clock P.M. I promised to go so we got ready and went. Mamma came home with us and stayed all night. Had quite a nice meeting. Twenty-two present. Organized Sunday School.

July 18:…They left us their spring seat to use going to Heren's and back. I ironed, fixed fence, fried a chicken and fixed a little lunch to take along. Got lunch and harnessed the horses. Left about 1 or 1:30 o'clock. Never got there until almost 6:30. Almost lost a tire clear off going down Buffalo Creek hill. We hammered it on with a rock and poured some water on it, out of Buffalo Creek.…

July 25:…Took the barrel expecting to get some water at Grandad's but they said their well was awful low so I wouldn't take any. As we came home, the horses were anxious to go. Clem and Elwin were standing up holding to that empty barrel and as we crossed the first coulee they both went out between the wheel and the box. I was sure scared. I don't see how they missed getting run over or wound-up in a wheel. Just struck Clem's hip a little and Elwin's back. They certainly got off lucky. They keep me in hot water all the time. They are so careless. Perhaps they will sit down from now on.

Sunday August 2:…The boys came back about 3 o'clock and said they had a big fire up there. They took some wet sacks and Will took a shovel and went with them. We went up on the hill right away and the whole country up there was on fire. Mr. McIntyre came for water and they ran up there and went to fighting fire…Will and the Kansas boys came about 6:30 or seven o'clock. They got the fire out. It was awful. The tall one lit his pipe and dropped the match was what started it—but he threw his pipe away and said he had quit smoking.…

August 7:…Smoke was thick this afternoon. Must have been quite a fire somewhere near. Wind blew furious all afternoon. I went up on the hill but could not see anything but smoke. Watered the cucumbers.

November 3: Election Day. Every man in the country is gone to town. Mrs. Berry came down this morning and did her washing.…

Harvesting Ice on the Yellowstone
Both Feet in the Stirrups

by William "Bill" Huntington

Born in Nebraska in 1876, **William Huntington** lived on Blue Creek outside Billings from about 1913. He was an avid rodeo performer, judge, and
promoter. The following excerpt is taken from his memoir.

When the temperature drops way below zero, it makes me think of the
old days when everyone put up ice. There wasn't any artificial ice plants or
automatic refrigerators in those days. If anyone wanted ice for the following
summer he got out and got it in below zero weather. Most everybody got
their ice from the Yellowstone River and stored it in large ice houses along
the river.

As soon as it got cold enough for the river to freeze over, everyone got
ready for the ice harvest. It was a very disagreeable job but about the only
work there was in the winter. It didn't take much equipment. A team of
horses, an ice rack fourteen feet long, a pair of tongs, plenty of warm clothes
and a lot of guts and you were ready to put up ice. The colder it was, the
better for the ice man for the ice was better and you didn't get so wet unless
you fell in the river as some of them always did.

The river isn't the best place to get ice as it freezes uneven. A lake is the
best place if there is one handy. When there was snow on the ice as there
generally was it had to be scraped off. Then there was an ice plow pulled by
a team that they used to mark the ice and then they would sock it down in
the ice to cut it on the mark. Sometimes they sawed the ice. They had to be
careful to mark it straight so the ice cakes would be the same size.

When it was all ready to go in the ice house there was a long wooden
trough that reached up into the top of the ice house. In the top of the ice
house there was a pulley and an iron frame that had a couple of prongs on
it that was put back of the ice. A horse was hitched to a long rope attached
to the pulley and about ten cakes at a time was pulled into the ice house.
They weighed about a hundred fifty pounds apiece.

It took several men in the ice house, especially if it was a big ice house.
They set the ice cakes on end just like bricks as close together as possible. If
there was some uneven cakes they had a spud bar to even them up. They
generally placed the ice four or five inches from the wall, packed sawdust all
around it and over the top to keep the air out. The ice house had to have a
drain to take care of any water that melted from the ice.

I remember one time we were putting up ice for Pete Yegen. The weather turned warm. He had a big crew working and wanted to get through while

the ice was good. He had a large platform built on the edge of the river, a trough to pull the ice upon the platform. The wagons would back up to the platform, push the ice in the back of the wagon. Several wagons could load at the same time. On account of the weather turning warm the water raised so we couldn't load at the platform. We had to go up the river about thirty yards and drive out on the ice to load. It was dangerous, but Yegen wanted to get his ice house filled that day.

The ice was thick but when you got loaded the ice would pop and make a lot of noise. There was a team broke through but we got them out without too much trouble. The only casualty was Mr. Yegen. He stepped in an air hole in the ice and got a cold bath.

I had a very heavy team, a Percheron stallion and a large Percheron mare. They weighed right at 3500 pounds and were worth a lot of money. I was worried that they would break through the ice but didn't want to be the first one to quit for all the teamsters was scared. I was doing a lot of business with Yegen Brothers and I knew that if anyone quit the whole crew would quit. I was sweating blood every time I drove out on the ice. Anyway, we got the job done and the ice house filled. We were all glad to be finished.

When I got home tired from wrestling those 150-pound cakes of ice, my wife took me in our bedroom to show me the new lace curtains she'd hung at the windows at the head of our bed. I admired them and went to bed early.

In the night I had a nightmare, dream or something as I hadn't had a drink for three months. I thought that my nice stallion had broke through the ice. I grabbed him by the tail and was pulling him out of the river when my wife shook me and woke me up. She wanted to know what I was doing upon my knees in the middle of the bed tearing up her new curtains. I told her I was sorry about the curtains but I'd sure pulled a good horse out of the river.

The Kiskis

by May Vontver

An immigrant from Sweden, **May Vontver** credited a high school English teacher in Nebraska with encouraging her to write. She taught for many years and served as a Superintendent of Education in Montana. Commenting on her often difficult life, she wrote, "My hopes and ambitions, such as they are after the years, center about the never quite dormant desire to write."

"Hadn't you better eat in the house today? It is cold outside," the teacher suggested.

Pretending not to hear her, the three Kiskis slipped silently through the door with their double-handled Bull Durham tin can. They stood in a knot on the south side of the schoolhouse and ate from the one tin. From her desk Miss Smith observed that they now and then put one bare foot over the other to warm it. This was the second time they had disregarded her invitation to eat in the house with the others. The rest of the children had drawn their seats into a circle about the stove and begun to eat.

Teddy Kirk at last decided to enlighten the teacher: "They have only bread in their lunch pail. That's why they won't eat with us."

Miss Smith made no reply. She suspected that the lunches of the group around the stove weren't very sumptuous either. She knew hers wasn't. The people with whom she boarded were homesteaders too.

"What about these Kiskis? Who are they?" she asked Mr. Clark that evening at supper.

"The Kiskis?—Oh, they took up their claim here last fall. They are pretty hard up. They have only one horse. Kiski hauled out all the lumber for his shack and barn with it. Thirty miles it is to Hilger. I was hauling wheat then and I used to pass him on the road, walking beside the load and pushing when it was uphill."

Miss Smith smiled crookedly. One horse in a country where four- or six-horse teams were the rule was somewhat ludicrous. It was pathetic, too.

"Now, now! You needn't look that way. Kiski broke ten acres with that horse of his last spring. Got the ground in shape and got it seeded, too. The horse pulled and the old man pushed and, by golly, they got it in." There was respect, even admiration, in his voice.

"They have eight children, though," Mrs. Clark broke in. "The two oldest girls are doing housework in Lewistown."

Eight children. That meant three at home younger than the ones at school.

"Have they any cows?"

"One, but she's dry now. It's pretty hard for them."

Miss Smith decided not to urge the Kiskis again to eat in the schoolhouse.

In school the Kiskis were painfully shy. Rudolph, the oldest, going on eleven, hid his timidity under a sullen demeanor. Once in a while, however, he could be beguiled to join in a game of "Pum-Pum-Pull-Away" or horseshoe pitching. He was a good pitcher. Margaret, next in age, expressed her shyness in wistfulness. Johnny, barely six, refused to speak. Never would he answer a question in class. Never a word did he utter to the children on the playground. He might, now and then, have made remarks to his sister and brother in Bohemian, but if so, he wasn't ever caught making them. Yet, he was by nature a happy child. When anything comical happened in school or something funny was said, he would laugh out loud with an especially merry, infectious laugh. It was plain that he observed and understood more than his usual behavior indicated. The teacher, mindful of her psychology texts, tried vainly again and again to utilize these occasions of self-forgetfulness by surprising him into speech.

At the beginning of the term, in September, every child had come to school barefoot. As the season advanced, the other pupils, family by family, donned their footwear, but the Kiskis continued to arrive barefoot, although it was now late in October and getting cold.

"Why don't you wear your shoes?" "Aren't your feet cold?" "Haven't you got any shoes?"

With their bare goose-fleshed feet, Rudolph, Margaret, and Johnny picked their way between the prickly-pear cactus without answering. But it was plainly to be seen that more and more the continued questioning and the curious staring at their bare legs and feet embarrassed them.

Gradually the weather grew colder. The cracked gumbo froze to cement. Still the Kiskis came barefoot to school.

Then the first snow fell. It was but a thin film; disks of cactus and tufts of bunch grass stuck through. Yet it was heavy enough to show plainly the tracks of the Kiski children's naked feet.

One day when John and Margaret had planned to reach school just as the bell rang, to escape the inevitable and dreaded comments of the others, they miscalculated the time. All the children were on the porch watching as the Kiskis walked, heads down, toward the schoolhouse.

"I don't see how you can stand it!"

It was the irrepressible Teddy Kirk speaking. The others left their remarks unspoken, for this time Margaret answered and there was defiance in her indistinct mumble.

"We like to go to school barefooted. We get there quicker that way."

She did not tell them that they had not come barefoot all the way; that at the hill nearest the schoolhouse, they had stopped and undone the gunny sacks wrapped about their feet and legs and hidden them under a rock. When they went home, they would put them on again, for no one else went their way.

But little Johnny wasn't as good at keeping his mouth shut at home as he was at school. He didn't know better than to tell that none of them had worn the gunny sacks *all* the day. Fortunately or unfortunately for the children, a little Old World discipline was exercised upon them. The next day they wore the gunny sacks *all* the way to school. They wore them all day, too.

Their schoolmates and their teacher after a while grew used to seeing the coarse string-bound sacks, but the Kiskis never became used to wearing them. No longer did Rudolph take part in the games. Margaret grew sullen and unapproachable like him. On pleasant days when the girls strolled by twos and threes with their arms about each other, Margaret stood alone in a corner against the wall. Sometimes they invited her to come with them; but she never answered. All recess she would stand there just looking at the ground. At last the girls quit asking her. Margaret made believe that she did not notice either them or their neglect. No longer did Johnny's laughter ring out in unexpected places. All three were creeping farther and farther into their shells of silence. Finally Rudolph ran away. After two days his father located him in a barn, where he had been hiding in the hayloft. Unless he had milked the cows in that barn he had had nothing to eat during his absence. He was brought home and made to go back to school.

In November the threshers came to Kiski's place. Because the field there was so small, they made that threshing their last job before pulling out of the country. Mr. Kiski hauled the wheat to Hilger and bought shoes and stockings for the children who attended school.

Other school children, the smaller ones especially, always proudly displayed their new shoes at school the first day they wore them. Several times that fall the teacher had been asked to admire the pretty perforations on the toes, the shiny buttons, or the colored tassels on the strings. But the Kiskis were almost as painfully conscious of their new footwear as they had been of the gunny sacks. They arrived with faces darkly flushed, sat down immediately, and pushed their feet far back under their seats. The teacher had hoped that to be shod like others would gradually restore their former morale. She was mistaken.

Kiski's cow had come fresh. The children had butter on their bread now. Miss Smith heard about it. She had occasion to pass by the children as they stood eating and she saw that it was really true about the butter. Yet the Kiskis would not eat with the others. They continued to go out at noontime. If the weather was severely cold or stormy, they ate in the hall, quickly. Then they would come in, without looking at anyone, and go to their seats.

As the four-month term drew to a close, Miss Smith's heart ached for the Kiskis. They had not learned a great deal from their books; she had been unable to supply them with the many bare necessities they lacked; and their own keen realization of being different had made their attendance a torture. They were so unapproachable, too, that she found little opportunity to show them her love and sympathy. She had had but one chance that she knew of to do so, and she was grateful for that one occasion, though it had not affected the Kiskis' silence nor changed in the least their subsequent conduct.

It came about in this way. Miss Smith had been late to school. There had been a heavy snowfall in the night, and she had not had previous experience in breaking trail. If she had not been new in the country, she would have known that wading three miles through knee-deep snow takes considerable time. When at length she reached the schoolhouse, the Kiskis were there standing about the cold stove. All were crying—even Rudolph. They had been too miserably cold and numb to attempt building a fire for themselves. As soon as Miss Smith had the fire crackling merrily, she took Johnny in her lap, undid the new shoes and stockings, and began to chafe the cold little feet. And when his crying still persisted, she began telling "The Tar-Baby." She had noticed early in the term that he particularly relished this tale. And sure enough, at the very first "bim" of Brother Rabbit's paw on the tar-baby's cheek, Johnny laughed through his tears right out loud—something he had not done for a month. Miss Smith decided to tell stories all day.

She felt justified in entertaining the Kiskis this way, for they were the only pupils who braved the roads that morning. She had a great fund of fairy tales and folk tales, and a gift for telling them; also she had that day an audience whom professional entertainers might well have envied her. Johnny leaned against her knee. She put one arm about Margaret, who stood on one side, and would have put the other about Rudolph, on the opposite side, had she dared. He was a boy and eleven. With shining eyes and open mouths they drank in *Cinderella, Hansel and Gretel, Snow White, The Hag and the Bag, Jack and the Beanstalk, Colter's Race for His Life,* and *Mowgli.*

Only to replenish the fire and melt snow for drinking water did Miss Smith stop. Her audience was too timid and self-effacing to make any spoken requests, but after each happy ending their eyes clamored, "More, more!"

At noon the water on the top of the stove was boiling. Miss Smith put condensed milk and a little sugar in it and brought the hot drink to the Kiskis in the hall. For out there they had gone as soon as she announced that it was dinner time. They accepted with smiles and drank every drop, but without a word. Miss Smith, too, stayed in the hall to drink her tea with them. Then the storytelling went on again, until three o'clock in the afternoon, when the teacher bundled them up in some of her own wraps and sent them home.

Going back to her boarding place, stepping carefully in the tracks she had made in the morning, Miss Smith reflected that should the county superintendent ever learn of her program for the day she would be in for a reprimand.

In such a case, she thought, she would defend herself on the grounds that since formalized education had failed noticeably to benefit the Kiskis, it was not altogether unreasonable to try a little informality. Anyhow, she was fiercely glad that the Kiskis' school term would include one happy day.

It was with sorrow and regret that Miss Smith made her way to the schoolhouse on the last day of the session. With the other pupils she had accomplished something in the way of progress, but the Kiskis she would leave embittered, shyer, and more isolated than she had found them.

She had just reached the shack and barely had time to pile the kindling into the stove when she was aware of subdued noises in the hall. She thought absently that it was unusually early for the children to be arriving. When the door opened a crack to allow someone to peer in, she began to wonder what was going on. Then with a rush the three Kiskis were at the stove.

With her unmittened purple hands, Margaret was thrusting something toward her. It was a small, square candy-box of pristine whiteness. A wide, pink silk ribbon ran obliquely across the top and was looped into a generous bow in the center.

"We brought you a present, Teacher," Margaret began breathlessly.

This time, however, Rudolph did not want his sister to be the chief spokesman. "There are fourteen pieces, Teacher. Two have something shiny around them. We looked."

And before Miss Smith had time to recover from this surprise a miracle came to pass. Johnny spoke, and he spoke in English!

"It is to eat, Teacher. It is candy."

Miss Smith said, "Thank you, children. It was very good of you to give me this."

She shook the stove grate vigorously. The ashes flew into her eyes. She had to wipe them.

"Open it, Teacher. Open it now."

The teacher took the box to her desk. The Kiskis followed and stood about her watching. There really were fourteen pieces. Johnny pointed out the two with tinfoil. Each of the fourteen reposed daintily in a little cup of pleated paper. It was a wonderful box, and Miss Smith was lavish with praises of it.

She held the opened box out to them. "Take one," she invited; and as they made no motion, "Please, do."

The three black heads shook vigorously. Johnny's hands flew behind him.

"They are for you, Teacher," they protested. "You eat."

But Miss Smith couldn't eat just then. More than anything else, she wanted to see the Kiskis enjoy the contents of that box themselves. She felt small and unworthy to accept their astounding offering. But again, how could she refuse to accept it and kill cruelly their joy in giving? It was a gift not to be lightly disposed of. An inspiration came.

"Would you care if I shared it? There is enough so that every child in school can have a piece. Johnny could pass it around when they all get here. Would you like that?"

"Yes, yes, yes." Their black eyes shone.

Johnny carried the box to his seat and sat down with it. Rudolph and Margaret hovered about the teacher, happy, eager, excited. Rudolph explained how it all came about.

"Anna came home from Lewistown last night. Margaret and I wrote her a letter once and told her to buy us a present for you. We were afraid she'd forget, but she didn't."

Teddy Kirk was coming. Rudolph and Margaret saw him and ran out on the porch.

"We brought candy for teacher. You are going to get some, too. Johnny has it. Come and see!"

Teddy was too taken aback to say anything. They led him in easily. The pieces were counted again.

Other children came. Rudolph and Margaret met each new arrival before he got to the door. To each in turn Johnny exhibited the box and its contents. He did not mind being the center of attraction now. He made use of his new-found speech, too.

"I am going to pass it around," he told them. "When the bell rings, I am going to pass it."

Rudolph and Margaret talked. They chattered. The other children kept still. They had to get used to these new Kiskis.

When the bell rang, a few minutes before time, everybody was in his seat. Johnny got up and passed the candy. Teacher saw to it that he got one of the shiny pieces.

Candy—candy of any kind—was a rare treat to everybody. These chocolates were very fresh. They had soft creamy centers. Some had cherries in them. The children had not known that sweets like these existed.

They took their time about the licking and nibbling. Delights such as these had to be given their just dues. There was no needless or premature swallowing. And to think that the Kiskis had provided it! The Kiskis were assuming importance.

The Kiskis ate candy, too. They beamed on everybody. They had had something to give and everybody thought their gift wonderful.

The sun shone. At recess the girls again walked about by twos and threes. Margaret walked with them. Teddy presented Rudolph with one of his horseshoes, and Rudolph began to pitch it. Edward, the other first-grader, found a string in his overall pocket and promptly invited Johnny to be his horse. Johnny accepted.

He trotted; he paced; he neighed surprisingly like a horse. Then he kicked at the traces a while.

"You should say, 'Cut it out,'" he instructed his driver.

That noon the Kiskis ate lunch in the schoolhouse.

Adventure: The Beginning
Montana Bill

by Spencer Norman Lauson with Dolores W. Boyles

Spencer Norman Lauson was born in South Dakota in 1901 and raised in Billings. He was a traveler, hobo, and college student between the ages of 18 and 35. He later worked as a petroleum chemist and building remodeler.

With my deep desire to get an education, came the realization that the world around me held so much to see and experience. How could I ever get to all those places I was reading about. When would I ever have the chance to leave Billings, much less Montana, or the States?

One late spring day [1923], when I was studying under a tree for the exams that would finish up the school year [at Billings Polytechnic Institute], a friend yelled from across the shaded campus.

"Hey, you want to see Jack Dempsey train?"

"Sure, just like I want to see the Tower of London," I replied, with a smirk.

"No kidding, he's going to be in Great Falls and I'm going up to see one of my friends that used to go to school here. Want to come along?"

Suddenly my world had expanded, at least as far as Great Falls. For me, even traveling a couple hundred miles was an adventure. And I wasn't going to miss it!

As soon as exams were over we started out. Ed was a mechanical genius, and it was a good thing, for the clunker we were driving looked like it had long since served whatever purpose it was put on earth for, and intended to retire shortly. The road we were taking was even more uncertain. We drove along the Alkali Creek Trail to the old Buffalo Highway, a poorly marked road where rusty, red directional tin signs hung from time to time on section line fences. It was difficult to tell just where we were. About a third of the way to Great Falls, the dilapidated old car decided that this was the place it would give up the ghost.

I sat on the ground next to the car and watched Ed as he poked his head under the hood to determine the cause of the car's demise. It was a desolate area. It would be luck if we saw another car passing this way for the rest of the day; for sagebrush and buffalo grass stretched as far as the eye could see. I could imagine, as I sat there wiping the sweat from my neck, what herds of now-extinct buffalo had thundered past this very spot decades ago, pursued by Indians on a hunt. Only the rustic tin signs identifying our road as "Buffalo Highway" reminded the traveler that vast herds of buffalo once grazed here.

"Got it!" Ed yelled out, as he raised his head from under the hood. "Just needs a bearing, and I think I can make one out of a lead washer."

"Boy, I hope so," I said, shaking my head. Staying overnight in this place didn't appeal to me, for I had seen a rattler stretch out around a rock and slither away as I watched in quiet horror.

The next hundred miles saw me perched on the front fender, holding an oil can to lubricate the bearing. It would be the only way we would make it, Ed had said. My hope was that disturbed rattlesnakes would not strike out at my dangling legs as we drove by. If this was what traveling was all about, maybe I wasn't cut out for it after all.

Mercifully, the red tin buffalo signs marking the dirt trail eventually led us into Great Falls, where throngs of people had gathered to watch Jack Dempsey train for a fight on the Fourth of July in Shelby, Montana.

Nicknamed the "Manassa Mauler" from a town named Manassa located in Southern Colorado where he was born, Jack Dempsey had compiled an impressive record of 50 victories and only two losses when he knocked out Jess Willard to become the heavyweight champion of the world. In Shelby he would defend his title against Tom Gibbons. Ed decided to stay in Great Falls to visit with a school friend, but after watching Dempsey train, I had to see the fight in Shelby. I caught a train to the prairie oil town, and when we pulled into the station an astounding sight met my eyes. A gigantic Chautauqua tent town had sprung up on the prairie. Fight enthusiasts slept in tents, railroad coaches, boxcars or bedrolls on the ground. Those who slept on the ground risked unwelcome guests with rattles on their tails. I was not going to take that chance and finagled a place in a boxcar.

By the next morning the tent town extended far out into the prairie. However, this enormous gathering of fight fans did not bring in enough money for the promoters to cover their costs. Unfortunately, many had come out of curiosity and had no intention of paying the admission fee, let alone $250.00 for a ringside seat. Soon the crowd outside the arena fence far outnumbered those inside. As they pushed and shoved, maneuvering for a better view, suddenly the fence collapsed and the freeloaders swarmed into the grandstand. I elbowed my way through the mob and managed to get a cherished ringside seat.

The fight was a long and drawn-out affair, Gibbons staying on the defensive most of the time as he endeavored to keep out of reach of the famous mauler. The crowd was disappointed that there was no knock-out and no blood drawn. Dempsey finally retained his crown through a technical decision, but Gibbons gained fame in spite of his loss. The promoters were the real losers in this fight, as it broke the whole community.

I guess you might say that the trip to Shelby was the beginning of my romance with traveling. As rugged and uncomfortable as it was, it was far better to strike out to someplace new than to wither and die in the small town where I grew up. I watched people get old there, never seeing anything different, never knowing there was another kind of world out there, and I wanted none of that.

A Trip after Cough Medicine

Daylight in the Canyon, the Memoirs of Eleanor Lynde

by Eleanor Lynde

Eleanor Lynde was born in Wisconsin in 1913. After her parents came west to homestead, she grew up in Hardin. During her family's long career in the sheep business, she faithfully kept a journal of their lives on the lonely, wind-swept prairies and mountains of eastern Montana. Following her husband Myron's death, she transformed these memories into *Daylight in the Canyon*.

Early the next morning, right after breakfast, Myron bundled into his sheepskin coat, tied his black silk scarf around his neck, put on his hat and buckled his overshoes. I handed him the mail, letters the herders had written, those I'd written to family members, Stan's precious letter to Santa, and of course the very important catalog order.

Myron said good-bye at the door. The elderly Bill Mills walked out with him. They talked a bit and Myron slid into the driver's seat and skillfully drove out the gate. It was six o'clock and just breaking day, and I felt good about him getting the early start. I stood at the window, watching him maneuver through the snow drifts until he was out of sight. I felt great love, pride and admiration, that he was willing to tackle this difficult trip for his family.

He told me not to worry, but how could I help it unless I kept myself busy? I washed clothes, baked bread, did some sewing, read to the children and cooked a nice supper.

Bill Mills had taken a lunch as he had to be out in the hills with the bucks, but he came in at six o'clock for supper. Both of us were worried about Myron and had hoped he'd be able to make it home by supper time. He hadn't, but I was determined to make pleasant conversation. The first words that rolled off my tongue gave me away, though: "I wonder if Myron made it to town okay?"

The same thing was on Bill's mind, and he answered quickly, "Oh! Mine (his way of saying Myron) is a real good driver. He'll make it if anyone can...but in all of this snow, I don't see how anyone could make it. The worst part is that the road goes through those deep coulees. They're blown full of snow and when it crusts like it is now, a pickup could drive out on it and drop through and then really be stuck. You know, my horse couldn't waller through it."

Supper was finally over and dear, kind Bill went to his bunkhouse. As I was picking up the dishes, I paused at the darkened window, hoping to see the pickup lights. I said some prayers for Myron and then felt better. That night, each time I got up to give the children their cough medicine, I'd look out; at twelve o'clock, it wasn't snowing. The wind wasn't blowing like it had been and the stars were shining. I wondered if it was a good omen.

The clear weather was more cheerful, but I knew that Myron could still be in trouble. I decided that if he hadn't returned by the next day, I'd have Bill ride down to the Grapevine Ranch and ask the cowboys to start searching the country.

I got up early for the usual six o'clock breakfast, but Myron still wasn't back. As I looked out the window, I was reminded that the children would be needing fresh underwear, so I hurried out to the line and got a handful of clothes to dry back of the cook stove. While I was out, I thought I saw a pickup on top of a high hill which was nowhere near the road. I couldn't imagine who would be up there among those boulders. I hoped it was Myron, although I knew he wouldn't be driving up there. But who else could it be? And if it was Myron, why was he so far off the road? Was he lost, sick, injured? I could hardly wait for Bill to come in, and I could hardly prepare breakfast for looking out the window every few minutes.

My vigil was finally rewarded by the sight of our truck pulling into the yard. Myron had been stuck so many times on his way to Hardin that he didn't get there until six o'clock at night. He went right to the druggist and got a large bottle of cough medicine, and fortunately our grocer was willing to stay open until Myron's large order was boxed up and loaded.

Stan, hearing his dad's voice, scurried into the kitchen. "Dad, Dad! Did you get my letter mailed to Santa?"

Myron grinned. "I sure did, Son. I had a lot of trouble, but I got to the Post Office and put the letter to Santa right in the mail slot."

Wearily he leaned back in his chair and talked about the past twenty-four hours. "As soon as I got gas and everything was loaded, I started back, hoping my tracks weren't badly blown in. It was dark by then. Some of the road was okay because I could see the tracks, but there were plenty of times I got stuck and had to dig out. On my way to town I noticed the wind had blown snow off the top of the hills and when I couldn't go through a coulee I'd try to go around it by going up in the hills. I made my own roads whenever possible, even though I knew that I could run into a boulder and tear up the pickup. That is why I was on the hill near here. Ellie, I sure was glad when I saw you out to the clothesline so early. I figured that the kids weren't too bad or you wouldn't be out there. You know, the cabin with the smoke coming out the chimney and you out to the clothesline was a beautiful sight. I knew everything was normal. These hotcakes are a mighty welcome sight, too. Let's eat."

Yes, everything was normal. Myron was home safely, a big bottle of cough medicine sat on the shelf, and a two month's supply of groceries was stowed in the cupboards and cellar. I said a prayer of gratitude.

Creating a New Community in the North: Mexican Americans of the Yellowstone Valley

by Laurie Mercier

Stories from an Open Country: Essays on the Yellowstone River Valley
William Lang, editor

Laurie Mercier is Program Director at the Center for Columbia River History and Assistant Professor of history at Washington State University-Vancouver. Mercier has researched ethnic and oral history in Montana, Oregon, Washington, and Idaho. She is the author of numerous articles on oral history, public history, and women's history in regional and national journals.

The Yellowstone River wets the richest agricultural lands in eastern Montana. Since the early twentieth century, irrigation projects and the nation's sweet tooth have made sugar beets the most profitable and enduring crop grown. Unlike agricultural products such as grain and livestock, which demand little more than the labors of a single family, sugar beets have required an army of temporary workers to thin, cultivate, and harvest the persnickety roots. Mexican Americans have provided much of this essential labor, yet their contributions have gone unheralded. This essay traces the history of the Mexican Americans who came to the Yellowstone as seasonal workers and created a vital ethnic community, which has persisted despite years of economic hardship, discrimination, and cultural and social change.

Long before Montana became a state, Hispanic explorers, trappers, miners, and *vaqueros* were among the first non-Natives to visit the region. After the United States annexed the northern half of Mexico in 1848, many Latin Americans continued to migrate to the north, but it was not until the 1920s that Mexico's dramatically increasing population and an expanding western U.S. economy combined to persuade millions of residents to seek work across the border. By 1930, more than one thousand Mexicans and Mexican Americans had come to the Yellowstone Valley.

Federally financed reclamation projects transformed the arid West in the early 1900s, including the Yellowstone valley, where Billings capitalist I. D. O'Donnell and other local businessmen invested in growing sugar beets, an expensive and labor-intensive crop. They incorporated the Billings Sugar Company in 1905 and built one of the largest sugar beet factories in the world the following year. A dozen years later, during the height of wartime agricultural demand, the Great Western Sugar Company bought the factory and encouraged area farmers to plant beets instead of wheat. Beets became a profitable investment up and down the Yellowstone, and Great Western became Montana's (and the nation's) largest sugar producer. Holly Sugar Company also built factories in the region at Sidney in 1925 and at Hardin in 1937.

Profitable sugar beet production required a reliable supply of low-cost labor, which the Montana labor market could not supply. Sugar companies began to recruit from areas where labor was more abundant and from groups of people who had been denied access to other kinds of employment. In 1921, Great Western's Labor Bureau in Denver recruited 385 beet laborers from "southern points" in Texas, California, Colorado, and Mexico for Montana farms. Two years later, the company reported that most of the 500 workers they imported were "of the Mexican type," the beginning of a seven-decade reliance by the beet industry on cheap labor from the American Southwest and Mexico. Government and industry worked together to maintain this employment niche for Latinos. Even when many Americans clamored for immigration restrictions in 1924, for example, growers lobbied for unrestricted movement of Mexican labor and Congress exempted Mexicans from new immigration quotas.

The Great Western Company cultivated its dependence on two ethnic groups to tend valley beets. In 1924, it brought to Montana 3,604 Mexicans and 1,231 German Russians to harvest a record 31,000 acres that year. But the company had different long-range plans for each ethnic group. Great Western loaned money to its German Russian growers, hoping to attract their peasant relatives, who could provide temporary labor for thinning and harvests and eventually become tenants and even landowners. This Company encouragement, along with kinship ties, community acceptance, and ready adjustment to Montana's climate, probably explains why 77 percent of the German workforce remained in the Billings district that winter, a sharp contrast to just 25 percent of the Mexicans. Company actions reflected American racial assumptions that European immigrants made more capable landowners than Mexicans, who many insisted were more suited to agricultural labor than farming.

The racist underpinnings of American culture, together with restrictive legislation and hiring practices, hindered Latino economic mobility, and the low wages made agricultural labor a family endeavor. Families migrated and worked together as a unit and sold their collective labor to farmers. This pattern of family migration and family wage-work shaped the character of the Yellowstone's Latino community and helped maintain fairly equal male to female ratios. It also stimulated the growth of a settled community. Sugar companies, which sought to maintain a stable workforce, promoted family settlement by providing transportation, labor contracts, and housing for families.

The Great Western and Holly Sugar companies created *colonias* near their factories to encourage Mexican workers to "winter over" in Montana. In 1924, the Great Western Company invested in improvements in the Billings *colonia,* which housed forty-two families. Mexican laborers built ten new adobe apartments, cindered streets, extended the water line, constructed a drainage ditch, and leveled and planted grass on the compound grounds. Severo "Sal" Briceno came with his family to Billings in 1928, and he recalled that the forty-odd adobe homes of the *colonia* each had one bedroom, a woodstove, and an outhouse. Briceno's family of nine spread into two of the small homes. Residents were responsible for upkeep, and the factory donated tar to patch pervasive leaks in the flat roofs. An outdoor water faucet served every five houses, and when temperatures dipped, Briceno remembered, "we'd have to go out there and make fires around it to unfreeze it."

As in other industrial labor arrangements, settled families fostered a stable workforce, and the *colonias* helped families remain and survive on their meager wages. *Colonia* residents could raise chickens, pigs and gardens to supplement their diets. The company also created a winter jobs program on the factory grounds, believing that in the spring "there would not be a big debt hanging over [farmworkers'] heads, making them more willing to work in the territory rather than to leave...in order to get away from their debts." The *colonia* provided a clinic and school for migrant children and unified the Latino community. Esther Rivera recalled that her father, Fred Duran, "used to talk about the *colonia* all the time. Everybody knew everybody. The people really hung together."

As the *colonia* provided the immigrants with a sense of community, it also isolated them from other residents, while their growing numbers also aroused prejudice. The Great Western Company campaigned against the baseless fears directed at its Latino labor pool. During the 1920s, the Company's annual reports emphasized that Mexican laborers had "solved the farm labor problem," that many were U.S. citizens, and that they were skilled workers. These reports concealed the racial tensions that predominated in white Billings.

During the first half of the century, people who spoke Spanish and/or were perceived as "Mexicans" faced great discrimination in Billings. Sal Briceno recalled that Latino children could not participate in the annual Kiwanis Easter egg hunt in South Park: "They had men on horses riding around that South Park kicking us out. There were a lot of kids that wanted candy, but they'd kick us out." Latinos were banned from the public swimming pool, segregated in theaters, and not allowed in restaurants. Signs above some Billings business doors read, "No Mexicans or dogs allowed." Mexican Americans knew racism's unwritten rules and the boundaries of acceptable behavior. Robert Federico's four aunts and mother had vivid stories of "where they could go and could not go." If they could endure stares and taunts, for example, they could venture into the local skating rink. But most places, such as bowling alleys, were off limits. Sal Briceno noted "they (whites) would have kicked me in the head with a bowling ball" if he had ventured there. Barred from most stores, Mexican Americans were dependent on their farm employers to do their shopping.

Farmworker families usually came as part of a crew or group of families recruited. Robert Rivera's family was part of a trainload of Californians who were recruited and promised "opportunities" in Montana during the 1920s. Once in Billings, farmworker families often stayed at the St. Louis Hotel on Montana Avenue across from the depot, while they waited for the Great Western Sugar Company to match them with farmers and take them to the farms. The Riveras and other families, who wintered over for beet planting in the spring, stayed in the *colonia* until the Company transported them once again to Custer, Hysham, Belfry, Joliet, and other places where farmers needed labor. The company also arranged credit at the local grocery until workers were paid and brought farmworkers back to the *colonia* at the end of the beet season. But with limited earnings, families faced many a grim winter. Rivera recalled that his family and most others took their beet earnings to Sawyer's on 29th and invested in bulk groceries:

> That's where most of the people traded, and if they had 3-400 dollars to spend on groceries for the winter, they would buy in big lots, flour by the 100-pound, coffee by the 25-pounds, lard by the 50-pounds, and as much groceries as they could afford they'd take in provisions for the winter. Of course when that was gone, that was it.

Some migrant workers developed lasting relationships with farmers and sought to renew their associations each spring, while some other families remained with farmers throughout the year and helped in feeding cattle and mending fences during the winter while they waited for the beet season to begin. As Robert Rivera noted, these arrangements helped sustain farmworker families and also initiate permanent resident status:

> If they wanted you to stay, a lot of times they would offer you the place to stay for the winter if you wanted to. Then the men would work for them...which was better than moving back to the colony, because once you moved back there was nothing to carry you through the winter.

Cowboys Don't Walk: A Tale of Two

by Anne Goddard Charter

Though raised as a debutante in St. Louis, **Anne Goddard Charter** was drawn to the simplicity of the West. She and her husband, Boyd, have ranched in Wyoming and the Bull Mountains. She helped found the Northern Plains Resource Council, a community-based conservation organization that advocates a strong connection to the land.

The Bull Ranchers Bunch-Up

The next day, Boyd and Bob Tully decided we'd better all get together to see how we could fight this [coal stripping in the Bull Mountains]. A meeting of ranchers was called at the Tully ranch. We decided we all had best work together and stick together and the best way to start was to become an organization. So we called ourselves the Bull Mountain Landowners Association, elected officers and agreed to present a united front to the coal company.

Bob Tully was elected chairman, and as I was the one living in Billings with the kids during the winter, I was elected vice-chairman. My job was publicity. The only thing I could think of doing was to call *The Billings Gazette* and give them the news that we had formed an organization, what our purpose was, and the names of our officers. I was referred to reporter Dave Earley who listened to my spiel, asked a few questions and then, silence.

Being a woman, I had to fill in that silence, so I blurted out that Lou Menk, chairman of the board of Burlington Northern had just bought a Bull Mountain ranch and we were considering (tongue-in-cheek) asking him to become a member. His ranch was actually outside the coal field but he was still a neighbor. Dave seemed to appreciate a good joke, and he asked me to bring him some maps the next day. When I presented him with the maps he informed me that Mr. Menk would have to decline our offer to make him a member of the BMLA.

"What offer?" I cried. "We haven't even talked to him."

"Oh but I did," said Dave. "I telephoned him to see what his reaction would be. He told me that he was a true conservationist at heart, but that his first duty was to his stockholders."

That incident provided us with about a year's-worth of publicity. Dave Earley followed up every aspect of our publicity and every story with a reference to "Menk in the middle!" This gave us confidence in our ability to be noticed and make a difference, and it kept up the momentum.

…Perhaps our most significant undertaking as the Bull Mountain Landowners Association was the Washington, D.C. adventure. As none of us had any previous experience in politicking, organizing or public relations, we were prone to do just about anything anyone suggested. We were told that hearings on strip-mine reclamation were being held by a House of Representative's committee and that we should try to get in on it. We wrote, received the reply that they were filled, but there would be another hearing later on. We were turned down for that, too. That made Boyd mad and he said, "Call Senator Mansfield and I'll talk to him." These were House hearings and he was in the Senate, but Boyd said that didn't make any difference. And it didn't.

Senator Mansfield got us in on the hearings. Our men suddenly had a lot of pressing ranch work, so three women were delegated to go. It was decided that Vera Beth Johnson, a young, striking looking rancher's wife, would explain the situation in the Bulls. Ellen Pfister, with a law degree, would tackle the actual reclamation problems. I, the grandmotherly type, would come up with a speech made up of "it doesn't make sense"—most of which could still be applied today.

Ellen did her homework, part of which consisted of ferreting out information from the Agriculture Department at Montana State University, which was reluctant to come up with information, as much of their financing for the research had come from mining companies. There was no "right to public information law" then.

In D.C., our initiation to the hearing was to sit through several hours of listening to Representative Steiger of Arizona harass those representing the Navajo Tribe in their protest against the infamous Black Mesa strip-mine. They were accused of agitating on the reservation, and being backed by communists. You could feel the hostility in the air of the hearing room.

When our turn came, it was getting close to the noon recess. All three of us wanted to get our two-cents-worth in, for by then we were fighting mad. Vera Beth was first up with a map, and all her best school teacher skills ready to present our situation. She noticed that Steiger was talking over his shoulder to an aide and was paying no attention, so she called out, "Representative Steiger, do you know where the Bull Mountains are?"

At first, there was dead silence, then the whole room dissolved in laughter and the press corps practically rolled under the table. The chairman rapped his gavel saying, "Mrs. Johnson, it is not customary for the witnesses to ask the questions. Please proceed."

Completely undaunted, Vera Beth proceeded and from then on we had everyone's undivided attention. No one seemed to mind that we ran over into the noon hour. Afterwards, the coal lobbyist came up and said, "You ladies should come more often, you do liven things up." The Chairman told Vera Beth she reminded him of his daughter, and Steiger said he guessed that if it was his land, he'd meet them with a shotgun. We began to feel good, and when our fellow believers began to gather around us, we felt better and better. We gathered for lunch to become better acquainted and became friends and helped each other through the years.

The Northern Plains Resource Council

While trying to save our land from mining in those days, things just seemed to happen. And so it was with the founding of the Northern Plains Resource Council (NPRC). The big event on the Bull Mountain Landowners Association (BMLA) agenda was to participate in the first coal symposium to be held in Billings which supposedly would present all sides in the coal controversy. We knew that the "front men" had been working eastern Montana even before they hit the Bulls, and they were getting some Xes on their dotted lines. We felt the need to get together with these other landowners to share fears and strategies. They undoubtedly would come to this gathering, so we'd have a chance to meet and talk with them.

In the meantime, we heard from Billie Hicks, a member of the Audubon Society who was on the planning board, that the "environmentalist" on the panel was from North Dakota's Knife River Coal Company, and that all the panelists would be industry men. We told her we'd get our own environmentalist, and she could assure that he got on the panel.

Cecil Garland, founder of the Montana Wilderness Society, accepted our invitation to be our environmentalist. But we were informed that the panel was full, and that it would be unfair to those giving up their valuable time to come to Billings to add anyone else.

When I told Cecil that they would not let him on the panel, he said not to worry. He'd come anyway, a day early, and if I'd gather a few interested people together, we could plot our strategy. About eleven of us met that evening, and we plotted and discussed. The need for an umbrella organization kept coming up, and finally, Cecil said, "Why don't you just form one?"

"How?"

"All you need is a name, officers, membership dues and a letterhead."

After much discussion, Ms. Pfister came up with the name Northern Plains Resource Council. She said the Northern Plains would be our territory, and if we called ourselves a resource council, we would not limit ourselves to just coal. She indeed had an eye for the future. We elected officers and each of us paid the five dollars dues to become the charter members.

The following day, the symposium began with formal introductions, but soon our strategy was clear: we were going to have our say and challenge every word spoken by the panel members. The panel members were constantly interrupted, challenged and argued with, not only by our group, but by the entire gathering. There were few passive listeners. Nothing was accomplished, but it generated a lot of righteous indignation.

After the meeting, we signed up lots of new members from all over eastern Montana and Wyoming for our Northern Plains Resource Council. We were becoming a community. This casual beginning was a far cry from the accusations made by the big eastern potentates that subversive outsiders, probably communists, had come in to organize and finance us.

Later Voices

Old Willows, Winter
Isabelle Johnson
oil on linen (1948)
Courtesy Yellowstone Art Museum
Permanent Collection, gift of the estate of Isabelle Johnson

Isabelle Johnson: A Life's Work

by Donna M. Forbes

Born in Nebraska, **Donna M. Forbes** moved to Billings with her family in the 1930s. She became director of the Yellowstone Art Center in 1974 and retired in 1998 after overseeing its expansion and transformation into the Yellowstone Art Museum.

I remember her hands. Tough, gnarled, arthritic. She was fond of looking at them. They seemed to represent the embodiment of her art; the means of making that nervous line that marked on canvas or paper this place she loved so well.

"A sense of place" has become the usual descriptive nod given to those visual and literary works that loosely fall under the category of regional. Yet no Montana artist since C. M. Russell has had such a profound sense of place as Isabelle Johnson. She saw this hard, rocky, handsome land with a painter's eye, and a rancher's sensibility.

It was a lonely business, being a painter in Montana back in the 50s and 60s. Isabelle had been warned, while studying at Columbia, that if she returned to her home, there would be no one to understand the artist's struggle, no one to discuss those intriguing complexities found within a canvas. She would have to be her own critic. Few rewards. Obscurity.

In varying degrees, all of this did happen. There were some friends to talk to—Bill Stockton, in particular. She and Bill had some wonderful, great, wild arguments that lasted far into the night when she taught at Eastern Montana College. I'm sure the young art students were mightily puzzled over the depth of information those two widely educated, formally trained artist-ranchers brought to the fray.

Never one to openly seek a market, Isabelle waited for the recognition her maturing work deserved. She would inwardly rail at an audience too far removed from the great art museums and centers of culture to have the depth of information her work demanded. The pervading local amateurism was a torment. But recognition did come in 1970 with a one-woman exhibition at Fort Worth's fine Amon Carter Museum of Western Art. The director, Mitch Wilder, came to the Johnson ranch one day at the suggestion of Terry Melton. He looked through Isabelle's studio work and saw the artist there. A show was arranged, the culmination of 25 years of painting, and remained the highlight of her life.

Isabelle was intensely proud of her "real" students, among them Ted Waddell, Jim Poor, Orlin Helgoe, me. We were the children she never had, and she followed our careers as carefully as any anxious mother, admonishing when she thought we had strayed from her high standards. With graduate study in art history complementing her formal art training, she could be wickedly accurate in her assessments.

The first Isabelle Johnson painting I saw, as a young woman back from a year's art study in New York, was *Old Willow, Winter* [page 187]. We had just met and Isabelle had invited me to the ranch to see her work. I had not expected to see painting like this in Montana. We became instant friends. To this day I cannot look at the Montana landscape without seeing those wonderful paintings. Our friendship lasted forty years as I went from student to, in Isabelle's words, "my boss." During the last decade, she would pull out paintings and ask what I thought. Should she sell them, were they worth keeping, or should they go into the bonfire? She knew the answers but wanted the dialogue.

A number of years after I became the Yellowstone Art Center's director, Isabelle and I discussed the importance of a home for her work. By that time she had sold seven paintings to the C. M. Russell Museum in Great Falls. The Yellowstone Art Center had purchased or been given several. It was imperative, I told her, that the body of her work be preserved intact as a legacy for Montana. The Yellowstone was building a major collection of Montana work from the 1950s forward. This would be a cornerstone of that collection. She seemed relieved to know that her work would be part of a museum.

Finally, all of her family were gone. Close friends visited daily. Our former long drives over the hills as she recounted the history of the Crow people, the Bozeman Trail, and the settlement of the Stillwater country, were shortened. She silently battled cancer, loss of hearing, a stroke—all of the signs of aging she refused to acknowledge. Her incredible good nature never flagged, nor her acerbic comments about art and artists. She read constantly, art journals, history. Her final project, *The History of the Stillwater*, was completed just before her death. Writing had replaced the painting she could no longer manage.

A Month of Sundays—The Best of Rick O'Shay and Hipshot

by Stan Lynde

Stan Lynde is a third-generation Montanan, born and reared on the rangelands of the Crow Indian Reservation in southeastern Montana. He is the creator, author, and artist of two highly acclaimed syndicated cartoon strips, *Rick O'Shay* and *Latigo*. He is also the author of two novels. Lynde is a recipient of the Inkpot Award for achievement in the comic arts and the Montana Governor's Award for the Arts.

White Shorts and Tennis Shoes
Sketches from the Ranch: A Montana Memoir
by Dan Aadland

Dan Aadland ranches and writes in south-central Montana. He holds a Ph.D. in American Studies and has been a Marine officer and teacher. His many equine articles have appeared in magazines such as *Equus* and *Western Horseman*. The following passage comes from his fourth book.

It has continued to rain. We appear to be getting a traditional set-in June storm, cold enough at our altitude to prompt a fire in the woodstove. Over several days three inches have come down, enough to keep things green well past the Fourth of July, so we take joy in that, even while edging toward cabin fever. Montanans do not do well when deprived for very long of their big sky. Also, relatives are visiting. It is nice to see them, but the rain makes it harder, for coming from territory totally paved, they haven't learned mud control. We do our best to train them in our nearly Oriental dedication to removing shoes in the "mud room," but this is difficult for them, and their shoes continually release squiggles of mud on the kitchen floor. It is a small thing, true, but I am stubborn and am certain I can train them. When they forget to remove their shoes I stare at their feet while I talk to them. Usually this works, but then I feel guilty. They are good people.

I have to get out of the house. Emily is not a very willing foul-weather rider, and I'm a lousy foul-weather host. She agrees that the cattle need checking (but she knows what I'm up to). I head out the door with apologies to the guests, my slicker under one arm, Tom Sawyer escaping from Sunday school. Major, too, is anxious to go. He is so wet that as I curry him I pull off sheets of water which splash down on my boots. But there is from time to time a brief lull in the rain, a thin spot in the clouds, a good omen.

Under the protection of the tack room roof, I take time to rag a coat of neatsfoot oil onto my saddle. Then I throw it on Major and we "light out for the territory." Even in the rain I am liberated. I wonder what I would be psychologically without this space around me, shudder, and force myself to think happier thoughts.

We slog through the mud up the wagon road to the top of the hill. I have avoided the steep trail on the side of Indian Coulee, a concession to safety. Major has not yet been shod, and I'd rather not go skidding down a sidehill. The rain has all but stopped, the hole in the clouds enlarging. And then it hits, just as I top out, the stubborn sun finally born again, grudgingly at first, the sagebrush flat bathed in yellow halftone. Then the theater lights come fully on and the range in front of me is as green as Ireland. I'm quite smug about my timing.

The cattle check is routine, at least at first. I check the salt trough, find the supply waning, worry for an instant about getting up here with the pickup and a resupply, muddy as it is, then remember the two-year-old mare I need to start in training. Nothing more quickly trains a new young horse to accept weight on its back and to ignore strange touches and sounds than to pack a hundred pounds of salt up the hill. I can get her to that stage in a couple days, put a sawbuck pack saddle and panniers on her, and throw a fifty-pound salt sack in each side.

The next thing to check for is the presence of the bulls, errant critters who sometimes look to the other side of the fence not just for better grass but for hotter cows. (The guys always think the girls in the neighboring town are prettier.) I quickly see three of the four. Breeding is still going steadily, for the cows are in small bunches, a bull with each, not scattered randomly. Far to the south there is a large black critter that could be a bull, but he is too far away to tell for certain, and I've spared my binoculars a wetting by leaving them home. So Major and I ride half a mile until we can see that, yes, this is the fourth bull.

It turns out to be a fortunate detour. Along the way we find a black baldy cow whose calf moves strangely, its head held just a bit to the side. We get up to the pair and I see what I feared—the calf has a nose full of porcupine quills. His face looks like a pincushion. From what I can see the steer calf has been spared the worst a porcupine can dish out, for his eyes look clear and I can see no quills through them. But he's a mess. Left unattended he will either starve or die from a quill working its way back into the brain. We worry about predators, but in some ways porcupines, rabies-spreading skunks, and marauding raccoons cause us more grief. All have their places in nature, I know, but I have little good right now to say about the critter that has caused my liberating ride to turn into actual work.

Oh, well. At least the rain has stopped. Before the work begins I shed my slicker and tie it behind the cantle. It is not yet all that warm, but by Montana standards the humidity is up there. Major's wet hide, heated up by the sun and his exertions, gives off clouds of steam. Were I a better cowboy and in condition to relish wrestling and tying this calf, I would rope it and pull out the quills with my Leatherman tool. But neither of those things is true, and the calf, born in February, already weighs about 300 pounds. Instead we'll cut out the pair and do our best to get them home to the corral. This will be touchy on such slippery footing, for the cow will have the edge on Major, who is barefoot and packing considerable weight.

It proves quite easy, however. The calf is enough affected by his condition to be rather subdued, and the cow is a good mother, sticking with him like glue. So the two line out down the wagon road. At the bottom of the hill we take them through a gate into the hayfield, down through a meadow, and soon have them trotting down the lane into the corral. In less than half an hour after discovering the calf, Major and I have brought them two miles in.

So now I need to get the calf into the alleyway which runs to the squeeze chute. This effort is hampered by what three inches of rain does to corrals—the mixture of mud and manure is a foot deep with the consistency of chocolate pudding. I feint this way and that, trying to get the cow and calf into the smaller pen, hear a sucking sound and realize I've left my overshoe-covered cowboy boot planted in the mud. I do a backward hop on my weak left leg and manage to insert my foot back into the boot. (None of the alternatives would be pretty.)

I know I should go to the house and get help, Emily and Steve, but I keep thinking I can get this done without the delay that would cause. So it's back and forth, slogging until the sweat runs down my face, flecks of mud and manure catapulted onto me by eight hooves every time I turn the cow and calf, my eyeglasses speckled with the stuff, my clothes covered, my disposition edging gradually in very violent directions, an involuntary stream of wretched language coming effortlessly from my mouth. And then I realize I'm being watched.

Visiting Relative is standing well back from the corral, where the gravel is good and there is no mud. He has been watching my frustration. He says, "Is there any way I can help?" He seems to mean it, and for a moment I'm encouraged, for one human standing in just the right place to keep the cow from running there would make this entire ordeal into a piece of cake. Then I look at him.

He is wearing a white knit shirt, white shorts, and white tennis shoes. He is spotless. No, he is more than spotless, he is squeaky clean. Alongside him Moby Dick would look small and dark. I swear I can smell his cologne. I look down at my decimated clothing, take off my glasses to wipe the droplets of brown manure into a translucent stain, and say back to Visiting Relative, "No, thanks a lot, but I'm certain I'll get it eventually."

And, of course, I do, and once the calf is in the chute pulling the quills is no big deal. And all along I think of just how right Thoreau was when he bragged about getting all the good things from his neighbors' farms without the work, the mortgage, and the worry. He can take walks across their fields, he says, for which the farmers can find no time. Visiting Relative will enjoy fishing in "my" river while he is here, something I will not have time to do, will take his family on several hikes, will kick back, drink beer, and relax. I will play catch-up on the work I missed during the rainy days. I do not begrudge him his fun, for this is his vacation and he works hard at his job. But standing in the mud and looking at him in white shorts and tennis shoes has been much like looking at a visitor from another planet. His offer to help, though sincere, is useless.

Those of us who stay on the land incur a social obligation, not just a business one. We are forever hosts to the extended family. At best, most ranches will only support a single family unit, so where do the brothers and sisters go? Los Angeles, Seattle, Cincinnati. And because a ranch is the ultimate home, it remains so to all, remains a place toward which part of the psyche of all who have known it inclines like the salmon to where it was spawned. This is understandable and good, for the ranch could be a lonely place without visitors.

Billings: The First 100 Years, A Pictorial History
by Anneke-Jan Boden

Anneke-Jan Boden taught speech and communication for many years at Eastern Montana College (now Montana State University-Billings). She was a founder and first general manager of KEMC, the National Public Radio affiliate for eastern Montana. She has published extensively in diverse genres. See page 117 for biographical information about **Ben Steele.**

The Line Camp
Ben Steele
pen and ink drawing (1973)
Courtesy of the artist

Ranchers constructed line camps at points distant from their own homes. The line camps provided safety from the blinding snowstorms and usually had been stashed with firewood and food supplies. (Caption to the drawing by Anneke-Jan Boden.)

Home

Kayaking the Full Moon: A Journey
Down the Yellowstone River to the Soul of Montana

by Steve Chapple

Steve Chapple is a journalist, screenwriter, and novelist. He writes regularly for *The New York Times, Conde-Nast,* and *Sports Afield.* He divides his time
between Billings and the Paradise Valley.

I once asked my own father why he never became a doctor. "They always
paid my father with bushel baskets of wheat or cucumbers," the Old Man
had said, and he laughed at the irony of what doctors have become.

...My grandfather Henry came to Billings from Toronto in 1889. Three
Montana families from Canada—the J. D. Mathesons, engaged in the newspaper business, the Pentons, who were ranchers, and the John Rixons, who
were in printing—wrote to Trinity Medical College, requesting a physician.
My grandfather was second in his class. It was eastern Montana's second
request for an Episcopalian physician. He wanted to go to Montana. This
was the way it was done.

Billings was a tent town on the Yellowstone then. I have a picture that
used to hang in my father's office. It is by L. A. Huffman, dated 1882. It
shows a short, single street. The south side of the street is empty and fades
off to the Yellowstone and Sacrifice Cliff, the same view Hemingway would
later have from a higher elevation. The north side of the dusty street is lined
by white canvas saloons: the Blue Grass, the Buffalo Grass, and the Bunch
Grass. It is not hard to imagine the clientele who would be attracted to
drinking joints with the names of vascular plants. Texas cattlemen were
driving their animals north.

"At this early state in the growth of Billings, the gambler, the dispensers
of strong drink, and women of the 'red light' were numerously represented
in Billings and plied their several occupations, brazenly," a Congregational
minister of the time claimed. What a string of moronic clichés only a
Congregational minister could come up with. Not that everything he said
was not true. But in what measure? And in what mixture? And who else lived
in Billings? My father was buried by a Congregational minister, but at heart
both men were Unitarians, if that.

Within a year the Northern Pacific had laid tracks through town. A
hundred thousand pounds of silver bullion was transhipped from the Judith
Mountains. The army of the plains needed resupplying. Farmlands were

opening, first to pioneers, soon to waves of immigrant sod busters. Tents
were folded. Buildings were built with lumber. A pretty good basin of oil
north and east of town would be discovered—but not for another forty years
or so, and not enough that Montana would become another Texas.

In 1887, two years before my grandfather arrived, there was a last Indian
scare. It was a strange one, since it involved the Crow, some of whom had
scouted for Custer on the side of the whites, against the townspeople.

A young Crow warrior named Wraps-Up-His-Tail went to the Bighorn
Mountains and fasted. In his vision he saw the Son of the Morning Star
sweep a sword through a forest. Trees fell. Wraps-Up-His-Tail understood
this to mean that if he wore a sword, soldiers would fall like trees before him.
In one account, Wraps-Up-His-Tail and his followers wore red flannel and
rode horses of the same color. They all carried swords. Wraps-Up-His-Tail
believed he was invincible because he was following his vision. He and his
band stole sixty horses from the Blackfeet, then returned to the Crow
Agency. They did not like the agent. They fired on his headquarters. Gen.
Alfred Terry was notified. He decided to proceed with caution. Citizens of
Billings called a meeting. Troops from Bozeman took the train to Billings,
but turned around. A fight was soon provoked.

Wraps-Up-His-Tail, who is now called Sword Bearer, made a "bravery
ride" before the white troops, perhaps with the expectation that they would
die when he slashed the sky with his sword. He was fired upon. His heel was
hit and so was his horse. He rode into the hills. He was taking a drink of
water from a creek. An Indian policeman named Fire Bear approached and
shot him through the back of his head, saying, "This is for getting all these
people in trouble."

My family never talked of any of this. The railroad came. The Old West
ended. Civilization began.

Dr. Henry encouraged his brother James to join him. James was also a
doctor. Henry and James sent for their younger brother Charles to dispense
their medicines as town pharmacist. They installed him in a tent. The tent
became a red brick building. The building became a landmark. "You Can Get
Anything at Chapple's." My father's first job was to discourage shoplifters and
to talk with old Spanish War veterans, to discourage them from buying legal
morphine. This was about 1905. My father felt sad for those old sheepherders
and cowboys, addicted defenders of democracy against evil Spain. Great-
Aunt Jennie came down from Canada and married a British cattleman named
Graham. Lou became county attorney. Tom Chapple started the furniture
store. Great-Uncle Charley invited Plenty-coups and his wives to lunch on

his front lawn when they came to town. Jane Rixon, Charley's wife, did not like that much, according to their granddaughter.

Billings was prospering. The town was named for Frederick Billings, a Vermont banker and Northern Pacific Railroad executive. His son Parmly and his nephew moved to the town that had offered up its name to Eastern capital in that optimistic if sluttish manner of Western towns wishing to guarantee their future. The Billingses owned a huge chunk of bottom land, as well as their interest in the railroad. "I would rather be mayor of the city of Billings than president of the USA," smiled Parmly Billings. "We intend to annex New York, and there is some talk of hitching on Boston." So these transplanted Vermonters had a Montana sense of humor, at least.

Parmly Billings died the year before my grandfather was elected mayor, a year after Judge J. R. Goss became mayor. It was Judge Goss who set up the town meeting that asked the troops to look into Sword Bearer's "rebellion," as it is called now. Judge Goss's only daughter married Uncle Lou, whose son Wreford torpedoed the first Japanese ship of World War II, the *Haro Maru*. Wreford was also sent to rescue Douglas MacArthur in the Philippines but was waylaid because his submarine, the *USS-38*, sank a Japanese attack ship near Mindanao. That much is in the *New York Times:* "WREFORD CHAPPLE, 83/SUBMARINE WAR HERO DIES."

Wreford's cousin, Charley, Jr., who invented the Isolette for preemies and grew up over on Yellowstone Avenue, maintained Wreford had actually rescued MacArthur, which I do not think is true. It contradicts the *Times*. My mother's version of the story, which I do not think is true either, contains one of those difficult-to-verify details that make history, not to mention the word of one's mother, always so imprecise. "Wreford's was the second submarine to reach MacArthur's position," says my mother. "They sent more than one, for MacArthur. MacArthur's furniture was there, his household effects, as well as several American nurses who had reached the beach with the general. MacArthur told Wreford to load the rattan furniture and leave the nurses. Wreford, of course, protested. He was told he would be courtmartialed if he disobeyed. He took the rattan."

Americans swoon for their heroes. I doubt that the truth about MacArthur and his furniture has probably come out any more than the truth about Sword Bearer. In an account that Judge Goss wrote, he says that the news that Sword Bearer and the Crow wanted to "kill off all the whites that were in this country" came "through an Indian girl who was staying as a servant in the family of Paul Van Cleve, ... she being a Crow herself...." One wonders why, since the Crow had allied themselves with the whites for generations, they would suddenly rise up like Sioux. The Salem witch trials were also started by a servant in a home. Hysteria serves a purpose, as often as not, and soon enough. In Massachusetts, the lands of witches were confiscated. In Montana, Indian reservations were further circumscribed.

Chicken Guts and a Royal Coachman

Yellowstone Reflections

by Roger Clawson

Roger Clawson is the winner of several national awards as a reporter and newspaper columnist. He spent his adolescence exploring the Yellowstone River bottoms and islands around Custer, Montana.

What's a boy raised on chicken guts doing feeding royal coachmen to the aspen? The thought rippled through my gray meat like a fingerling chasing hellgrammites.

Standing up to my shinbones in water too cold to drink, I flicked my wrist. Forty-seven feet of hollow core fly line rose from the water and curled over my shoulder. Flicking my wrist again, I shot the big curl toward a glassy patch of blue water in the lee of a boulder.

POP!

The line cracked like a bullwhip, shooting a $1.89 dry fly into the ether.

Muttering a few of those seldom-heard disparaging words, I re-rigged. After snagging an aspen on this side, an aspen on the other side and a cockleburr bush 15 yards behind me, I managed to drop a fly on the flat water behind the boulder.

A trout broke water, swallowed my fly, spit it out and thumbed his nose at me.

Nine dollars and 37 cents worth of flies later, I hit the blue patch again. Another strike. This time I managed to set the hook before the fish could cough it up. I jerked the line so hard that the 3-inch rainbow trout flew 36 feet into the air. Not everything that goes up must come down. The fish became entangled in tree tops among a cloud of artificial insects from earlier casts. Another fisherman, one of those guys with a .5 ounce split bamboo rod and spider web for leader, waded past. "Hey," he said, "look at the fish in the trees." "What trees?" I growled.

The next fish I hooked may have weighed 3 pounds. It may have weighed 1 pound or 14. Who knows? I only know that I gave it such a case of whiplash that it might still be waiting its chance to sue someone.

The royal coachman is a delicate creation of feathers and thread on a hook, counterfeiting an insect native to England. It does not belong on the Yellowstone. Likewise, this canoe flier has no business on the business end of a fly rod.

Playing Isaac Walton with a graphite rod was a clear sign I had forgotten my roots. I was putting on airs, pretending to be something I wasn't.

The Old Poacher raised me better than that. The Old Poacher raised me on ripe chicken guts and corrupted beef liver. He taught me the fine art and basic science of catfishing.

First, we would fetch the guts. Refined folks might call this commodity "poultry entrails" or "offal." Fly fishermen in their tweed caps and latex boots could not be compelled to say the word if they had a creel full. But we called 'em "guts." Next, we stopped by the railroad yard to collect a half ton of scrap iron from the junk pile.

Then, with the bait in the open air of the pickup box (so it could breathe) and us inside the cab (so we could breathe) we were off to the river. At river's edge, the Old Poacher would build trot lines of heavy cord with double ought hooks and great chunks of iron as anchors.

He baited the hooks and slung the weights into the water. The sinkers made splashes that scared the beaver. Then he settled back, rolled a Bull Durham cigarette and spun stories until catfish the size of newborn calves found our lines.

Catfishing and flyfishing are as different as England and Montana, as different as Prince Charles and the Old Poacher. One is not better than the other. They're just different.

Both the Prince and the Old Poacher were products of birth and environment. The Prince entered the world under the right pelvic arch and was destined to be king. The Old Poacher was born in a dirt farmer's cabin and was reared to believe it is a sin, but not a crime, to kill the king's deer.

The Old Poacher might have been a fly fisherman had he lived further up river. But he lived in Custer, and that was reason enough to gather chicken guts and scrap iron on a Saturday morning. Custer's stretch of the river was and is catfish country. Big cats, from 2 to 20 pounds, are channel catfish. Stone cats are dark little fellows that seldom beat 8 inches. Black bullheads, and (less common) yellow bullheads are chunky fish that seldom top 1 pound.

The noble and native cutthroat trout once ranged downstream to the Tongue River at Miles City. Today, he can be found in only 5 percent of his former range. Agricultural, industrial and municipal pollution are only partially to blame. Part of the cutthroat's problem is the species' lack of discrimination. At Big Timber the native's identity is lost in a mixed gene pool. Mixing with brown and rainbow trout, the cutthroat disappears in a muddle of hybridization.

Brown and rainbow predominate from Big Timber downstream to Billings where warmer water species begin to flourish. Meet the mystic ling.

On the middle Yellowstone ling fishing is neither sport nor food gathering. Ling fishing is a ritual.

A long, green, eel-like fish, the ling spawns under the ice in February. The majestic violence of spring breakup triggers the primordial instinct of the ling fishermen who migrate to the strand with buckets of minnows, gas lanterns and an ample supply of good lies.

A ling fishermen would never ask another, "Did you get your limit?" The question would be akin to asking a parson how many of his prayers were answered. Ling fishing is a form of worship.

Smallmouth bass, native sauger and walleyes predominate below the mouth of the Bighorn River. Of the three, the walleye has the biggest following. Walleye fishermen have their own magazines and lobbying organization. In state capitals they are a redneck, grassroots force to be reckoned with. On the river they are a bunch of good ol' boys slinging metal at the fish, trading lies and sharing cold beer.

Walleye, smallmouth, browns and rainbows are all imports. Even the cutthroat is a relative newcomer, having slipped over the divide into the Yellowstone drainage in the past million years.

Of all living things that walk, swim, fly or take root along the Yellowstone, none is older than the paddlefish.

In the 1800s anglers occasionally snared large fresh water fish they called "spoonbilled cats." This living relic from eons past is older than the river. More than 60 million years ago, paddlefish spawned in streams that no longer exist. The species was 40 million years old when the Yellowstone was born. In historic times, the paddlefish spawned throughout the Mississippi drainage.

Dams drowning rivers reduced the spawning areas to six, with the lower Yellowstone the hottest of all. Close your eyes pilgrims. Now, picture this. A dry fly fisherman, a purist who has never touched a nasty angleworm or nightcrawler, transported from his blue ribbon stretch of the upper Yellowstone to Glendive.

At the Intake diversion, he opens his baby blues to see men armed like gladiators, chunking treble hooks and sparkplugs at the flood. "Who are these Neanderthals?" he might ask.

Here, fishing is neither art nor science.

It's combat. With a long blunt tail and tiny mouth, paddlefish range up to 90 pounds.

No one knows why, but paddlefish were not caught or at least not report-ed in the first half of this century. The Garrison Dam on the Missouri blocked migration of the big fish in 1953. Nearly a decade passed before the first of the young paddlefish above the dam reached maturity and began to plow upstream to spawn in the Yellowstone. When an angler caught one in 1962, the paddlefishing caught fire and 60 were taken within a week. Nearly all the fish were male. The slow-maturing females appeared in the early 1970s.

Today, almost 5,000 fish averaging 50 pounds each are taken in Montana every summer. Glendive shops offer one of the finest selections of deep-sea fishing gear to be found in a small city more than 1,000 miles from salt water.

Sun Dance: The 50th Anniversary Crow Indian Sun Dance

by Michael Crummett

Michael Crummett is a free-lance photographer and writer from Billings. His book, *Sun Dance: The 50th Anniversary Crow Indian Sun Dance,* received the National Benjamin Franklin Award for Best Book on a Multi-Cultural Topic in 1993/94.

The little Crow Indian baby lay dying. At ten months of age, he had hardly grown and was as small as the day in June, 1938, when he was born. He had ceased eating and drinking, and the outlook was grim.

His parents, William Big Day and Annie Lion Shows Big Day, were at a loss. They had adopted the baby from Cecelia Lion Shows on Father's Day, 1938, to give him a fresh, healthy start. In the traditional Crow way, a sick or troubled child is adopted by another family in order to provide a new beginning. From Pryor, Montana, they took their child to Billings, some thirty miles away, where they hoped the white doctors would remedy his illness. Instead, the physicians diagnosed their son with double pneumonia and informed the parents that he did not have long to live.

With tears and disbelief, the couple returned with the boy to their log cabin. Patches of dirty, crusty snow still dotted the landscape around this Crow village when the local Catholic priest was summoned to administer last rites. In desperation, William undressed his failing son and took his limp, naked body out into the sharp mountain air. Greeting a new day and a rising sun, Big Day held the child heavenward and asked *Akbaatatdia,* the One Divine Being, to spare his only child. "If you will let my boy live," he prayed, "I promise I will bring the Sun Dance back to my people."

Within four hours, the infant began to drink water. Soon he was eating beef soup, a thin, nutritious broth. Miraculously, William's son made a full recovery and regained his health completely.

Faced with such a traumatic experience, William Big Day's vow to (sun) dance again was a natural response for a spiritual Plains Indian. In the 1800s the Sun Dance was a culturally paramount, supremely sacred ceremony of religious purification and renewal. Over the course of four days and three nights, Sun Dancers prayed to the Great Spirit, abstained from food and water, fluttered under the sizzling summer sun, suffered physical torment from self-inflicted "piercing," and trilled through eagle bone whistles in an effort to transcend the actual confines of the Sun Dance lodge and reach a most-personal spiritual realm. Self-denial, bodily pain and an endless stream of tobacco-smoke prayers to the Almighty were offered as a testimonial of the individual's genuine purpose of attaining good health, locating buffalo, gaining greater power over an enemy, stealing horses or manifesting revenge.

Big Day witnessed his first Sun Dance in 1938, and actually participated during the summers of 1939 and 1940 at Fort Washakie, Wyoming. Under the revered Shoshone medicine man, John Trehero, whose Indian name was Rainbow, William had several moving experiences. For one, he discovered a large lump coming through his lower ribs and became very ill on the second day of the ceremony. He could not move and could not dance because it hurt so badly. Rainbow finally got him up to the Sun Dance Center Pole and began doctoring William with his medicine feathers. By the time the treatment was complete, the lump had vanished and Big Day was able to dance back to his station, then finish the grueling ceremony. Both men had a vision and acknowledged that, had it not been for that Shoshone Sun Dance healing, William would have died by spring. "I found out," William affirmed, "that this Sun Dance was a great and powerful thing."

...In the summer of 1941 William Big Day kept his promise to *Akbaatatdia* and conducted the first Crow Sun Dance since 1875. For sixty-six years, the Crows had abstained from this sacred ceremony for reasons ranging from the federal government's policy of assimilating all Indian people, to white reservation missionaries denouncing the indigenous religious practices as evil and pagan, to internal tribal reassessment of the ceremony. But since the life of his baby boy had been spared (which coincided with these other influences in his spiritual development), Big Day's vow would be fulfilled and his place in Crow Indian history indelibly imprinted.

...The Crows' first Sun Dance in Pryor, in 1941, was actually William's fourth. Shoshone Medicine Man Rainbow had been invited to help Big Day with all of the ensuing responsibilities. Participating were twenty-three dancers, one of whom was Anglo but married to a Shoshone woman. On the first day, William's vision about the passing of the medicine feathers became a reality. According to Big Day, "John Trehero got up and gave the feathers to me, and said, 'I give these feathers to you. You can help your people when they are sick. You can doctor them in the Sun Dance, and in everything that they might need help—help them with these feathers. The power of the Sun Dance is through them feathers.' Then I was standing towards the sun and raised my hands to the sun, and thanked Him for finding a way (for me) to help my people." After that first Sun Dance, Big Day was convinced that "some kind of life came back to the Indian again!"

In 1942, William Big Day participated in the second Shoshone-Crow Sun Dance in Pryor, sponsored by Frank Hawk and conducted by Tom Compton, another Shoshone Medicine Man. In addition to sickness, the abiding concerns of this ceremony, held against the backdrop of World War II, were the prayers for peace and for the safe return of Crow soldiers fighting for the United States on foreign soil. From 1941 to 1946, there were nineteen Sun Dances, half of which took place outside of Crow Agency, tribal headquarters of the Apsáalooke or "Children of the large beaked bird." During this period the Sun Dance was firmly re-established among the Crow Indians; it has been conducted regularly ever since.

In the summer of 1991 a very special Sun Dance was held in Pryor, at the exact spot where the first one was conducted fifty years before. The historical significance of this ceremonial was that it marked the Golden Anniversary. It was exceptional because Heywood Big Day, the medicine man who sponsored and conducted the 1991 ceremony and dedicated it to his father, was the same person who, as a baby boy near death fifty-two years before, was the inspiration for William Big Day's reintroducing the Shoshone Sun Dance to the Crow in 1941. Heywood was a living testimonial to the strength of the Sun Dance tradition, truly an unbroken circle of love, spiritual rejuvenation and cultural rededication.

poetry by Donna Davis

Montana native **Donna Davis** is an award-winning poet and actor, some-time philosophy professor, and quondam attorney. In 1997, the Montana Arts Council awarded her an Individual Artist Fellowship in Literature for her poetry.

March

You can't trust her.
She's counterfeit,

pretending to summer
like the bastard to the throne.

She feigns the sway
of the greening bush,

but she's winter's accomplice.
Slut that she is, she invites

the thrust of tulips and
pink and purple hyacinths,

then wags her frosted finger,
as much to say, "Naughty,

naughty, not just yet."
She'll whisper to

your most private parts
and lick your solar plexus

and just when you're ready
to say yes, yes,

she'll stand akimbo,
one hip jutting,

and dare you to join her
above the hardblown clouds.

And when you say no,
she'll shine and shine
and leak into real spring.

In the Days of Rock 'n' Roll

In the Jeep we
bop to the beat
my son and I and I
tell him as we tap and snap,
feet and fingers giddy,
I can remember this
the first time
around and he says,
so can I, and I laugh
and his eight-year old
voice climbs, I'm serious,
I was there, too, inside
you while you danced
at the Armory,
because

didn't you say I
was once your egg, so I
did ride in you since
forever, swirling around
blind but I learned the beat
of Buddy Holly and the Beach Boys
the throb of Louie, Louie
and I knew midnight
by the slow dance
that smoothed shut the fun
and how you loved to dance
with Danny, second best
dancer to his best pal
Hal with the hot car and smooth
moves and why he dated Sallie Jo
because her sister got p.g.
and he figured like sister,
like sister — not the p.g. part,
just the doing it —
and how we walked one day

all the way to his house
on the edge of town, me

all snugged up inside you
and you not even suspecting
I'd ever show myself
with a face, you not ever
wanting kids, only a pony
(but boy what a ride
you had when I first
became me, whole,
and you at last wholly you)
because nobody slugs a pony and
there'd be nothing to hide

and especially after seeing
Hal's house which you thought
at first wasn't his, all small
and rundown, his fat wheezy
mother with her dirty
hair, the grey echoed in her
fleshy arms and flowered house-
coat out on the porch
in an old busted La-Z-Boy
and wondering how could she
especially when her son
was so cool with his white
socks and Bass loafers
and Beatle cut and nice
even teeth and then we

went home and you made sure no
one could wonder about us so
you got straight A's and
never ever invited anyone
over to our house, huh, Mom?

Resolutions for the Coming Millennium

The woman with no bones resolves
to find courage elsewhere.
I offer her my spine; she declines.
She'll grow her heart so big
that ribs become unnecessary.
For protection. I resolve to emulate her.

As I become more mountain-like, I resolve
to make a talus slope. This should serve.
To slow the assaults on my summit.

Hock-high in snow, the white horse stands
with a pinto and a roan. I glance back
for a second look. There is no white horse.
I resolve to let cease
the impossibility of being me.

Like the fabled Tibetan waterfall, I am a constant
with no constancy. I am hidden, but do not hide.
Thus I have no need for resolutions.

I sleep with an owl under my pillow and resolve
to be wise. Or feared. Or foolish. I practice
turning my head 15 degrees more each hour. One
revolution per day with ebb and flow and stasis.

I breathe and in this one breath, I shrink
the world.   in   hold   out   pause
In the next, I am become the world
in   hold   out   pause   and all
that was and all that is and what will be
resolved

Nature's Graces to Gathering Places

Creeker: A Woman's Journey

by Linda Scott DeRosier

Linda Scott DeRosier was born in the upper room of her grandmother's log house at Boone's Camp, Kentucky, and spent her early life in eastern Kentucky. She is the 1999 recipient of the Frances Shaw Writing Fellowship, granted to support her work on a novel. She teaches psychology at Rocky Mountain College.

Nature was hard to miss in my home country. What with the floods, the humid heat, and the paucity of bottomland, I often viewed her as somewhat less than kind. But she sent flowers to take the edge off. The summers of my youth were filled with a remarkable array of flowers, both indigenous and cultivated, that seemed to surround every house in my community. The scent of honeysuckle always takes me home because it grew wild everywhere in my home county. On the bank directly across from my house, Aunt Exer fought the dread honeysuckle—which we called "the weeds"—with her climbing roses, but it was pretty much a losing battle. Wild honeysuckle is the kudzu of eastern Kentucky. As children, we loved to chase each other through the honeysuckle thicket by the creek. Some adult, usually Pop Pop, would always check for snakes in the weeds before we were allowed to cavort in there.

At the edge of the weeds across the creek in front of our house, a huge stand of immense orange tiger lilies multiplied each year and held their ground in the face of the honeysuckle onslaught, while purple flags prolifer-ated every which way on the side of the hill that bordered our backyard. Momma planted red and white gladioli in her bed in the side yard, along with sweet williams, peonies, spiderlegs, and cannas, but she was never able to get a climbing rose to do a thing, even though she routinely put in new ones every year....

Nobody back home could tell me the proper name for spiderlegs, and I could never get any to grow from the seeds Momma gave me; so that was one favorite I was unable to carry with me from the hills. Then about five years ago I saw some spiderlegs blooming in a nursery and learned their proper name (cleome). Since I have been able to name them, I have bought cleome plants each year and even raised a few of my own. Most of the ones I have raised have not felt particularly welcome in Montana's cool, dry, and short growing season and have refused to grow tall or to return on their own. A good part of my heritage is in my flower bulbs and seeds that I have carried with me as I have moved around the country. Two deep-purple irises and a white peony—homegrown, all—grace my desk even as I write this piece.

It has been interesting to watch the descendants of the flowers of my homeplace adapt themselves to the soil and climate of a new land while I have also been learning to deal with the different environment. I think some-times that I am much more tolerant and flexible about my expectations of my flowers than I am of my expectations of myself and other human beings. After I moved to Montana in 1988, it took seven years for my peonies to bloom. I continued to feed them and neither cursed them, spat at them, nor displayed any other signs of impatience or disappointment. I wish I could be as patient with human nature as I am with my physical environment.

As we learned to appreciate different aspects of nature—from floods to flowers—we also had to learn how to harness nature to our own ends. In most families, women learned one set of accomplishments, men another.

Since my daddy had no sons, I was required to master some skills clearly in
the male realm. Growing up as a country-wife-in-training and as Daddy's
"boy," I learned many skills that would serve me well if I should ever need
to breed, raise, kill, and cure my own meat; or grub, plow, and otherwise
prepare a field for planting; or sow, hoe out, and harvest vegetables; or cook,
can, and preserve those fruits of my labors. With small variations, we shared
an unwritten calendar, which marked the proper time to put in one crop or
another. For me, Valentine's Day is far more likely to bring back memories
of sowing lettuce and planting onions than remembrances of romance. In
case you ever need to know…you always put in your lettuce and onions on
February 14.…

Although back then I may not have been the most willing worker in the
world, I feel a lot stronger now in the knowledge that I can take care of
myself because of having taken part in all those life-preserving duties. Let me
admit that I have not done most of those very basic tasks since I left home
at age seventeen, and I hope I never have to do them again. In the sixties and
seventies, when many of my academic friends and colleagues longed to
return to the land, my suggestion was that if they had ever lived on the land,
they might not have been quite so nostalgic for it. Trying to keep a coal fire
banked so that it will last the night and not burn dangerously high, as well
as having to break the ice frozen on the top of the water bucket in the
morning, instills a powerful appreciation for central heating; and just a few
times of carrying last night's full chamber pot to the outdoor toilet as day
breaks makes indoor plumbing most welcome.…

My dear husband, the original tree-hugger, will probably shoot me when
he sees this account, but he has no idea how very close to nature some of us
were forced to be. He grew up in a small town in Connecticut. If he wanted to commune with nature, his family drove to the shore or to the
Berkshires. Therefore he is concerned for every snail darter and tree owl on
the planet. Although it is not true that I would lay four lanes of blacktop
across Yellowstone Park and call it progress, I am not too far away from that
position. Town folk live in places where nature has been so long domesticated that they don't know her for what she is. Living close to the land taught
me that nature can be—indeed, usually is—a mean mother.…

There is a comin'-home spirit that is an essential part of growing up in
Appalachia; if you grow up there, you never doubt where home is. I carry
that spirit of place, and I perpetually call upon that spirit to address every
new experience in my life. I live in Montana now, and I deeply appreciate
the beauty of my adopted home. But much of what I love about this place I
never would have noticed had it not been for my growing up on Two-Mile.

The house I live in now is nestled under 400 feet of rock cliff. I suspect that, once you look beyond the tiny green handkerchief that is my backyard, not much about the two-hundred-foot field of boulders that leads up to the rock face—or the cliff itself—has changed since man moved in. I probably spend more time than I ought to looking at those rocks, watching the morning sun gradually overtake the butte that lies to the west, and later watching the purple shadows of evening shift as the boulders play hide-and-seek with the setting sun. At night those rocks turn white and seem to glow in the moonlight as I sit on my back porch and think about all the folks who have come and gone while those old rocks have stood guard. In a now-you-see-it-now-you-don't world, those rimrocks are now-you-see-'em, now-you-see-'em…now-you're-gone. The ridges of home tell different tales from my rocks, but I would never have noticed one without the other. I learned to look for and to think about such things on Two-Mile, with Pop Pop telling Sister and me about old-growth timber long before either of us could make any real sense of such a lesson. You cannot grow up as close to the land as I did and not notice your natural surroundings, and you cannot grow up Primitive Baptist without seeing time stretched out before you and behind you and pondering the world's meaning and your own. I know, for example, that I have been extremely lucky in this life: lucky to have been born into a time and a place where folks may not have had much in the way of material things to pass along, but they handed down a sense of belonging that cannot be taken away even by disapproval or hostility.

Ride with Me, Mariah Montana

by Ivan Doig

Born in 1939, **Ivan Doig** is one of the state's premier writers. His memoir, *This House of Sky* (1978), a finalist for the National Book Award, recounts his coming-of-age in central Montana. He currently lives and writes in Seattle. The following excerpt is taken from the last installment in his trilogy dedicated to Montana's centennial.

Billings begins a long way out from itself. Scatterings of housing developments and roadside businesses and billboards full of promises of more enterprises to come began showing up miles ahead of the actual city. The Bago and we four were rolling in on the freeway that runs shoulder to shoulder with the Yellowstone River, then the Yellowstone shied out of the picture and snazzy profiles of hotels and banks against the rimrocks became the feature.

"The Denver of the north," Riley crooned in an oily voice as downtown Billings came up on us. "The Calgary of the south." He waited until we were wheeling past a petroleum refinery that was obviously functioning much below capacity. "The Butte of tomorrow?"

"Mmm, though, look what the light is doing," Mariah put in. There in the late afternoon sunlight, the cliffs rimming the city were changing from baked tan to a honeyed color. Then and there I formed the opinion that held for the rest of our time in Billings, that if you had to have a city this was an interesting enough place to put it....

The Holiday Inn was quite the extravaganza, whether or not you were about to get your nuptial knot tied there.

Walk in as the four of us were doing and the lobby vastly soared all around you; in fact, that cubic center of the enterprise at first encounter seemed to be universally lobby, a hollow square the entire six stories to the roof and equally out to the perimeters of the half-acre carpeted-and-plantered space. You had to wonder whether the architect remembered to put on motel rooms, until you discerned that the half dozen beige facings that ran all the way around this atrium at equal heights apart like the ribcage of the building were actually balconies, with room doors off them. The place had a lot of other ruffles, too. Up one side of the whole deal shot a glassed-in elevator shaft outlined with sparkly dressing room-like lights the full altitude to the ceiling. There, natural light descended through a skylight, I suppose for the sake of the trees—some of them fairly lofty—in eight-sided containers, beige, plunked near the middle of the atrium. At the far end of the expanse was a waterfall, no less.

I fingered my bowtie. A tuxedo was a new sensation for me. Beside me as we trailed the Mariah-Riley vanguard into the assemblage, Leona behaved like she went to weddings in the atrium of the Holiday Inn every day of her life.

True, she had been a little surprised to come into the Bago with the groceries and be informed by Riley we were going to a matrimonial function. "But I thought you two were waiting for the privacy of California. I don't have a thing to wear and—"

"Mother, it's not Mariah and me, it's"—he consulted his notebook—"Darcy and Jason."

Which didn't help Leona get her bearings any. "Do we know them?"

"That never matters with these two," I edified her about journalism....

Riley still had something monumental on his mind as Mariah balanced against him to grimly work her feet back into high heelery. The moment she was shod again, he gave out another big goofy smile and said:

"You know, we could make this a double header."

Witless witness though I was to Riley's sudden new shenanigan, I caught his drift before Mariah did, her photographic attention already focused back into the wedding throng like a riverjack trying to figure out just where to dynamite a logjam. *Doubleheader, hell,* the recognition hit my dismayed brain, there went the *ballgame.*

The object of Riley's intentions tumbled rapidly enough, however, to what had just been put to her. Her head jerked around, eyelids fanning, as she a little wildly sought verification in his face. "Get married, you mean? Here and now?"

"Yup, now and here," he corroborated with utmost good cheer. "All we'd have to do is arrange for the minister to hang around until Darcy and Jason scoot off to their honeymoon. Why, we've even got dear loving family on hand," he dispensed along with a generous wag of his head toward me and then one in the general direction of wherever his mother was mingling. "How about it, Mariah Montana?"

I honest to God had the impression, right then, that even Elvis in triplicate stopped spinning, for the longest of moments, to watch whether Mariah was going to endorse Riley's inspiration to hightail to the altar. So much for my campaign against. No, reason and history and minimum common sense never stand much chance against the human impulse to dart off and do it.

"N-No, no I don't think this is the time and place," Mariah declined nervously, to my surprise, not to mention Riley's. "Getting married in this"—her eyes did a loop-the-loop to indicate the infinite reaches of the Holiday Inn lobby—"while we're doing a piece here would seem kind of, mmm, tacked on, don't you think?"

What I thought, not that anybody was running a poll for my opinion, was that now they could derive a sample of what they were letting themselves in for by remarrying. Blow up at her, left, right, and sideways, I mentally urged goddamn Riley: insist it's now or never, matrimonially, because that way you'll come in for a nice reminder of the spikes that spring out when Mariah stiffens her back. Jump him, the dressed-up motel romeo, for treating marriage like the decision to go get an ice cream cone, I similarly brainwaved Mariah. Get out the big augur, each of you, and remind the other of how you caused the wind to whistle through the holes of that first marriage.

But see how Riley can't even be trusted to be his normal aggravating self? He fixed his two-tone gaze on Mariah and, in the same soapy mood as when he'd strolled up, grandly allowed: "A woman who knows her own mind, just what I've always wanted. California is fine by me, for us to get official." And off he went to sop up some more mood of the occasion, humming a little Mendelssohn....

I still can't account for the next event. I mean, there I was, dutifully keeping my nose out of Darcy and Jason's event, trying to blend my plum-tuxed self into the maroon backdrop of the atrium rug, when the bald guy emerged from the crowd and came straight at me as if he was being led by a dowsing stick.

Actually, the guiding instrument sat on his shoulder. The videocam in fact might have been mounted permanently there, the way it led the guy shoulder-first as if he was doing some kind of walking tango across the floor.

"Hi, I'm Jason's uncle, Jim Foraker. You must be from Darcy's side of the family."

"Just mildly acquainted, is all."

"I'm making a video for the kids," he said, bombardiering through the camera eyepiece onto my visage. "When Jason and Darcy get up into the years a little, it'll be kind of a kick for them to look back and see who all was at their wedding, don't you think?"

Especially when they try to figure out who the hell I am. Before I could retrieve my tuxedoed bearded self from posterity's lens, however, Jason's videoing uncle let drop: "I've got the sound package on this machine too, so how about saying something? Just act real natural. Tell the kids maybe what it was like at your own wedding?"

Which one? tore through my mind first. Shirley, when our young blood was on perk day and night. Marcella, everlasting but lost to me now too. My God, it gets to be a lot, to have to publicly pick and choose among sorrows. Darcy and Jason replaying on their golden anniversary in the year 2039 will have to be the ones to report whether I flinched, tottered, trembled, or just what. But whatever was registered by the videotape constituted only an emotional fraction. I felt as if I was coming apart, the pieces of my life I most prized—Marcella, the ranch, our life there together, our astonishing offspring Mariah and Lexa—cracking from me like streambanks being gashed away by rising water: yet at the same time I needed to hold, to not buckle under even to those heaviest thoughts, to somehow maintain myself in the here and now. Atrium extravaganza or not, other people's occasions deserve their sorrowless chance.

So. I had it to do, didn't I. Squaring myself in Jim Foraker's frame of lens to the extent I could, I began.

"Every wedding is the first one ever invented, for the couple involved. So I won't go into any comparison of this one with my own. But I can tell you a little something about after. I don't know whether a shivaree is still the custom"—some manner of mischief was; out in the parking lot I could see young guys tying a clatter of tin cans on behind a car with JUST MARRIED! DARCY ❤ JASON soaped all over it—"but after Marcella and

I got hitched, everybody in the Two Medicine country who was mobile poured in to the ranch that night."

Cars and pickups all with horns honking, it was like a convoy from the loony bin. People climbed out pounding on dishpans and washtubs and hooting and hollering; you could have heard them all the way onto the other side of Breed Butte. Of course the men laid hands on me and the women on Marcella, and we each got wheelbarrowed around the outside of the house clockwise and tipped out ceremoniously at the front door. Then it was incumbent on us to invite everybody in for the drinking and dancing, all the furniture in the living room pushed along one wall to make enough floor for people to foot to the music.

Luckily there is no limit to the congratulations that can be absorbed, and Marce and I were kept giddily happy by all the well-wishers delivering us handshakes and kisses on the cheek. Leave it to our fathers, though, to carry matters considerably beyond that. Lambing was just starting, and under the inspiration of enough wallops of scotch, Dode Withrow and Varick McCaskill formed the notion to go check on the drop band for me; as Dode declared, "Mac and me all but invented the sonofabitching sheep business." It was a mark of the occasion that Midge Withrow and my mother did not forthwith veto that foray, but just gave their spouses glances that told them to come back in somewhat more sober than they were going out. First Dode and my father had to flip a coin as to which of them got my working pair of overshoes to wear to the shed and who got stuck with two left ones from the discards in the corner of the mud porch, and then there was considerable general razzing from the rest of us about how duded up they were to be lamb lickers, but eventually the two of them clopped off, unbuckled but resolute, toward the lambing shed. Busy as we were with our houseful, Marce and I lost track of the fact of our sires traipsing around out there in the Noon Creek night, until we heard the worried blats of a ewe. Coming nearer and nearer. Then the front door flung open and there stood the volunteer over-shoe brigade, muck and worse shed-stuff up the front of both of them to their chins—Dode had been the one who drew the two left overshoes, and it had been that awkward footwear that sent him sprawling face-first; my father, it developed, simply fell down laughing at Dode—and a highly upset mother sheep skittishly trailing them and stamping a front hoof while they wobbled in the doorway declaring, "By God, Jick and Marce, you can't afford not to hire us," each man with a lamb held high, little tykes still yellow and astonished from birth: the first twins of that lambing season.

Finishing that telling, I sought how to say next what it still meant to me, that shivaree of almost forty years before.

"I suppose there must have been a total of a couple of thousand years of friends under our roof, Marcella's and mine, that shivaree night. A lot has happened since; the toughest part being that Marcella isn't in this life with me, any more. But that shouldn't rob what was good at the time. Our shivaree was utmost fun, and by Christ," I nodded emphatically to make sure the lens picked up this part, "so is the remembering of it. Darcy, Jason," I lifted my champagne glass, just a hummingbird sip left in it by now but any was plenty to wish on, "here's to all you'll store up together, starting now."

Montana Apocalypse: Extremism and Hope in the American West

by Ken Egan Jr.

Western Futures: Perspectives on the Humanities at the Millennium

Stephen Tchudi, editor

Born on the shores of Flathead Lake in 1956, **Ken Egan Jr.** teaches literature and writing at Rocky Mountain College. He has served on the Montana Committee for the Humanities and received Fulbright grants to teach American Literature in Greece and Slovakia. The following passage anticipates major themes in his forthcoming book on Montana literature (University of Nevada Press, 2002).

A recent controversy in Montana has reminded me of what's at stake in this struggle between extremism and hope for the soul of the West. Lynda Bourque Moss, the energetic director of the Western Heritage Center in Billings, proposed American Heritage River designation for the Yellowstone, a precious, meandering, life-giving thread on the high plains. Moss, along with many others living along the river, assumed that this was a win-win situation as local citizens could designate specific sites and projects for funding, and the region would benefit from a federally-funded River Navigator who would help implement the local initiatives. The director went out of her way to emphasize that the Navigator would have no authority to impose or enforce federal regulations in local communities. Yet the result was a firestorm of fear and protest. Of course the idea merited tough discussion, possibly even final rejection. But citizens poured venom upon the idea and its proponent. Why are people in the West so quick to explode into something approaching paranoia? How have we been so hurt, so emotionally maimed, that we resort to shouting matches in lieu of reasoned debate? Can we stop insisting that our way is the only way? Can we figure out a way to "decenter" ourselves, to see from another's perspective, even briefly? I turn back to the books to absorb whatever hope, whatever trust I can. Let's see what we can turn up.

Rick Bass's *The Book of Yaak* (1996) and Spike Van Cleve's *40 Years' Gatherin's* (1977) make an improbable, even wacky pairing. Surely they would have little to say to each other. These two writers seem to inhabit mutually exclusive universes: one is a recent immigrant to the state, while the other is a third-generation Montanan; one seems to represent the political left, the other the right; one inhabits the terrain west of the continental divide, the other the landscape east of the divide. Yet both writers show what a connection to place means for Western citizens: relationship, deep time, community, family, hope. Both writers have a tremendous amount at stake: for Bass, his precious, irreplaceable, irrecoverable Yaak Valley; for Van Cleve, his precious, irreplaceable, irrecoverable "Melville Country." Both men are willing to fight fire with fire to protect something so important, even resorting at times to the name-calling that marred debate on the status of the Yellowstone River. But both are looking for common ground, looking for a way to bridge the divide that separates them from their ideological rivals. Bass, for instance, dwells upon his connection to timbering practices: "I can say that I use wood, and love much about the culture of logging. I love the rip of a saw, the muscularity of it—the smell of wood, the sound and sight of wood....These to me are as much a part of the culture and a part of the wild as the lions and bears and wolves"....Or as he puts it with admirable terseness in his "Conclusion": "I believe the simplest and yet most inflammatory belief of all: that we can have wilderness and logging both in the Yaak Valley." You can't accuse Bass of biocentrism. And I suspect Spike would immediately appreciate Bass's desire to live simply and well in his cabin in the Yaak Valley. After all, Van Cleve describes the first three years of his marriage "at the head of the creek" as among the happiest of his life: "We lived well and happy....We just knew we had to be careful of what little we had, so we did fine, because in my book 'poverty' depends an awful lot on a man's state of mind, not just what he's got...."

But despite these common grounds, Bass and Van Cleve would disagree fervently on the status of wolves in the region. If Bass describes the wolf as a semi-mystical, potent embodiment of wilderness, Van Cleve sees the animal as a predatory force best eliminated from the range. We're at the heart of the matter here. For all of the intense potential conflicts in this region, none is so public and so polarized as the environmentalist/rancher debate. But I deeply believe that this is a false dichotomy, a false choice. We don't have to allow one or the other perspective to have the final, complete word.

What would these two say to each other? We can only guess from their books, but I bet they would begin with good hunting stories, and then share stories about encountering bears in the wild, and then tell about special places in their home terrain, and then (only then) talk about what they're trying to preserve and how they would set about it. They may have to work through language, through what Bass derisively calls "semantics." The word "environmentalist" can instantly send many Westerners into a streak of cussing. But here's a little secret that too few appreciate: many Montanans act on environmentalist principles while barely able to utter the "e" word. And Bass, for all the stereotyping of left-wing agitators, can sink his teeth into the earthiness, the practicality, and the humor of Van Cleve. When all is said and done, these two would share a blood knowledge that could bypass the superficial political divisions.

Of course, there are plenty of forces out there that don't want this kind of healing, this form of rapprochement. It often serves political and economic institutions to keep the pot boiling, the anger raging. If citizens engage in the hand-to-hand ideological combat typified by our most extreme movements in the West, then they likely won't direct their scrutiny toward companies that seek to exploit Montana workers and resources. But there's another force at work here, one deeper and more insidious than overt political and economic interests: the very stories we tell ourselves, the narratives that form our lives. We seem drawn to plots with a classic rising and falling action: begin with conflict, bring that conflict to a climactic resolution, then clean up the loose ends with a satisfying close. More than that, we currently seem to prefer tragic or darkly comic plots, typical of what observers have aptly called a "Gothic America." We are caught, then, in a web of story-telling that drives us apart, or drives us toward open conflict. Our own history and traditions of storytelling reinforce this cultural tendency. No wonder Westerners often incline toward conspiracy theories, the assumption that there's some kind of plot out to get us. It seems an almost inevitable pattern. What I propose here is, by contrast, prosaic, low key, quiet, undramatic. I'm proposing (along with many more gifted thinkers and writers) that we stop shouting, stop hurting each other, stop falling into the trap posed by apocalyptic tragedy. Wallace Stegner wrote that the West is the native land of hope. We should live up to that charge.

Joseph Kinsey Howard once asserted, "The key to happiness for an individual...lies in completeness as a human being, rather than in competence in a particular field; and the happy community is the many-sided, fully functioning community of neighbors to whom democracy is not so much a word as it is an instinct." We have witnessed manifestations of this possibility in this region recently:

Item: During a conference on A. B. Guthrie, Jr.'s *The Big Sky*, Lee Rostad, a rancher and writer from Martinsdale in central Montana, and Annick Smith, a rancher and writer from Missoula, engage in an intense debate about the relationship between environmental consciousness and ranching. While few issues are resolved, it feels like the beginning of a dialogue that matters, a dialogue that might just lead toward understanding, even community.

Item: A radio program discussing writing by and about Westerners runs for thirteen weeks during the fall of 1997. The program is carried on NPR stations throughout the Northwest. Listeners phone in and converse with writers, scholars, and other callers. The conversations are spirited, heartfelt, and illuminating. Something like community has formed through the airwaves.

Item: During a graduation ceremony at Rocky Mountain College, Janine Pease-Pretty on Top, Crow woman and [then] president of the Little Big Horn Tribal College, delivers a memorable address to graduating seniors, urging them to recognize the natural and the spiritual as central to their lives. She then receives an honorary doctorate. The ceremony concludes to the beat of Crow drummers. It seems fitting.

Light of the Feather: Pathways through Contemporary Indian America

by Mick Fedullo

After growing up in the suburbs of Philadelphia, **Mick Fedullo** received an M.F.A. from the University of Iowa's Writers Workshop. He is an adopted member of the Crow Whistling Water Clan and has been given the name Storyteller. He now lives in Pryor, Montana.

I arrived in Billings on a blustery day in March, picked up a rental car, and was blown onto Interstate 90. The winds were fierce, and luckily at my tail; had I been commandeering a schooner, I'd have made the forty-eight-mile trip to Hardin in half the time it took. Along the way I marveled at the high plains—my first encounter. Not at all the level nothingness I'd expected—the flat plains, in fact, sprawled out farther to the east. Here, the land rolled up and down and gave one a feeling of elevation, of being close to the sky. Nothing was level, and that amazing sky, with its racing cumulus flocks, was everywhere. Okay, I may as well get it over with and say it—the sky was big, or perhaps, through some sleight of land, it just looked that way. Whatever the case, I'd never seen a bigger sky.

they all been when they were needed? The paramedics loaded the man into the ambulance. They left Jose's jacket lying on the ground. He slipped between the observers and picked it up.

He strained to hear what the patrolman was saying until he remembered the Christmas party and his Christmas candy. As he headed down the street toward the school, he noticed the tracks where the car had spun its wheels making its get away. There, beside the tracks was a billfold. Jose picked it up.

Jose turned to run back and give the billfold to the paramedics, but the ambulance was already rolling away, lights flashing. Should he give the billfold to the school principal? Of course. The principal would see that it got to the owner. He stuck the billfold in his jacket pocket and ran on toward the school.

Jose was startled by the approaching lights of a police car. Two policemen jumped out. One caught his arm and demanded, "What are you runnin' from? Were you involved in that mugging back there?"

Jose tried to back away.

"Speak up. Why were you running?"

Finally Jose managed to get the words out, "I'm late for the party at school."

"He looks too young," one of the men said. "The people back there said there were three teenagers."

"I guess you can go on to your party," the other patrolman said as he put his hand on Jose's shoulder. "Wait! What's this?" He pushed Jose into the headlights. "There's blood on his jacket! Fresh blood! He was involved in the mugging!"

The other man pushed Jose against their car and searched him.

"What's this? Is that *your* billfold? What's your name? Come on, speak up!"

Jose only mumbled and tried to pull away.

"Where's the money? And where are your accomplices? Talk up. The more you tell us the easier it'll go on you."

Finally Jose burst out. "There were three men. They took off in an old blue Ford with two bumper stickers."

The patrolmen shoved Jose into the back seat and headed for the police station. At the station they asked Jose a lot more questions. He gave them the best description he could.

"All right," one of the patrolmen said. "We'll take you home and check with your parents as soon as we get your name and address."

…Just then two more patrolmen and a woman came in the door. "That's him!" the woman exclaimed, pointing at Jose. "That's the boy that did it!"

A patrolman grabbed Jose roughly and held him while he asked, "Are you certain?"

"Yes, I'd know him anywhere. I'll never forget him!"

Jose shook with fear and anger as the patrolman gripped his arm more tightly.

The woman went on, "I saw the whole thing. It was right in front of my house. I was scared to go out of my house, but this boy ignored the muggers and came running. He knew just what to do. Even checked his pulse and gave him CPR. Had him revived before the ambulance I called could get there. If it wasn't for him, poor old Mr. Davis would be stone dead."

The patrolman released his hold on Jose while he discussed the details with the woman.

Jose backed slowly between the men, then when no one was looking, he slipped out the door.

As Jose walked to school the next morning he looked closely at his jacket. His mother had cleaned it lovingly. No one would suspect that stain was blood. As the bell rang he slipped into his seat. Flint leaned over and whispered, "Jose, you should have been at the party. It was great. And they put two apples in our sack of candy! What happened to you?"

"I had something better to do," Jose answered.

The teacher was staring at them. "Will you boys please stop talking and listen?" She held up *The Billings Gazette* to show them the headlines. "Yesterday a man was mugged, not three blocks from our school. He was knocked out and had quit breathing. But a young boy happened to be coming down the street and gave him CPR. Like the nurse taught you, remember?" She turned the paper and read to them, "After the young hero saved Davis's life, and gave the police enough information so they were able to catch the muggers, he slipped away in the crowd, without telling anyone who he was." She looked up at the class. "And they think he might be a student in our school! Doesn't that make you proud?"

All the students gasped, then sat up a little straighter. But Jose just slid down a little farther in his seat and grinned to himself.

poetry by Tami Haaland

Tami Haaland, a third-generation Montanan, teaches English at Montana State University-Billings. Her poetry has appeared in *Calyx, Intermountain Woman, Alkali Flats,* and *Ring of Fire: Writers of the Yellowstone Region.* In January 2001, she won the 14th Annual Nicholas Roerich Poetry Prize for *Breath in Every Room,* forthcoming from Story Line Press.

national historical landmark. The inscription of Captain Clark's name and the date on the huge pillar beside the Yellowstone, about 30 miles downstream from Billings, is considered the only remaining physical evidence, on site, of the Lewis and Clark Expedition.

In these pioneer-style floats, a fascinating assortment of craft can be seen skimming, twisting, bobbing and occasionally capsizing down the river. They come in all sizes and shapes, including bright modern boats, makeshift rafts, inner tubes, kayaks, rubber life rafts, canoes and even a dugout in '66— though not for long. Sun shades, balloons and flags brighten the flotilla.

Anything can happen on the 126-mile jaunt. Craft are grounded, sent spinning in whirlpools, slammed against rocks and bridges and temporarily side-tracked in irrigation canals. One was lost briefly under a log jam. In '66 a midwest family on vacation took to the river to avoid highway traffic, but it didn't work. Their vessel struck a junked, submerged car.

The hazards are sunburns, sore backs and three-day stubbles.

Fish and Game Department personnel are constantly on guard in patrol boats and a search and rescue unit is always standing by. Ham radio club members lend ship-to-shore services. Children under 12 must wear a Coast Guard-approved life preserver at all times, and each adult must have one in the boat.

People are beginning to realize that the river is vital to recreation and transportation. There has been much cleaning up from the boundary of Yellowstone Park to Pompeys Pillar. The entire stretch has been designated a state waterway by the Montana Fish and Game Commission.

City councils, Jaycees, rod and gun clubs, businessmen and individuals along the route have launched clean-up programs, made long-term plans for park and campground development, planned boat launching areas, created access areas and removed water hazards.

The event is held in early July, when the river is most suitable. As a rule, the peak of the spring run-off is over by then but the river is still quite high. Because of heavy snow pack in the mountains and a late, wet spring, the Yellowstone was still rolling at near-record depths in '67 when the River Rats ran.

Perhaps it was above normal in 1806, too. At any rate, Clark and his men over-estimated it. Their notes indicated big boats could navigate it to the mountains, and even for some distance up two tributaries, the Bighorn and Clarks Fork.

Although it is not rated highly for transportation, it is a blue ribbon trout stream for about 100 miles. It is also proving itself as a float stream. It offers enough white water to zip the boat along and make it exciting but not dangerous.

The early explorers made their own maps. Now a detailed map of the river from Gardiner to the mouth of the Bighorn is available. Prepared by float fan R. E. Burdge, it is both helpful and interesting, pinpointing side channels, bridges, roads, ranches, camping areas and historic sites.

This July 12 [1968], hundreds will put in at Livingston to see the "Yellow Stone" and camp along its banks as the early explorers did. Jaycees from Livingston, Big Timber, Columbus, Laurel, and Billings will sponsor the outing again. They will send the group off with an early breakfast at Livingston, provide sandwiches at lunch stops, entertain them at night and transport their sleeping bags or other equipment to the campsites.

Anyone can join the fun any place along the route in whatever craft he chooses. It is not a race. Just remember your life preserver and sunburn lotion, and be prepared to get wet.

Wind Walker

by Terry C. Johnston

Terry C. Johnston was born on the plains of Kansas and immersed himself in the history of the early West. His first novel, *Carry the Wind*, won the Medicine Pipe Bearer's Award from the Western Writers of America, and his subsequent novels have become bestsellers. Until his untimely death in March, 2001, he lived and wrote in Billings.

Titus Bass's eyes were wet, tears falling down his leathery cheeks as Flea laid the burlap shroud across the crook of his left arm. "You stay with your mother," he instructed his oldest son. "Sit with her. Do anything she needs of you. I…I must do this alone."

Not able to choke out anything more, Scratch dragged the reins to the right and heeled the horse in a quarter turn. The animal slowly carried him away from the smoking rubble that remained of Fort Bridger on Black's Fork in the valley of the Seedskeedee. The stars were still in bloom early that morning as the sky began to gray in the east. Just the faintest hint of rose at one spot on the horizon. A reddening, deepening, bloody rose that so reminded him of the smears running up and down the newborn's body, of that blackening pool of blood there beneath his wife's buttocks as her legs quivered in pain and exhaustion while she delivered the tiny lifeless body.

The boy had never breathed.

Scratch let out a long sigh, watching the thin, gauzy wisp of breathsmoke trail from his mouth as he began to sob again. This tiny son of his had never taken a breath, never known the simple joy of tasting life in his lungs.

First Maker breathed His spirit into each of us, he thought as he started the horse upstream toward the lion's head rocks where he and Gabe had waited out the Mormons' sacking of the fort. So it was the Indians of these mountains believed. The Creator of all blew His breath into the mouth and nostrils of every newborn at the moment of emerging into the world so that the child gasped with the powerful spirit that infused the infant's tiny lungs and made the babe cry out with life.

But where had the First Maker been for this child he clutched, here in the crook of his left arm, just beneath his broken heart? Where was this all-powerful Creator, this Grandfather Above, whose place it was to watch over the tiniest and most helpless of creatures? Where had the First Maker been when Mary and Toote sat staring down at the child's lifeless, blue-tinged body, lying limp across Shell Woman's arms until Bass desperately shouldered Mary aside and took the child into his own hands, pressed his open mouth over its tiny nose and lips...where had the Creator been as he desperately fed his tiny son the breath from his own body?

With that one hand gently laid on the babe's chest, Titus had felt each of his breaths make the tiny chest rise. After each attempt, Scratch had stared down into the wrinkled face, looking for some flicker of the eyelids, some cough and sputter, some bawling response as the legs and arms would start to flail...but instead his child lay still and lifeless, no matter how he breathed into its lungs or rubbed its cold, blue body. So helpless, so goddamned helpless as he had started to sob, his tears spilling to mingle with the thick, milky, blood-streaked substance smeared all over the limp newborn.

Titus had pressed the tiny body against him as his head fell back and he let out a primal wail that shook him to his very roots. As he rocked and rocked and rocked there by his wife's knees, Waits-by-the-Water cried, clutching Mary and Shell Woman, clawing at their arms in grief, finally burying her face in the Shoshone woman's lap. Finally Bridger came up and knelt beside him, put his arm around Bass's shoulder.

"Let me take 'im, Scratch. I'll hol't 'im for a while."

"No," he had growled, like a wounded animal with its paw caught in the jaws of a trap—hurting, angry, and preparing to chew off his own foot to free himself.

But this was not the sort of pain he could swallow down and be shet of it. No bloody chewing through the gristle and bone, fur and sinew, would make this loss any better.

"G-get me something to bury the boy in, Gabe. Just you do that."

Bridger had risen there beside him and moved with Shadrach off to locate the charred pieces of those once-used flour sacks. He had brought them back and showed them to Mary and Toote. When Titus nodded that they would do, the two women had slowly inched away from Waits, while Scratch went to sit at his wife's shoulder. Propping her against him, Bass laid their stillborn son in her arms and rocked them both in his.

"Day's comin'," Bridger said before he turned away with Shad and the women to see to the burial shroud and to give them privacy. "Couple hours, maybe three at the most."

"I'll go when you're done wrappin' the boy up," Titus whispered.

"What if it's still dark out there?"

"Even if it's dark, Gabe, I'm gonna do this right by the child."

Holding her, embracing both of them, from time to time he asked Flea to bring in some more firewood. Waits-by-the-Water felt as cold to him as the tiny stillborn. He knew she had to be freezing, shaking the way she was. Just keep the fire going so she did not die on him too. He didn't know what he would do if that happened...couldn't possibly go on without her. Wouldn't even want to go on without her, even if he could.

Strange now that the light of a new day was coming, brightening out of the east at his back, even though he felt his own spirit withering, shriveling, darkening like a strip of rawhide left out in the elements to dry and twist and blacken. Should have been that he went to bury this little body after dark, with the coming of night instead of the start of a whole new day. The way life had of giving a man a new chance all over again every dawn.

Miles upstream on the far side of the rocky outcrop, he found the tree that had several high, thick branches. Titus dismounted below its rustling leaves touched with a gentle breath of breeze every now and then. He shuddered once at a chill gust, pulling the flaps of the old, stained blanket capote together. This was always the time of day when it was coldest, just as the sun was deciding to raise its head into this gray world of little color and contrast. Sitting there, still and silent except for the occasional snort of the pony, or the creak of cold saddle leather beneath him, Bass listened to the wind sough through the leaves of that tree—wondering why the wind blew now, this holy breath of the First Maker...wondering why that life-giving breath of the All Spirit had not entered his son's mouth.

Damn, but he didn't want to grow bitter. Not here and now holding this boy's tiny body. Not when it came time for a father to do the only thing a father could for his stillborn son. He did not want to get hard and crossways with the First Maker, not now because in the last handful of years he had been sensing more and more that spirit breath move through him as it never had before. Maybe only because he was getting older. Maybe most every-thing he'd cared about before just didn't matter any more, while some things meant more than they ever had in his life.

No, he did not want to become embittered, even though he so convinced himself that he possessed the power of that spirit in his own lungs that he could breathe its wind from his body into the lungs of his infant son, giving the stillborn babe a breath of his own spirit wind. But he had found himself helpless in the face of death. Every bit as helpless as he was in understanding why the First Maker had refused to save the baby. And Lucas too. Why had young life been snuffed out in its innocence…when men like Brigham Young and their evil flourished?

But, that wasn't for him to know, was it? Not…just yet.

Titus kicked his right foot free, gripped the round saddlehorn the size of a Mexican orange, and slid down from the horse's back. A gust of wind tugged at his long, gray hair, nudging that single, narrow braid he always wore—and carried a moan to his ear. An eerie, melancholy sound strangely like the final sigh a man makes as the last air in his lungs comes whispering out in a death rattle. Drawn by that moan's direction, he turned slightly, made to look at the high slope of loose talus that had torn itself away from the foot of the rocky cliff. Jagged seams and fissures streaked down from the top of that ridge.

One of them would be the most fitting place for the tiny bundle.

Turning back to his pony, he untied the short length of buffalo hair rope looped at the front of his saddle, laid the shroud on the ground, and quickly knotted together a sling so that he could carry his son on his back. He stood and studied the slope covered with sage and juniper, scattered with loose rock and talus shale, knowing he would have to use both hands to make the climb if he was ever going to reach the crack he had selected, that fissure where the wind would enter at the top of the ridge, moan down the entire length of the crack, then whisper out at the bottom, making the sound of some language he did not understand. But a sound that continued to call to him nonetheless.

Planting his foot for that first step, he immediately slid back down. Clawing with his hands, he managed to hold on for the most part, but as he made a little ground, he always seemed to slide back, losing more than half of what he had gained. Eventually he found that if he kept himself low, digging in with his toes and crabbing up on his knees, he didn't lose so much. The sun was beginning to warm the air, and he had begun to sweat inside the blanket coat by the time he reached the bottom of the narrow fissure. There on a ledge less than six inches wide he set a knee, dug in the heel of the other moccasin, and balanced himself as he turned slightly, slowly slipping his arms free of the rope loops.

For a long, long time he cradled the body against him and let the tears flow as the sobs wracked his body with spasms. As the sun emerged from hiding, he eventually blinked to clear his eyes and turned to peer over his shoulder at the coming sun. The very top of that bright, glowing orb was spraying the horizon with a luminous, orange iridescence. Scratch turned back, pivoting on that one knee, and raised the bundle toward the crack in the rocks.

Turning the tiny body sideways, he managed to get the infant back more than a foot, as deep as his elbow. When it would go no farther, he quit nudging and pulled the arm out of the fissure. As his left hand clutched a fingerhold in a nearby seam, Titus leaned over and grabbed hold of the first of the loose rocks around him, one no bigger than his own hand. He stuffed it into the fissure. Then another. Again and again he shoved loose rocks in after the burlap shroud, pounding each one in with the succeeding rock so they wouldn't easily come loose with freezing and thawing, freezing and thawing across untold seasons. Finally he had all the rocks the fissure could hold.

He had buried his son within the folds of the earth, here in these free mountains.

poetry by Danell Jones

Danell Jones is a writer, teacher, and scholar who lives in Billings. Her work on Virginia Woolf earned the Bennett Cerf Writing Award from Columbia University. Recently, the University of Colorado at Boulder awarded her the Jovanovich Imaginative Writing Award for poetry.

ONE FORWARD, TWO BACK

I
The neighbor watches
coffee in one hand
outrage in the other

you can't walk there, she keeps thinking
you can't walk

but I swan by
my dress caught up suddenly
against the onion sky
like an emperor

II
the uncertain mixture of twilight and midnight loosened
only the strange woman who wants to leave
I think of mighty promises
and keep moving

III
Stop for once: my vision returns
Stop again: the townspeople talk about us at night, at dawn, all day
Stop here: their rumors and our love visions

IV
If, in sifting through the world
he is smiling
go back

V
An excellent conscience surfaces this rubble
the way lovers have been alive in each other
the way bluebottles agonize a traitor's bones
Tomorrow, do you suppose
we will be scattered among a hundred cities
this sperm of love
scattered

VI
Finish up
and come back home
forget Babylon
it only tempts crowds

later, when you've written all about it
smoked a lot of cigarettes
visited all your friends with their big Jupiter eyes
then, return to the little house of opposites

walk slowly
clutching your blue jacket
bring your shoes, your wine
your briefcase full of receipts

we will sit on the porch
& listen for the new-laid eggs of wild hens
& pull the dainty ferns from the hem
of your blue traveling suit

No Queen Mary

Reaching Port

by Keith Jones

Keith Jones was born in Wyoming in 1917. In 1959 while living in Billings, he announced to his family that he would build a sailboat to take him around the world. Despite losing his first craft at sea, this son of the arid high plains fulfilled his dream. The following excerpt provides a glimpse into that remarkable adventure.

Rosemary says the adventure started the day I came home from work and asked if she would like to take a trip around the world. She immediately had visions of the *Queen Mary* tied to a New York dock with colored ticker tape billowing out in a light breeze coming in gently from the sea. She imagined bon-voyage flowers and cards filling the stateroom, our friends sipping champagne, giggling and laughing, and finally the call, "All ashore that's going ashore."

Thus, I couldn't understand her look of surprise and dismay when I told her of my plan to spend my spare time for the next ten years building a sailboat about thirty-six feet long. By the time it was finished, our four children would be out of college and we would be able to take off from work to tackle the world.

Women are funny. It surprised me then how much sweet talk, hugs, squeezes, and that sort of thing it took to get her to realize what a wonderful way of life I had planned for us. But she's pretty smart; she came around to my way of thinking in about six months.

Sometimes it surprises me that I dared to think of it. Neither of us were deep-water sailors. I had been born and reared on a Wyoming ranch and left it at age seventeen to go into construction in Alaska. The closest I'd been to the ocean had been as a Seabee during World War II, and I'd spent all that time at a base in Hawaii. Rosemary hadn't been that close. Born and reared in Montana, mostly in the Billings area, she hadn't spent any time out of the state. I had returned to Thermopolis after the war and we met when I moved with my two children to Billings after my first wife died. Rosemary also had two children from a previous marriage. In 1950 we merged our two families, and after her father died we took over the family mobile-home business in 1961.

First, I had to find a marine architect with a set of plans we could afford for a boat capable of going around the world. We wanted one that would be comfortable, yet small enough so that I could handle the sails, pull up the anchor, and do the hundred other things that need to be done when your life depends on you and your boat's performance.

For an architect we found Edwin Monk of Seattle, Washington. As time went by I could see that he had more common sense in his little finger than some men have in their head.

Next, I needed a place to build the boat. Montana is cold in winter and I needed a building. An old garden space on the back of our lot provided the place, and by scrounging up "cull" two-by-fours from small sawmills, I built a shed twenty-four by thirty-eight feet from stacked two-by-fours. Since it was barely large enough, I had to put a big window at each end where planks could be run through before being cut off. Eventually the bowsprit protruded out the front window. The building looked like an old barn, but the neighbors were a kindly group and didn't raise any objections. The city fathers also waived a few building restrictions when I promised to keep the area cleaned up and to turn it back to a garden within ten years.

Rosemary is an income tax accountant. Each tax season, I would wheedle as much money as possible to buy lumber. It is hard to comprehend the amount of lumber that goes into a thirty-six-foot sailboat. It is even harder to come up with the money to pay for it.

I used Monk's recommendation of vertical-grained fir for all the deadwood, fore and aft timbers, keelson, stem, and what not. The planking was of Alaskan yellow cedar. The ribs were of white oak and the masts of Sitka spruce. What beautiful timbers, all straight-grained. When a plank was lying flat, I could sight along the grain from one end to the other for all twenty-four feet, then turn the plank on edge and again follow the grain end to end.

My only qualifications were five years in construction in Alaska and three in the Seabees. When I stopped to think, I wondered if I had not been somewhat insane to think I could carry out this project. I found the answer to my qualms was simple: Don't think about it. Work. Work. Work. Don't think.

The next nine years became one of life's small bonuses. I would come home from the mobile-home lot, eat supper, go out to the boathouse, pat the boat a couple of times, and go to work. Talk about relaxation. Of course, many times I did not know the next step. I was completely in the dark, for instance, on how to bend eighty-eight two-by-two oak ribs, some of which were supposed to wind up looking something like a piece of spaghetti.

At the End of the Rainbow's Run Lies a Memory of Gold

by David Karnos

David Karnos teaches philosophy at Montana State University-Billings. He has published a well-received book on the vocation of philosophy, *Falling in Love with Wisdom*. He participates actively in the Billings and Montana communities, including previously serving on the Montana Committee for the Humanities. He is also a fanatical fly fisherman.

As I turned the corner of the last switchback, my foot felt ease in taking leave of the accelerator which had been its mate the past three hours. Ahead lay the "last-straight-run" and the pull-off where my worldly vehicle would be deposited, a new outer wading skin donned, and a path.

With the drive over I began to relax and enjoy the sunrise, the crisp air, the lightness…and the closer I came to that path, the lighter I felt. Everywhere, my gaze floated over things; not touching them, just gliding. But then I made the turn onto the walkway, and there wondered for a moment whether I had chosen this particular fishing trip just so that I could take this walkway again. Or had I come here once again to challenge that particular rainbow which had so deftly taken my tippet last year?

…Noticing that my once gingerly gait had disappeared,…I turned…to the trees for salvation…, and so wandered down the lane of magnificent boughs and limbs which invariably drew me to their heights and then down again to those subterranean depths whence springs the well which nurtures roots through roof. In me, I thought, this well gives shape to my own unique style: remembering. For without memory I could always be severing my roots and would lose that source of nourishment which allows me to grow upwards, outwards and thus capable of even looking ahead of myself. And without gathering these sources, I could never follow those signs along this pathway—turn left at this tree, right at this bush—which issue in the promise of the rainbow for which I brought this creel. So too, it is a matter of ingathering; of remembering my origins and traditions which give me a lifeline, a weight, gravity and body—and afford me a flyline, a weight forward, tippet and rod.

Fortunately, I remembered these things and my creel, as I recognized the last signpost of the pathway—a turn right at "anthill-rock" and duck below the "big-pinegate-limb." Fortunate, because in the world of flashing neon signals I often forget what signs mean, and so pass by many golden opportunities in life.

There must be different kinds of forgetting. For instance, there is the natural, forgetting of yesterday, and most of the things which happened in it from one millimicrosecond to the next; a forgetting of the normal immediately forgivable and forgettable mundane world. To be sure, I remember such details if called to account for them, or if reminded of them by others, but without emphasis they will disappear as will the whole day. As only something significant will be remembered, so most of my days pass by, vanish and find forgetfulness and this, too, can be fortunate.

Unfortunately, there is an unnatural form of forgetting. I forget to give gifts, because hoarding life's creels is often more pleasurable than remembering the source's graciousness. I forget former loves, perhaps because they were never caught and hoarded. I forget former hates because they nourish memory's ulcers. Such forgetting is not natural; it demands my cooperation, my repression, my resistance to remembering, my incasting and controlling; for the penalty of letting these matters go free into memory is often painful guilt. Too often, this forgetting neglects what should be given honor.

Liberation from these consequences of repression has often been the point of repentance and its religious sense of forgiveness. To forgive is to forget what one ought not remember with honor; it is to memorably close off the future from its recurrence. Thus, we can move forward in this life only because our guilty past is forgiven and eternally forgotten. The meaningfulness of a pact is suppressed for a future whose signposts we can neither read because we have no familiarity with the language yet, nor follow because we have not yet walked the pathway.

However, if we ask the question, *"What does lie ahead in the future?"* we may become reminded of a third kind of forgetting: forgetting that we shall be forgotten someday. Because we cannot stand the thought, we repress it. Much like the swaying silence of these trees along my pathway, our classic literature attests to this question. It tells kings and wanderers how they must find and face being forgotten, how they must move from the horizontal position of mundanity to the vertical height of sovereignty, and how, through their suffering, they must find repose in what is right and true. Ironically, our common mundanity cannot stand the thought of death, so we insist that the dead be buried lying down, resting, and therefore not active, troubled or agitated. Such anxiety reveals the resistance every human being has to being pushed into the past, for surely it is a superficial view to say that our anxiety about death is simply a fear of the process of dying, because although that process can be agonizing, it can also be very soft. Rather, I think in the depth of every anxiety of having to die is the dread of being forgotten.

People often say they choose nature, and fishing trips, because they lose themselves there. But what they mean is that they find themselves by being rid of the garbage. It saddens me that some people dread being forgotten so much that they must mark their own trails with undying flowers; or, even here alongside the ever changing banks of this river, with their aluminum security deposits. Such dread is echoed, perhaps, by that sedentary angler who cannot fathom the purpose of my fly-casting. Why repeat the same motion over and over, he asks, if you can get there with one quick, calculated shot of the weighted lure? To me, it is well to feed out the line, to constantly stretch toward what is anticipated and near-to-hand.

Then, is there anything which can keep us from being forgotten? In the religious sense, only the projected certainty that we are all known from eternity and that we will be remembered in eternity can save us from the horror of being forgotten. That projection is a fishing trip whose streambed these waders will not likely traverse. But though we can choose to believe that we will not be fogotten by others, we can forget ourselves and like Dorothy struggle along the yellow brick road until we come to remember that sense of directedness which brings our true home to mind. Whether or not we remember all these things in life is not important; that we do not forget ourselves is infinitely important. And so, now, do I preserve myself in realizing that whether or not my creel is filled at the end of this particularly delightful rainbow's run, I will return home with sparkling memories of this day's journey.

Prairie Pastoralism and Predators:
"Keeping the Wolf from the Door"

by Tim Lehman

Presented to the American Society for Environmental History 1997 Biennial Meeting

Since 1990 **Tim Lehman** has taught American history, including western America and environmental history, at Rocky Mountain College. He has published articles and a well-received book on American agricultural policy.

Predators are among the hardest animals to love. Aldo Leopold's encounter with the "fierce green fire" in the eyes of a dying wolf, and the subsequent transformation in his thinking from game management to a land ethic which appreciated predator as well as prey, has come to stand for a larger social transformation into the age of ecology. Donald Worster, Lisa Mihgetto, and Thomas Dunlap have explained aspects of this societal re-valuation of varmints at the national level. Because of or in spite of this exemplary scholarship, a popular version of the story has emerged which is suspiciously linear and progressive. The story begins with a longstanding cultural antipathy for predators, reinforced by European folklore traditions such as Little Red Riding Hood, literary expressions such as Willa Cather's chilling tale of the wolves who ate the bridal party, and the views of promi-nent conservationists such as Theodore Roosevelt, William Hornaday, and George Bird Grinnell. These older views gradually gave way to a social Leopoldian epiphany, and now wolves are being reintroduced into Yellowstone. My interest in the topic comes from talking with ranchers who are still "unenlightened," who have not changed their minds but have now become a political minority. My purpose in this essay is to explore the formative years of Montana's attitudes towards predators, with an eye to ambiguity and complexity. Predator encounter stories from early Montana reveal a variety of possible outcomes and attitudes, with the dominant view shaped by the particular historical circumstances of open range livestock grazing in the late 19th century.

The first Montanans, perhaps because they had few domestic animals, felt no animosity towards predatory animals. The South Piegan band of the Blackfeet Confederation had many wolf songs which were sung to bring good luck on special occasions, especially before a long trip. The path to the spirit world, according to Blackfeet legend, was through the Milky Way, which they called the Wolf Path. Blackfeet hunted wolves to use their skins for ceremonial purposes and as camouflage when hunting buffalo, but the Blackfeet oral tradition had no mention of fearing wolves as a threat to human life. According to a modern rendition of a traditional saying, "The gun that shoots at a wolf or a coyote will never again shoot straight." Oral tradition has it that in the pre-reservation era two Piegan warriors, Red Eagle and Nitaina, were returning from a buffalo hunting trip when they found a wolf pup who was the lone survivor of a flooded den. Nitaina took the pup home and raised it, even though the parents returned and howled for days. According to Red Eagle, "Wolves are not like dogs, you know; a dog father knows not his own children. A wolf marries, and he and his wife live always together until death. When children come, he hunts for them and brings food for them while the mother goes out to hunt and run around and keep up her strength. Ah, they are wise, true-hearted animals, the big wolves of the plains. And what hunters they are; they never suffer from want of food."

Nitaina named the wolf pup Laughter and raised it, training it to do chores around camp and even to follow along on horse-stealing raids against the Sioux and Cheyenne. This wolf encounter narrative ended with humans happy and the wolf free, as eventually Laughter left camp for a mate, but had friendly visits with Nitaina for years afterwards. Red Eagle not only respected wolves, but attributed human characteristics to wolf "families," especially the loyalty and intimate caretaking of mother, father, and children. The wolves' superior hunting ability Red Eagle considered as evidence of these family values, not as an indication of cruelty.

The first European-American explorers in Montana viewed predatory animals with a mixture of wonder, curiosity, and occasional fear. The Lewis and Clark expedition encountered grizzly bears, wolves, and "prairie wolves," or coyotes. Their descriptions provide interesting details about pre-settlement distribution and behavior of these predators, as well as reveal attitudes towards these animals that were in marked contrast to later views. Along the upper Missouri, soon after entering into the semi-arid high plains and not far from the current Montana border, Captain Lewis saw, shot, and described a "prairie wolf," neither fox nor true wolf. The expedition saved the skin and bones to return east for scientific study and so provided the first scientific description of the coyote *(Canus latrans)*, which according to Lewis and Clark was in 1805 a somewhat elusive high plains predator and scavenger. Much more common for the expedition was the true wolf *(Canus lupus)*, which Lewis reported to be smaller than the eastern wolves, with color variation from "blackish brown" to "creen [cream] colored white." Whereas the "prairie wolf," or coyote, barked and denned in burrows on the treeless prairie, the larger wolf howled and sought tree cover, according to Lewis. He also reported that their prime food source was old, young, or sick buffalo, and that the wolves were "faithful shepherds" accompanying every herd. The expedition encountered an abundance of buffalo, antelope, elk, and deer while passing through the plains of eastern Montana, and these ungulates, as well as the wolves who accompanied them, were extremely tame, according to Lewis. On one occasion Captain Clark got so close to "great numbers" of "fat and extreemly gentle" wolves which were feeding on buffalo carcasses that he was able to kill one with his spear.

While the wolves caused the expedition no fear of bodily harm, the same was not true for the grizzly bear. Lewis and Clark encountered the "brown grizly" bear along the upper Missouri shortly before entering Montana, and were at first excited about this fearsome bear which the Indians had described. Their initial confidence soon turned to respect and eventually dread as they experienced numerous close encounters and found the bear difficult to kill. On one occasion a hunter shot a grizzly bear through the center of the lungs, after which the bear chased the hunter for half a mile, then walked a mile in a different direction and dug a two feet by five feet bed in the earth and was still "perfectly alive." After reporting this incident, Clark commented: "these bear being so hard to die rather intimedates us all; I must confess that I do not like the gentlemen and had reather fight two Indians than one bear." In what might be thought of as the first predator control effort in Montana, Lewis was so angry at frequent grizzly bear visits during the portage around the Great Falls of the Missouri that he ordered his men to sleep with their weapons at hand and loaded and organized a brief bear hunt to keep the animals away from camp and his men safe.

Other travelers along the upper Missouri and Yellowstone Rivers reinforced these views of prairie predators. George Catlin, while visiting the Indians of the upper Missouri River, noted that wolves were the constant companions of buffalo herds:

> There are several varieties of the wolf species in this country, the most formidable and most numerous of which are white, often sneaking about in gangs or families of fifty or sixty in numbers, appearing in distance, on the green prairies like nothing but a flock of sheep. Many of these animals grow to a very great size....At present, whilst the buffaloes are so abundant, and these ferocious animals are glutted with the buffalo's flesh, they are harmless, and everywhere sneak away from man's presence; which I scarcely think will be the case after the buffaloes are all gone, and they are left, as they must be, with scarcely anything to eat. They always are seen following about in the vicinity of herds of buffaloes and stand ready to pick the bones of those that the hunters leave on the ground, or to overtake and devour those that are wounded, which fall an easy prey to them. While the herd of buffaloes are together, they seem to have little dread of the wolf, and allow them to come in close company with them.

Other early visitors to Montana, from Prince Maximilian to trapper Osborne Russell to naturalist John James Audubon, commented similarly on the abundance, variety, and behavior of the wolf. Based on these accounts, contemporary wildlife specialists estimate that there may have been as many as two hundred thousand wolves on the western plains in the early nineteenth century. All accounts agree that wolves were no danger to humans, that they were surprisingly afraid of even a solitary person, and that they were well-fed by preying upon primarily buffalo but also elk and antelope. If wolves were a "pest," as sometimes noted, it was because they forced travelers to hang meat high, to bury bodies deep, and to guard camps closely.

Prologue

The Bluejay Shaman

by Lise McClendon

Lise McClendon writes fiction and tone poems and teaches writing in Billings. Her mysteries, *The Bluejay Shaman, Painted Truth* and *Nordic Nights*, feature her series detective, a Jackson Hole art dealer and Norwegian-Montanan, Alix Thorssen. Besides writing and the state of Montana, the loves of her life include her husband and two sons.

The Tetons scratched the summer sky, still sporting a hint of orange from the long-gone sun. Rough and hard, the mountains proved man's impermanence. Women's too.

When I pointed my old car north, leaving behind the gallery in Jackson, the hum—the hymn—of the road gave me the feeling my life was going somewhere. Being on the road was like that, a trickster highway. Somewhere in the distance is happiness, satisfaction, whatever it takes to feel good. Over that rise. Just a little farther.

The mountains were quiet, sleeping. They never looked the same twice but they always sounded like peace to me. But I crossed the pass into Idaho and drove north. For a Norwegian, a purity fills a northern mission, like the search for the Holy Grail. The lights shine bright in the North.

I grew up in Montana but my northern mission wouldn't bring me back my childhood. Montana had changed. The mountain ranges still sprang up from the prairies like gopher tunnels in a rich man's lawn. Cowpunchers still tried to live out their fantasies. And some of the original inhabitants, the Indians, remained.

But sure as I'd left, some other folks had moved in. The people I met in Montana were older but not necessarily wiser. That happens to a lot of us. But they should have known the wheels of time go in one direction only. You can't fight it.

Try as you might.

poetry by Bruce K. Meyers

The late **Bruce Kemp Meyers,** born in Ohio, taught poetry and writing at Eastern Montana College (Montana State University-Billings) for twenty-five years. He was also a gifted actor, singer, and photographer who collaborated on articles about his world travels with his wife, Christene. He is remembered in the Bruce Kemp Meyers Poets Corner and Garden on the MSU-Billings campus, and by his many students for his wry wit, sharp eye, and consummate kindness.

A Poem

A poem starts this way:
   so he says and I says
    and the words land
on a flower of words and
   that's how it begins.

Newton's Toes

Imagination sighed in Newton's toes,
Fluttered languid in the grass
Beneath the tree. Rain

Was on the corn some days,
But how it got there wasn't clear.
It was a mystery, like corn.

And then a breeze came up.
An apple struck his peaceful head
And wiped the smile away.

He watched as corn rose madly,
Water sought its level,
Rain prepared to fall as ever.

His feet were dumbstruck
As imagination held its breath
And rode the rapids

To his head, the very bone
The apple struck. He rose
Enlightened, too excited to be sad,

Surveyed the land
And that was gravity.

The Naz as Green Grocer

And the Lord came stomping across
   her still waters
And he stopped and he stared
   at her big blue eyes
And he said, "Linda:
Here is THE WORD."

She took the mackerel and
    the pumpernickel
And she said, "Lord:"
She said, "Lord:
Do I marry the fish or do I marry
    the bread?
Do I marry the fish or the bread?"

No, he said.
No: you marry the water, he said,
    the waves and the lightning sea.

(And turning he said with a smile
    and a wink,
"Leave the fish and the bread for me.")

poetry by Christene Cosgriffe Meyers

Christene Cosgriffe Meyers, a fourth-generation Montanan, has written fiction, poetry, and music all her life. She has traveled the world and writes about her adventures for travel and airline magazines, as well as for *The Billings Gazette,* where she serves as arts and entertainment editor. She is also a musician, gardener, and lover of pets and theater.

Seasonal Change

Surrounded by used grass, second-hand fall
We stop to rest our shadows on telephone poles.
Instead they look uneasy there, and wave.
Shucked, autumn huddles under trees.

Indian summer, mad guest staying late,
Whistles gay tunes through her teeth.
She was melting oranges and sugar cherries
When the notice came: evicted.

Frost was melting on pumpkins.
We were confused.
Still we believe:

Carrots in July.
Chrysanthemums in August.
Stray leaves on November trails.

When we look again our shadows are shrinking.
We slap them on, shiver once, then go.

The Frontier Myth

by Robert C. Morrison

Robert C. "Bob" Morrison is a native Montanan, artist, and teacher. Director of the Billings Public Schools Art Program in the 1960s, he became Professor of Art at Rocky Mountain College and was head of the department until his retirement in 1987. His art works have been widely exhibited and collected throughout the United States. He was a founding member of the Yellowstone Art Center (now Yellowstone Art Museum), the Billings Art Association, and the Montana Art Association.

The fact of our publishing a Western issue raises one question right away in the mind of the editor: is there anything left of the Old West? For a good part of the twentieth century the producers of popular art have been engaged in creating a body of myth and legend about the frontier. Indeed, we have reached the point where stories and images of the Wild West are almost pure folklore, composed of stereotyped characters larger than life and of exploits in which the heroic is commonplace.

This is all very well—folklore is folklore the world over, and it is presumably a good thing for any culture to have heroes to worship; but we note with some uneasiness that many people who live in the West today show signs of believing that the legendary Old West was the real Old West, and further that life in the present-day West still bears a family resemblance to the high and far-off days of the frontier. This is, of course, a satisfying belief. Merely by accepting it the Westerner assumes a certain stature—he himself can be a tiny bit larger than life. In addition, the belief that he is in reality living on the frontier helps him to rationalize the political disappointments and the economic deprivations of his region. But is there any truth to it? Is there really anything left of the Old West?

Those who travel through the plains and mountains are not likely to see any obvious inheritance from the frontiersmen of the past century, nor to detect any but the most superficial and tourist-oriented interest in regional history. The land, to be sure, still exists; roads and fences cannot diminish the majesty of the Western land—but the view from an airplane or from an automobile on the six-lane freeway is an abstraction, hardly more real than a panorama on the movie screen. This is not the land known by those who walked on it and lived from it.

Where the land is not abstract it is likely to be concrete, for the urban areas of the West are growing rapidly, and within and around them problems grow apace. While they are perhaps not yet the clotted horrors of the East, the cities of the West are managing an ever-closer approximation, in terms of noise, smog, crime, congestion, and ugliness.

Wild animals of various kinds are still part of the country; hunting and fishing are recreation for many, natives and visitors alike. But the ecological balance has been permanently upset. Game animals and fish are managed by the states as a resource and their "harvesting" is considered an industry, while other wildlife survives extinction only in game preserves and neglected corners. Some species—the "varmints"—have been deliberately extinguished: the prairie dog is gone; the coyote, the cougar, and the wolf are extremely rare; the eagle and the rattlesnake have retreated far from the habitations of man.

The horse, also, survives only as a curiosity. Those Westerners who keep horses do so mainly to keep alive the romantic tradition, and, to be sure, the sight of a herd of horses cantering over the prairie land, manes and tails flying, can stir even a cynic. The fact is, however, that the rancher who is raising cattle on a great expanse of semi-aridity can afford only a limited amount of sentiment; the horse is an anachronism, a toy, for which there is no use or need in any but a dude-ranching operation.

Without a horse, the cowboy becomes a ranch-hand who is a good deal more familiar with wrench and grease-gun than with sixshooter, and is as likely to be found at a PTA meeting as in a saloon on Saturday night.

The Indian problem is yet with us; it is possible that the Indian is the only element of the frontier myth still a real part of the West today. But the problem is certainly not the same as it was a century ago; the need now is to help the Indian to find a place in twentieth-century society, to guide him toward independence rather than to fight him into subservience.

On the face of it, then, there is virtually nothing left. Though the foregoing description of the present day-West is much over-simplified, it is substantially true—the old frontier exists only in fiction. And yet...

Yet the Westerner stays, often at the expense of his economic and cultural well-being, and in spite of the rigorous climate. Is it possible that, regardless of the erosion of so much of what was unique and vivid in the Old West, there remain among the inhabitants of the West vestiges of those traits of character which made the frontier what it was? Call it rugged individualism, or plain wrong-headedness—it would seem the only explanation for many of us who insist on living in and loving this part of the country.

The Prodigal Returns
Will James
pen and ink drawing (1921)
Courtesy Yellowstone Art Museum Permanent Collection, gift of Virginia Snook
Reprinted by permission Will James Art Co.
(See page 43 for biographical information.)

poetry by Kathy Mosdal O'Brien

Kathy Mosdal O'Brien was raised on a ranch near Broadview. She is a second-generation American, fifth-generation teacher, and granddaughter of homesteaders. Following a twenty-five-year career of classroom teaching, including a stint at Miles Community College, she served as the curator of education at the Western Heritage Center in Billings.

Hard Red Winter

Out here
your mistakes
can kill you.
It's that simple.

Not enough gas.
A dead battery.
One bad cut.
One dumb move.

Everything else falls apart
when the mistake is first.

In the winter,
pack blankets and dry food
and a coffee can candle
behind the seat
and don't take it out
until ~~spring summer~~
Don't take it out.
If you get stuck
and it's blizzarding
stay in your outfit
until morning
or until they find you.
The only live ones they find
are inside.

Everything takes longer
when it's cold.

Fill up your tank
and take spares
for the things that might break.
Take along a crescent wrench

and water.
If you get lost, afoot,
follow the cowpaths
down to the water.
They know the easiest way
to get there.
Follow the water
down to where the people are.
That's where it goes from here.
Or find a fenceline;
it will take you to a gate.
That will give you a road
to follow down to where the people are.
That's where it goes from here.

Everything is harder
to do when it gets dark.

Plan ahead a little.
Tell somebody when to worry
if you're not back,
and where you'll probably be.
If you're pinned or bleeding a lot,
you'll want them to find you.
Attract attention.
Honk the horn, fire some shots,
start a fire
with something that smokes a lot,
especially if it's summer.
Somebody will come.

Everything makes something else happen
when you're out here.
It takes all winter
to get calves and wheat
even ready to grow in the spring
and they're both
a lot tougher than people.

Maybe you have
to live here all your life
to live here all your life.
Out here
your mistakes
can kill you.
It's that simple.

Helen

It was probably '35 or so
and company came for dinner.
Beans and bread was all they had
and not a lot of that.
Once they'd eaten and leaned back
she cleared away the plates.
She brought out the heirloom bowls
and gave one to each guest.
Then, to each in turn,
she gave another gift:
cardboard glasses, red cellophane lenses.
"Now put them on," she said.
Then, to each in turn
another bowl of beans.
"Now," she said and smiled again,
"now they're strawberries!"

poetry by Sally Old Coyote

Sally Old Coyote lives in the rain shadow of the Rocky Mountains. She was raised on a homestead south of Billings-Laurel until she was seven years old, when drought, grasshoppers, and Mormon crickets forced her family to leave the dryland farm. Despite hard economic times, she avidly pursued her education and became a revered teacher at MSU-Bozeman. She has written poetry and prose—both fiction and nonfiction—about Montana's high plains.

:SUMMER IN MY CHILDHOOD

I remember days
When there were no shadows
By eleven o'clock.
The sun was so hell-hot it burned
Right through our thin shirts,
Except where the crossed suspenders
Of our overalls left a paler X on our backs.
We walked fast on our heels
Across the dirt yard to the well,
Because the rest of our bare feet
Couldn't bear the heat of the dust.
The well was dry!
The water sank out of sight
In the long summer drought.
When my dad walked in his fields,
His eyes pleaded
As he searched for some sign in the sky.
Mom cringed as she looked at her garden,
Green in the moment of May,
Curled and brown by June,
Not a pea blossom, not a tassel promise of corn.
There was no relief when the sun went down,
Its afterimage burned through the night
And reseized our sere world at dawn.

Bough Down to Spirit of Christmas

by John Potter

Award-winning Chippewa Indian artist **John Potter** has been drawing and painting since he was three years old. The Wisconsin native holds a degree in illustration from Utah State University. His work hangs in private collections from coast to coast. He is an editorial artist and columnist for *The Billings Gazette*. He enjoys the outdoors and wildlife.

Ahh, nothing gets me in the holiday spirit or instills that jolly Christmas mood in me more than new fallen snow, brightly decorated homes, and icy city streets festively adorned with one fender-bender after another.

Hey! Hang up and drive the car!

Actually, the one thing that gets me into the Christmas spirit, aside from coming to fisticuffs with another shopper over the last "Psycho-Wrestler Barbie" doll on the shelf, is the wonderful Festival of Trees gala.

I love the Festival of Trees, probably because of the word "festival" itself, derived from the Latin "feast" (meaning "to eat a lot") and "ival" (meaning "what's for dessert?"). And of course, I love looking at all the beautifully decorated trees donated by generous businesses, organizations and individuals throughout the Billings area.

But did you know that the first Christmas tree did not originate with the Festival of Trees?

Nope. See, about 1200 years ago an English missionary named Winfred (who later had his name legally changed to "Boniface," because all the other missionaries called him a sissy), came upon some Druids about to sacrifice a young prince tied to an oak tree. Winfred having had too much caffeine, and desperately trying to prove his manliness, boldly stopped the sacrifice and cut down the oak.

Then, suddenly, a young fir tree instantly appeared where the oak had stood, which goes to show that one should never mix cold medication and caffeine.

The sacrifice formerly known as prince, terrified, ran for his life. Winfred, fearing for his own Yule log, turned to run too, but the Druids grabbed him and tied HIM to the young fir, thus making Winfred the very first Christmas ornament on the first Christmas tree.

The Druids then placed a star atop the tree, representing the Star of the East. The very same star that led the three wise guys to Bethlehem to lay gifts before Baby Jesus, after carefully removing the price tags, of course.

So, come on out to the Festival of Trees at the MetraPark Expo Center today. See first hand how the tradition of the Christmas tree has evolved over the past 1200 years. Visit Santa's Workshop, decorate some cookies and bring 'em over to me at the Artists' Reception! I'll be there right after I crash the Teddy Bear Picnic.

All the money over the weekend-long festival goes to support The Family Tree Center—The Billings Council to Prevent Child Abuse. Through their efforts and the educational programs they provide, The Family Tree Center offers a gift to the community that has no price tag.

When Wallflowers Die

by Sandra West Prowell

Sandra West Prowell is a fourth-generation Montanan and the great-granddaughter of early pioneers. She is a cofounder of the Montana Authors Coalition and liaison for the Rocky Mountain Chapter of the Mystery Writers of America. She has published three Phoebe Siegel mysteries.

Memories slumber in dark recesses. We bury them in the coffins of our minds and think of them no more until a sound, a smell, a word resurrects them and uncovers them to the light. They live again. Embarrassment turns to laughter, grief to solace. But murder? Murder remembered tortures and haunts and bruises the soul. It lives a parallel life to disconnected events and people that somehow pick up the stench.

No one knew what Ellen Dahl Maitland, the lone heiress of one of the largest fortunes in Montana, was thinking in the early-morning hours of June 1, back in 1968, but they pieced together some of what she did. Ellen hadn't gone to bed as early as she usually did, but instead curled up in a chair with a copy of Rosemary's Baby *she had checked out of Parmly Library two days before. She read well past midnight. At some point in the wee hours of the morning she placed a brass owl bookmark ten pages from the end, walked upstairs, drew a bath, and soaked there for the next two hours.*

Sometime after that, she sat down on the stool in front of her mahogany dressing table and pulled a pair of black-net nylons up her legs and attached them to the snaps hanging from her black garter belt. She was not wearing panties. A long-sleeved bolero jacket of see-through red nylon completed the ensemble. Last, she donned a full-length London Fog raincoat. There was no rain in the forecast.

Ellen left the house around five-thirty a.m., spoke briefly with the paperboy, backed her 1968 red MG out of the garage, and drove off. Her whereabouts until two-twenty that afternoon are undetermined, but it was then that she showed up at the Bunk House Motel, a sleazy pay-and-lay off I-90 and 27th Street South. In what passed for an office, and supposedly checking in alone, she placed twenty-one dollars on the counter; a room was hers for three hours. The clerk, Gummy, remembered her recoiling as she breathed in the scent of stale booze and cigarettes. In his statement he described her as a classy bitch. He asked no questions. Curiosity was not a job requirement.

At three p.m. on that day in June, I was unwillingly dropped off at a friend's house a couple of blocks east of South Park. Dressed in a poufy, blue satin implement of medieval torture known as a party dress, I joined a group of my preadolescent peers in Tiffany Barber's backyard to celebrate her birthday.

I'd been bought off: Wear the dress, attend the party, and when the party ended my father would pick me up, take me home to change clothes, and then head to the banks of the Yellowstone River for a couple of hours of fishing. Just the two of us. Those times were rare and I cherished them. The lives of cops encroach on their lives as husbands and fathers, wives and mothers.

By four o'clock I had weathered the ceremonious ripping-open-of-the-packages as the blond, sausage-curled, porcine-faced Tiffany sneered at each present and tossed it casually aside, gorged myself on bad cake and melting ice cream, and fended off a kiss-attack from Jimmy Canero with a well-placed kick to the crotch. I mean, I really had a crush on this guy and had to let him know. I'm sure he thought of that as he writhed on the ground.

Everyone was full of anticipation. The piñata that hung from a cottonwood limb was begging to be destroyed. Mrs. Barber called us together and laid down the law: sticks could only be swung overhead. Anyone violating this rule would be disarmed. With blindfolds in place, sticks clutched in a two-handed grip, we went to work.

The image of Ellen Dahl Maitland's assailant must have been mirrored in her eyes just before the first blow from an undetermined weapon fell across her face with a rage strong enough to fracture her right orbital socket and explode her eye. Carpenters working on the roof at the opposite end of the motel from where Ellen's face and skull were being rendered to a mass of bone fragments, torn tissue, and blood, heard nothing, saw nothing. The sounds of their Skil saws and hammers drowned out whatever screams there might have been.

We peaked in a frenzy within seconds. One after another our blows made contact with a hollow thwack. I took my best shot at the piñata, lodging my stick inside it. My hand vibrated as someone else brought their weapon down on mine. The stinging sensation it caused coursed through my palm. I tugged at my stick, trying to free it, and lifted the blindfold just as the donkey erupted, spilling its contents onto the ground. The deed was done.

The injuries had been too numerous and too savage and too anatomically traumatic to leave any semblance of her plain, haunting beauty. Ellen Maitland's face was obliterated, the damage so thorough it was impossible to determine the weapon or the number of blows she had received.

By five p.m. the party was breaking up. I'd been sitting curbside for what seemed like a long time when sirens cut through the still summer air one block west and shrieked south toward the Interstate. A half hour later my mother showed up. The only explanation I got was that Dad had been called into work.

It was a strange week at my house. We saw very little of my dad. There were hushed late-night conversations between him and Mother as she brought his saved dinner from the oven and sat with him while he ate. I remember catching her crying one afternoon and asking her what was wrong. She mumbled something into her handkerchief and waved me away with her hands. I was just young enough and selfish enough to resent anything that took my father's attention away from me and brought my mother to tears.

It wasn't a hard week to remember. Five days after Ellen Maitland died in a love-for-sale motel, Sirhan Sirhan shot and killed Bobby Kennedy at the Ambassador in L.A. The front page of *The Billings Gazette* dedicated itself to national mourning and relegated a local tragedy to the back of the paper.

Now, twenty-seven years past that June day, on a biting winter's night, my telephone rang, and as soon as I answered it, Ellen Maitland reached out from the grave and put a stranglehold on my life.

The call came at the same time I was anticipating that my clogged sinuses were going to blow off the front of my face. I'd had my shot of NyQuil and was bundled on the couch watching the sing-along version of "Grease," doing my best to sing along.

"Ms. Siegel?"

"Speaking."

"This is Bob Maitland."

"Okay."

There was a pause. "Do you know who I am?"

"Of course, Mr. Maitland…"

"Bob, please."

"I know who you are, Bob." Who the hell didn't know who he was; the golden boy of the state Republicans, and only the most popular political figure in Montana since Mike Mansfield. Rumor had it that he was about to announce his run for governor. "What can I do for you?"

"We need to talk. I had a conversation with a friend of yours, Maggie Mason. She encouraged me to call you."

"Okay."

"Are you all right? You sound a little…"

"If I sound like I'm dying, Bob," I said and emphasized his name, "that's because I am dying. I have a combination of Ebola and hantavirus and probably don't have more than a few hours to live."

I could hear him chuckle. "Bad stuff. I had it a while back. It took me a long time to shake it."

"That's comforting. What's on your mind?"

"Maggie said you're about the best investigator around. Are you up for a little business?"

"Depends on what it is."

"I see no problem with that. Would it be possible to meet at my home?"

"Why not? Let's make it before noon."

"Eleven tomorrow morning?"

"Sure. Directions?" I wrote them down as he gave them. "Great. Can you give me an idea of what this is about? I should tell you upfront that I don't do child-custody cases, bedroom windows, personal injury, or—"

"My wife was murdered twenty-seven years ago. It remains unsolved."

"After twenty-seven years?"

"The book is never closed on a murder case."

"I'm aware of that. Where's law enforcement in all this?"

"After this much time, who's interested? Those initially involved stayed with it for a long, long time. Some retired, some just gave up. Now and then on the anniversary of her murder or if some hotshot journalist does an article on unsolved crimes in the state, something'll show up in the paper. That could change."

"How so?" I tilted my head to the left to see if I could give my right sinus some relief. It didn't work.

"Can I be frank with you?"

I was silent. As soon as prospective clients say words to that effect, I know I'll get partial truths.

"I was questioned at length, and, to some, I'm still a suspect. I was never charged, but many people read guilt into the fact that I had retained an attorney. Now I find myself with the same problem I had back then."

"Which is?"

"Let's just say there are some creative conversations taking place among my political enemies. The potential spins that could be created…well, they're overpowering."

"Sounds like it."

"In a nutshell, they have every intention of digging this up if and when I announce my candidacy for governor. But let's save it until tomorrow. You sound like you could use a good night's sleep. Eleven, then?"

"I'll be there."

I hung up and immediately dialed Maggie Mason.

"Maggie," I said after she answered. "Bob Maitland called."

"Oh, good, I was hoping he would. You sound like shit."

"I feel like shit. Tell me about this guy."

"Bobby?"

"You call him Bobby? Just how well do you know him and in what sense?"

"Let's see, I know he has a mole on his ass and his two most favorite words are 'oh baby' said in rapid succession. Bobby and I had a thing a few years back. No big deal. He's one of the good guys. We need him, Phoebe. We need him as governor. I'm behind him all the way, and you know I loathe those political pricks. Besides, maybe I'll write a kiss-and-tell book and make my fortune."

"Don't hold back." I blew my nose and immediately went into a coughing spasm. "You are one sick woman, Mason."

"Me? Listen to you. God, are you taking anything for that?"

"If it can be swallowed or inhaled, it's sitting right in front of me. Tell me more."

"Do you remember the murder? It happened in sixty-eight."

"No, I don't. Fill me in."

"I know nothing. Wait, I take that back, I've heard fragments. Something to the effect that he had been married and was widowed early on, but nothing substantial. We dated for seven or eight months, and it wasn't until near the end of that time that he told me about her. I was shocked to find out she was Rosella Dahl's daughter. "

"Ellen Dahl Maitland, daughter of the dragon lady. Damn, I do remember that."

"Dragon lady? What the hell are you talking about? Are you running a fever or something?"

"Dahl's House. That Gothic structure down on Division Street. The trip when I was a kid running around town on Halloween was to make a stop at Dahl's House. It was a spooky place. Complete with its own crone."

"You're regressing, Siegel. I'd really like to stay on here and relive your childhood with you, but I've got a brief to finish. Hear Bob out and let me know how it goes. I owe you one."

"If I live to see the sun come up, I'll do what I can."

"If I were you, I'd get to bed. You really do sound like hell."

"You realize this virus is virulent enough to travel through phone wires? Now you're infected. They're breeding inside you as we speak."

"At least someone's getting a little. Good night, Phoebe."

The line went dead.

The NyQuil was taking effect. I stretched out on the couch and pulled the blankets I had piled on top of me up under my chin. The amber glow from the fireplace licked the walls and shadow-danced around the room. Memories teased the fringes of my consciousness. I remembered the day: Tiffany Barber and Jimmy Canero, the piñata, and how we bludgeoned it over and over again. Our frenzy abated, we turned and walked away. So, apparently, had Ellen Maitland's killer.

poetry by Sheila Ruble

Sheila Ruble grew up in Colorado. In 1974, she and her husband moved to a small ranch north of Billings, where she presently teaches English horseback riding. Ruble's poetry and photography reflect her close connection with the natural world. She also teaches poetry in rural schools as a Writer's Voice Poet on the Prairie.

Weaning

Single file, cattle trail
down from the forest service permit
into the home pasture,
dark Angus against an incandescence of aspen.

Calves break formation
gambol high tailed,
giddy with youth and ignorance
of the gates about to shut upon them.

In the thin, fine air of fall
yellow quakies tremble
as the cows lumber, heavy bodied,
towards certain separation.

I am battered by their bawling.
Calves press against the corral fence
while their mothers drift, unwilling,
back into the tall meadow grass

driven to feed
next year's young, already curled
deep within those heaving,
sorrowful flanks.

Benjy's New Home
by Bonnie Scherer

Born and raised in South Dakota, **Bonnie Scherer** moved to Billings in 1969 to work as a surgical nurse at Deaconess Medical Center. *Benjy's New Home* emerged from her own close encounter with a rabbit who took up residence in her front yard. She has inspired and encouraged many people across the nation with her writings on the trials, tribulations, and victories of a cancer patient, stemming from personal experience. She has often served as a writer in schools in the Billings area.

Bill McCracken, her brother-in-law, is an illustrator from Mobile, Alabama.

Benjy
by Bill McCracken
watercolor (1989)

The shelter of the forest was the only home that Benjy had ever known and now that was being threatened by what man calls "progress." Benjy was afraid. Why, just this morning Benjy's mom had lined up all his brothers and sisters in a row and told them it was time they all moved out of the forest and into homes of their own. Even Benjy's mom and dad would be moving out of their lovely forest home.

The bulldozers would be marching in by the end of the week, trampling down everything in their paths. Their forest would be cut in half by a super, four-lane highway. With the highway would come traffic and civilization. The forest would no longer be safe for Benjy and the other forest creatures. You see, Benjy was a beautiful, cottontailed rabbit. He was sandy brown with just a touch of gray to give him almost a silvery glow. He had a set of magnificent pink ears, a tiny pink nose, coal black eyes, and the biggest white cottontail you have ever seen. Benjy was just about as perfect as any rabbit could be.

Although Benjy felt a bit sad and afraid about leaving the forest and his family, he knew in his heart that this was all a part of growing up and he couldn't help feeling excited about the prospects of what lay ahead of him. Benjy was so glad that Grandfather, who had lived in many places and seen much of the world when he was young, had often told the family many wonderful stories about his experiences. They had talked many times about the different places that had been Grandfather's favorites and not surprising at all was the fact that they were all in Montana. Now Grandfather's experiences would help each of the family members choose a new home.

Mom and Dad Rabbit were heading for Farmer Thompson's acreage outside of Bridger. They had found a perfect spot behind Farmer Thompson's big red barn. A wooden crate, half hidden in the tall grass, would be their new home.

Benjy's sisters and brothers would be hopping over to a wonderful place, the Special K Ranch. They knew they would be happy there for they had heard Grandfather speak many times about the special care and attention he had received while he was living and working on the ranch. They were all so excited they could hardly wait until tomorrow when they would leave.

Benjy, being the inquisitive one, had decided he would be moving to Billings. He knew it would be risky to live in the city, but he had been told by Grandfather Rabbit about a neighborhood on Alderson Avenue that had the biggest Colorado Spruce Tree he had ever seen in the whole entire State of Montana. The branches of this wondrous tree touched the ground in such a way that it made a perfect place for a rabbit to live, especially a small cottontailed rabbit. Why, he had even heard that the neighbors were all very friendly and would see to it that he was well fed. Grandfather said there would be a fresh supply of carrots, lettuce, alfalfa, and his very favorite, delicious red apples. No more green sour apples for him! Benjy went to sleep that night dreaming about Alderson Avenue and delicious red apples.

In the morning they all excitedly packed their belongings, said their goodbyes, and left the forest for their new homes. It was going to be a good day, Benjy just knew it!

Mom and Dad Rabbit moved in with Farmer Thompson, and although it was a well-known fact that Farmer Thompson preferred to raise sheep, fancy chickens, and canary birds, Mom and Dad Rabbit fit right into the routine of farm life. Farmer Thompson was a kind and gentle man and made their life in the wooden crate very comfortable and safe. They didn't even miss the shelter of the forest—well, not too much.

Benjy's sisters and brothers were welcomed with open and loving arms to the Special K Ranch. They even had their very own hutch, which was a new word for them, in a building that housed many different kinds of rabbits they had never seen before. With all their new friends, and the wonderful care they received from those who live at Special K, they could not have been happier.

Benjy found his tree on Alderson Avenue and everything that Grandfather had said was true. The food was great, the neighbors friendly, and he loved the excitement that city life brought. Why, the black Scottie dog that shared the same yard didn't even bark at him! He also met some cousins, the Jack Rabbits. They lived at Terrace Gardens and were so big and strong Benjy could hardly believe his eyes! It must have been the peanut butter and jelly sandwiches that kind Mr. Erichsen left them to eat every day that made them so awesome.

Since he knew Mrs. Erichsen personally, Benjy would ask her to make some sandwiches, too. Maybe he would grow as big as the Jack Rabbits.

Looking back, Benjy thought how afraid he had been when he first found out that he had to move. He was so happy to find out that, although moving certainly caused changes in your life, those changes could be wonderfully new challenges that could make your life exciting.

Benjy wrote to Mom and Dad Rabbit and his sisters and brothers every week and they all got together at each others' homes during all the important rabbit holidays. Yes, life was good and Benjy was a very happy and well-loved rabbit. It seemed to him that even the folks on Alderson Avenue were happier and more friendly with each other because he had made his home under the magnificent Colorado Spruce Tree.

Arcadian Idyll

by Jess Schwidde

Iowa-born **Jess Schwidde** served in the infantry as Battalion Surgeon in
North Africa and Europe during World War II. He established the first neu-
rological service in the Billings area in 1955. He credits his interest in writing
and poetry to the writers of the Billings Art Association for their willingness
to encourage and assist beginning writers.

The ancient cabin is nearly concealed in a forest of weeds, a ramshackle
windmill the only other visible, surviving structure. Adventurous vines clasp
once-freely-moving parts in perpetual arrest. An abandoned homestead is a
sad and desolate sight; but today there is life about this place, much life!
Indeed, this weed patch is soon to witness one of its more curious spectacles.

Faithfully following an old black bellwether, billows of hungry sheep harvest the spring grass. Tolerant of alterations in elevation and climate, they are
still wearing their fleecy winter coats. A veteran collie anxiously insures an
orderly march.

An excited herder suddenly bursts from the shack into the bright
sunlight. The flock churns in a brief nervous panic. Elated, eyes squinting,
Dell Stark examines this newly discovered treasure of dusty books clutched
in his arms. Unusual for a herdsman, he ignores a buzzing nuisance in his
path. Lady's convincing bluff sends the snake slithering under a ledge.

Dell smiles as he selects a small leather-bound volume with a red silk
bookmark. He climbs to a nearby stump, pauses, and in a slow panoramic
survey contemplates his flock. "Merinos," he says aloud, "Good wool but
poor mutton." He often wishes the reverse were true.

Holding the book before him in both hands, arms extended, his resound-
ing voice calls to his band: "Man, that is born of woman, hath but a short
time to live." Two thousand heads raise as one in unbroken attention. For
this single moment he is the world's foremost evangelist! "He cometh up,
and is cut down like a flower," he booms. Heads drop and the sheep return
to eating. Lady paces nervously, awaiting the signal to push on. The herder,
however, lingers, dreading the final curtain descending on this pastoral
tableau.

The Reverend Dell Stark reckons all preachers experience occasional
problems with their congregations. He is aware that these hollow-horned
ruminants, cousins of goats, were preferred subjects for sacrifice in ancient
ceremonials. Little wonder they become wary with matters ecclesiastical.

The sinking sun interrupts his reflections and reminds him that one hour
of daylight remains. Filling and lighting his pipe concludes the ceremony.
With reluctance he abandons his pulpit.

Dell and Lady urge the animals to water and a familiar, protected coulee. Contented, with full stomachs, they will cuddle close together until morning. Lady is fed and praised and assumes her post as night guard. Taking his flask from a pack, Dell drinks individual salutes to compliment his mother, his dog, his sheep and his home on wheels.

The sun hovers on the crest of the Big Horns. Whistling, he picks a path to his wagon. It's a grand life, he thinks to himself; and his day is not finished! After supper he will start a new book. He has long wanted to read *Pilgrim's Progress.*

Alien Seas

by Andrew M. Seddon

A native of England, **Andrew Seddon** has been a physician at the Deaconess Billings Clinic since 1990. He has published more than eighty fiction and non-fiction pieces, including his first novel, *Red Planet Rising* (1995). He is an active member of Science Fiction and Fantasy Writers of America.

[*Alien Seas* is set in the year 2090. Julia Allen is a molecular geneticist at a national research agency in Washington D.C. She has recently been awarded a position on the first manned mission to Saturn's moon Titan. Born in Billings, she returns home to tell her parents the news.]

Julia leaned her head against the cool plastic of the narrow aircraft window beside her seat and tried to still her racing thoughts.

"Trying to kill God," that's what her mother would say. Guaranteed. She could almost hear her mother's voice carrying on a sustained monologue. Her father—she hoped—would be pleased by her selection to the Titan mission. She crossed her fingers.

The hypersonic jet dropped out of the navy blue of the cloudless sky and spiraled towards the waiting landing pad kilometers below. Julia's stomach lurched as it always did during a descent. She craned her neck to see past the swept-forward curve of the wings and glimpsed ground crew moving like ants near the terminal before the jet's changing position blotted out the view.

The late afternoon sun reflected off the wingtips. Despite his promise, Steven Emerick hadn't managed to book her a morning flight, and her conscience hadn't allowed her to commandeer a NAIBMR plane for a personal visit.

A swirl of dust skimmed across the vast Montana plains and parted, leaving the dull tan of fall scrub in its wake. Here and there a strand of pine trees followed the course of a ravine or crowned a low hill with a green circlet. Mounted in a setting of yellow cottonwoods, the silver-blue thread of the Yellowstone River trickled towards the distant Missouri.

Julia could already smell the sagebrush and taste the dryness of the air.

"Lemme see!" The young boy in the middle seat pushed against her, ignoring his mother's urging to be polite.

Julia leaned back.

The boy planted a hand on each side of the window and jammed his nose against the plastic. "There's nothing!" he exclaimed after a moment. He flopped back into his seat and pouted.

His mother flashed Julia a tolerant smile. "I'm sure you'll like it, Joey..."

Julia resumed her former position.

Billings sprawled along the course of the Yellowstone, embracing the river in a tight clasp. Julia could almost understand the boy's disappointment. Compared to one of the massive megalopoli such as Dallas-Fort Worth, Washington-New York-Philadelphia-Boston ("NewBos"), or Phoenix, Billings was a mere village.

But Julia liked it that way. She wondered how the city would cope with the Clearances. As NorthAm struggled to deal with the twin burdens of pollution and overpopulation, the Clearances were sounding the death-knell for small towns and villages. Move the population—six hundred million— to the cities and restore agricultural and wilderness lands: that was the plan. The East Coast and what the Quake of 2041 had left of the West had undergone massive relocation, with the South and Central following suit. Montana struggled to remain one of the last bastions of a vanishing way of life.

Would it work? Nobody knew. Some said the Earth was doomed by an ecology too devastated to recover.

With a gentle bump, the jet settled down above the Rimrocks.

The Remora

by Aaron P. Small

Born in Brooklyn in 1923, **Aaron P. Small** received his Ph.D. in English from the University of Denver. He taught mythology and comparative literature at Eastern Montana College (now MSU-Billings) from 1955 to 1985. In 1994 he received the Literacy Award from the Montana State Reading Council. *The Remora* is his first novel.

Sylvia and Bernie walked down to where her parents were sitting and joined them, and the congregation seemed to sense the bar mitzvah beginning. Then the rabbi came down with young Max. Rabbi Rosenfeld had a special yarmulke, a long black robe, and his tallis or prayer shawl, and little Max wore a dark blue suit with a brand new tallis his father had given him in the Jewish tradition. A chair especially for Max had been placed behind the lectern. Max sat there. The rabbi began the services with a prayer in Hebrew and the congregation followed responsively with portions in English. Mr. and Mrs. Gluckstern looked at each other, but said nothing.

After more responsive reading, some in Hebrew and some in English, more prayers were said, including the Shema, the central prayer of Judaism. The deep voices of the men and the strident voices of some of the women intoned the Shema: *Shema Israel Adonai Elohenu, Adonai Echod*—Hear O Israel, the Lord our God, the Lord is One.

More prayers followed, and then the rabbi motioned to two men in the congregation who came forward and opened the ark, lifted out the Torah, and gently placed it on the lectern. The man facing the congregation tilted the scrolls so the other could untie and remove the velvet covering. Once opened, the Torah revealed carefully hand-written Hebrew characters. Rabbi Rosenfeld unrolled the scroll until he reached the portion of the Torah that fell on Max's birthday, reading aloud to himself until he arrived at the section he wanted Max to read. With the love a teacher displays toward his prize student, the rabbi handed Max the Yod, the silver pointer in the shape of a hand with the index finger extended. Max moved the Yod from right to left across the Torah and read in Hebrew, then transliterated the line into English. The rabbi stood behind him and silently mouthed each word to make sure there were no mistakes. Max read with the fluency of a yeshiva student. When he had to chant, his voice cracked, characteristic of puberty.

Some members of the congregation quietly repeated the words as they went along with the reading, some just watched and smiled. The visitors, who numbered about half of the people present, watched Max with amazement or looked across to other non-members who shook their heads in disbelief.

Bernie was called upon to read from the Torah. He walked toward the lectern, picked a tallis from a rack, placed it across his shoulders, and approached the Torah. He put his hand lovingly on his son's shoulder, and Max looked up at him. Bernie lifted the end of the tallis to his lips and touched the Torah with that piece of the tallis. He recited portions of the Hebrew, followed by Max's reading. Then Sylvia's father was called on for an aliyah. For a man in his seventies he moved with alacrity. Wearing his own tallis, he moved the end of the tallis to his lips and then to the Torah. In a husky voice he read the Hebrew and looked with pride at his grandson. A sudden undertow of whispering arose from the congregation. A picture of three generations displaying their love for the Torah was there for all to see, like a moment of time frozen. A son, a father, and a grandfather, all sharing the holy book. Bernie and Mr. Gluckstern took their places in the seats up front and Max, stretching to look over the lectern, began his sermon.

"Rabbi, Mom and Dad, Granma and Granpa, members of the congregation, and friends, I want to thank you for all coming here today and taking part in my bar mitzvah. In the eyes of the Jewish community I am now considered a man. Whenever there is a minyan needed for a kaddish, I can be counted as one of the adults. But it means more to me than that. I really am lucky. There are so many Jewish boys my age around the world who are denied a bar mitzvah because they are too poor or are in a country where the government does not permit it. But in this *goldeneh medina*, as Granma and Granpa call our wonderful country, we Jews can practice our religion without fear of persecution. I hope that I can carry on the tradition of my parents and grandparents...."

His determined eyes peering over the lectern, his voice cracking, little Max Rifkin continued to laud his country and his good fortune. Many of the women reached for their handkerchiefs, their eyes wet with tears. The older men and women who had come here as immigrants painfully recalled the deprivations under which they lived, the sufferings that made them seek new hope in the United States.

The bar mitzvah ended with the rabbi saying the benediction, his hands raised and outstretched. He asked the people to remain seated until the Rifkin family could get downstairs to greet all of the people present. The sounds of *mazel tov* arose from all over the sanctuary, like balloons at a birthday party. Little Max was being hugged and kissed by his mother and grandmother with such fervor that his yarmulke fell off his head onto his shoulder. The entire family walked down the center aisle to the basement steps and took positions immediately behind the door. To the left in the far corner was a card table covered by a white tablecloth and containing five large bottles of kosher wine and dozens of glasses. On the right side of the room were tables with chopped chicken liver, corned beef, pastrami, kosher pickles, Jewish rye bread, honey cake, pound cake, nuts, and various kinds of candies. Directly in the rear were two people in the kitchen serving coffee and tea. Sylvia, Bernie, and her parents stood and greeted the people as they entered the room, accepting with obvious joy the compliments showered on them. Little Max was busily filling a plate with chopped chicken liver, rye bread, and pickles.

"*Mazel tov,* Sylvia and Bernie. Some little man you got there."

A Northern Cheyenne Morning

by Bently Spang

Bently Spang is an enrolled member of the Northern Cheyenne tribe and was born in 1960 at the Crow Agency Indian Hospital. He is a visual artist, writer, and curator and outspoken advocate for Native issues. He currently resides in Billings.

My brother and I have always been close as siblings go. And though we were both born, along with my older sister, on the Northern Cheyenne reservation, we were raised in such far-flung places as Alaska and Seattle. We moved every two years for much of our childhood as my father sought transfers that led to promotions in his job with the Bureau of Indian Affairs (BIA). We were BIA brats and this constant uprooting as children forced us to rely heavily on each other as best friends and confidantes, especially my brother and I. Born two years apart, our closeness growing up made us more like twins, each sensing what the other was thinking or feeling at any given moment without having to verbalize. And despite being raised away from "the rez" for much of our childhood, we both knew it was home for us. It was as if our mother's umbilical cord was replaced, at birth, by one attached to this place on the earth. In those years away from the rez we returned often to visit family here. No other place felt like home, not like this home.

While away from the rez, our parents, childhood sweethearts who had grown up on the rez, kept our hunger for this place, for our culture, alive with countless stories. Each time we returned to visit, these stories were supplemented with still more stories from my uncles and grandparents; ancestral stories, hunting trips, childhood stories, and, of course, ghost stories. The ghost stories, mostly told at night, were our favorites and they would sit you in a grandparent's lap quicker than you could say "ha ho." They were so darn scary because they were so true....

We fed from these stories for months after returning to our suburban home in Seattle or to the converted army barracks in Mt. Edgecumbe, Alaska. They became legends in the telling and re-telling. For all its appearances of abject poverty, the rez was a magical place for us. The abandoned cars sprinkled across the land transformed into chariots of fire, and my grandmother's outhouse was a trickster's paradise. And we knew from our own experience those rugged HUD houses were filled with loving families and a fierce, Northern Cheyenne pride. It was that same fierce pride that re-filled both my brother and me. It runs through the veins of this place on the earth, our homeland, carrying with it stories of the happiest times in Northern Cheyenne existence as well as some of the most difficult. Our history is embedded in the dirt of this land. We are it and it is us. The Northern Cheyenne heart belongs in this place and no other.

In equal parts along with pride, a deep gratitude to our ancestors also inhabits the Northern Cheyenne heart. Were it not for the efforts of two of our chiefs, Little Wolf and Dull Knife, and the intellectualism and courage of others in the tribe, we would not have been standing in that clearing wallowing in the beauty and marveling at the stillness. Most Northern Cheyennes know of the heroic efforts of our people in getting us back to our homeland. As punishment for exterminating Custer and his troops at the battle of the Little Bighorn, my ancestors were sent to Oklahoma. They braved a harsh winter and thousands of troops, escaping to return here on foot, in the winter of 1877. Disease, a humid and unforgiving climate, and the cruelty of the soldiers only fueled their homesickness for our land and quickened their steps getting back here.

Standing there with my brother, both of us cradled in the arms of this tiny box canyon, these thoughts filled my consciousness, soothing me as they always had. But I still couldn't help thinking something was different this time. Then it hit me: this canyon was situated within shouting distance from a special place, one that we had just recently discovered. Earlier that summer my dad, my uncle, and I had ridden horseback just a mile or so from this place. On a high grassy flat, tucked away in the trees, we had discovered an old camp my ancestors had used. We were always finding evidence of my ancestors on our rides—teepee rings, lookout posts with remnants of old campfires—but this camp was unique. There were at least twenty-four teepee rings, the biggest camp we had ever encountered. Oftentimes, we were lucky to find one lone ring of rocks barely visible, half buried in the rock ground that marked a winter camp.

The placement of this camp was brilliantly chosen, too. It overlooked an old cavalry trail, the wagon ruts still visible today, but was virtually invisible to those on the trail. They could thus monitor the movements of the military with relative obscurity. The camp bordered the high country where game was plentiful, and the creek bottoms below the camp almost certainly, at one time, held abundant fresh water springs. Everything they needed was right at their fingertips. I remember, that day, feeling a deep sense of respect for their intellect, their ability to pull all these elements of survival together in such a poetic way.

And standing in that clearing with my brother, I realized that most certainly they had stood in this clearing at one time also, probably on a hunt, marveling at the raw beauty of this place and feeling their hearts swell just as we were. I closed my eyes and I could almost feel them around me, my ancestors, smiling at my realization and nodding their approval. I opened my eyes and I could see, could feel, that all the materials in that place—the trees, the rocks, the plants—had stories to tell. They had seen so much of life come and go in this tiny Northern Cheyenne canyon: the hopes and joys of a nation, the hardships, the gratitude of a successful hunter able to feed his people; perhaps they had even witnessed the genocide leveled against my people—man's inhumanity to man. I could feel that here were literally hundreds of stories just waiting to be told, hanging in the still, crisp air of that Northern Cheyenne morning.

It would be a lie to say I didn't cry that morning. Fat tears rushed to my eyes as I thought of just how close my steps were to those of my ancestors at that moment. It seemed to me that each tear sliding was a story being told, dropping back to the earth to germinate and grow again, to find its way into the next Cheyenne to be shed again. I cried with joy for the sacrifices made for me so that I could stand there in that place and cry. I cried with anger for the relatives taken from me by man's greed, and I cried with sorrow for those same relatives whom I would never get to meet, never laugh with and tease, never feel the warmth of their hug and their joy in seeing me. The tears came in a rush that startled me, a powerful grief held me tight for a moment, then passed. "They call us angry Indians," I thought. "Aren't you over that yet?" they say. "If only they really knew what it felt like, if only it were that easy to forget," I thought. Guess I wouldn't be Cheyenne then, I smiled to myself.

Wiping the tears, I looked at my brother, knowing tears were in his eyes, too. His back was to me and his big frame shook as I imagined the same emotions running through his heart. He turned to me, fingertips delicately wiping the tears from his eyes and smiled at me through the tears, chuckling at the startling rush of his emotion. "Did you feel it, too?" he said. I smiled yes. "They were here weren't they?" he asked. I nodded.

The true power of that moment lies in the trees and the rocks of that little canyon, another story waiting to be told. Nothing moved as we stood there, no crash of a big buck as it spooked out of the cedars, running up into the canyon, no turkeys running up the hill ripe for the picking. It didn't matter, though; there was no disappointment in either of us; we had found what we were looking for.

I hugged my brother tightly, feeling like a child against his big, barrel chest. He lifted me off the ground like he always does, proving his physical mastery over me and simultaneously getting even for my torturing him as a child. I accepted this with a grunt, as I always do. Setting me back on my feet, he proceeded to encapsulate our entire experience that day in one pithy statement: "We belong to this place," he said, his outstretched arms carving a circle into the air. I stopped the tears this time before they welled, nodding. "Yup," I said, unable to think of a response that came even close to the beauty of the words he had just uttered.

poetry by Shirley Steele

After migrating to Billings from her native Ohio, **Shirley Steele** discovered she had become a western writer. She has taught English at Billings Senior High School, conducted poetry workshops for adults and children, and taught poetry classes at Montana State University-Billings and Rocky Mountain College. She has served as Writers Chair for the Billings Arts Association and as State Writers Chair for the Montana Institute of the Arts. In 1992 she and her husband, Ben, received the Montana Governor's Award for Distinguished Achievement in the Arts.

MONUMENTS

The relics stand
idle,
monuments to dusty days
and hard-scratch times.
Children wade
through cheatgrass and Russian thistles
to ride on rusty running boards.
Behind phantom wheels
they mouth motor noises,
driving imaginary cargoes
to forgotten elevators –
monuments
to small, warm western towns
that somehow died.

MY FATHER DANCED

I remember how my father danced
every dance in the barn
in the old Bull Mountains.
Everybody danced in the barn
in the old Bull Mountains –
the old, the young, and the children
but my father danced every dance –
danced with all of the ladies,
danced with all of the children.
The fiddler only played three songs.
He played "Over the Waves" and "Mountain Home"
and "Turkey in the Straw."
My father danced them all
over and over again all night long
in the old Bull Mountains
and I watched until I fell asleep
on the bench along the wall,
watched my father dance every dance
in the barn in the old Bull Mountains.

Crazy Mountains: Learning from Wilderness to Weigh Technology

by David Strong

David Strong, a native of Livingston, teaches philosophy at Rocky Mountain College. He has published widely on the philosophy of technology, including co-editing an important collection of essays for the University of Chicago Press. The following excerpt typifies his combination of skillful storytelling and rigorous thinking.

The vast expanses of central Montana have an edge and a suddenness. Along the Yellowstone River, sandstone rimrocks line the horizon. Beyond these rims, the flats, benches and swells of the high plains, arid and mostly treeless, yet gold in autumn with prairie grasses, define a precise division between a yellow earth and a youthful sky. As a boy I was told that "Montana" meant land of the shining mountains. Mountains, especially the Crazy Mountains, seem to explode here into the blue as a child might draw them.

...While fishing the Yellowstone without much luck one early May, I fell to contemplating the Crazies, bright with new spring snow against a cloudless sky. I followed a ridge up from the foothills to where it disappeared, suggesting a passable route to the peak behind it. And so I awoke early at Rock Creek trailhead in the middle of July. Before I was ready to leave, a farmer appeared on his four-wheeler to check the irrigation ditches nearby. I enjoy the playful headshaking that goes on between people bent over shovels and people bent under packs, each pretending not to understand how the other "could do that sort of thing."

Leaving the trailhead, I soon left the trail, too, for the ridge, and by late morning stood at the top. I saw I could not get to Fairview peak from there, the connecting ridge was a smile of sheer cliffs, but a new route opened up to the north and so I hiked down into the cirque below, followed the stream down and up another to its headwall, crossed it, another down and up, and I was at Crazy Lake to camp for the night. It had been a long day, and the mountains had impressed me with their moodiness. The Crazies gather and they scatter. The peaks, ridges, and canyons twist off every which way and, so, too, does one's mood when hiking in them. At times I soared with the view; other times, feeling weak (sometimes I don't eat much while backpacking), I clung to a hard-won truth: "Mountains have tops." But at the top, amidst cirques, peaks and ridges, there is so much rock and the rock is overwhelmingly grey. I like shrubs and trees, meadows, dark earth, meandering streams and the fragrance of bottomlands. High in the Crazies even the lakes can be surrounded entirely by grey rock, and more than once I thought: next time I will choose a place with more life.

I had just poured a cup of coffee next morning when the sun's first rays fell on the lake and me. Suddenly again I knew why the Crow people prayed to the sun, smoked the sacred pipe, and acknowledged the four directions and Mother Earth at sunrise. The Crazies teach me to be alert to the joints of the day. We would do well to pause and linger before what gathers. Yet when I began to ascend a steep ridge out of the cirque my oppressive mood returned. It seemed to hang in the air. But I kept climbing, thinking, "rhythm...rhythm." That helped.

Changing moods, changing weather, the sun and clouds played chess with one another. Reaching the ridge top near Crazy Peak, I waited a few hours to discover if the clouds would clear or settle in. They did neither, so I worked my way down through the cliffs, letting my pack go first over the tougher drops, glad I hadn't known how hairy the cliffs looked from below. I decided to camp in an alpine meadow above Pear Lake. After a brief afternoon thundershower, the sky began to clear. "I won't put up the tent," I thought. Then at twilight I noticed a small sheet of mist, a mere clue, drifting in from the north, a long way off. "Better put up my tent." Before I had it up and got the camp in order, the valleys below had filled with an ocean of white fog that now rushed toward me, bending up and flowing down the ridges, surf of a fast rising tide. Soon I could not even make out the pass behind me and I had to check my bearings by the way I had set up the tent. That night a blast of wind that crackled the fly of the tent awakened me. The stars were out.

I did not sleep well, dreamed of an avalanche....Tired, I fell fast asleep at dawn. When I woke, the clouds overhead, now coming from their usual southwest, were dark and heavy. As I finished rolling up my tent the rain began, hesitated and then stopped. Groggy, not eager to begin the climb to the ridge or to cross the large and possibly dangerously steep snowfield, I stopped packing to make my morning coffee.

In the few minutes it took to boil water, the sun came out, the sky cleared, and my mood lifted. These peaks, meadows, lakes, this sunlight and sky filled me with light and life. Some shy and wary spirit in me could relax here, wander out freely without threat or fear. This clean, vast country danced my dance. Its distances were my distances. Its peaks, my peaks. Its beauty, my own. This country allowed me to breathe, to be. "This is exactly the right place. Whenever you go out of it, which ever way you travel, you fare worse." This is the way the world was created: these morning lit peaks, meadows, lakes, this newly cleared sky, this freshness, my joy; nothing out of place.

...Just being. Not very self-conscious, not pretending, simply corresponding, just being. Slinging this pack on my back I feel I am lifting the great song again. Feels good to be in my boots. Rock, dirt, boot, foot, leg and muscle join without gap—belong to each other, belong here. This morning I move through these trees resolute. Sharp-eyed, lion-like, I prowl this unpathed landscape, not knowing where I am or where I am going. Walking firm, hands bending branches out of the way, feet not missing a step. I am wild again. I am made for this place and this place is made for me.

Being, not thinking. Not saying, just being. I follow this landscape like a song. Watchful, moving, being, not rigidly destined. Moving with things calling out to move. Branches and clearings show the way. Here is the elemental, the wild, the old. Here are well-worn clothes with a comfortable fit. Here I become one of the old people.

All or Nothing

by Gary D. Svee

Tales of the American West, Richard S. Wheeler, editor

Gary D. Svee, a native Montanan, lives in Billings with his family. He long
served as editorial-page writer for *The Billings Gazette.* His western, *Sanctuary,*
received the Spur Award for Best Novel in 1990. The short story from which
this excerpt was taken received the 2001 Spur Award for Best Short Story.

They stood in light spilling from the front window of the Board of Trade
Cafe. Lars had come earlier than most, nodding to some of the regulars as
they arrived. "Cold," one said, the word riding a cloud of vapor into the
light. Nobody replied, words too precious to waste in the brittle air. Every
day they came to this corner in the dark—bank clerks, insurance salesmen,
farmers and railroad workers, all caught in the winter of their Depression.

A farm truck, black as the men's prospects, edged to the curb, idling as
the man inside evaluated the circle of men. The window squeaked down,
and the man peered out. Light and shadow the face was, eyes hidden from
the men.

"Picking beets," the man growled, his voice colder even than the air that
crept under the men's collars. "Two dollars a day and soup. All or nothing."

All or nothing. Bet your body could hold this old man's pace for a day.
Win and you got two dollars. Lose and you got nothing.

Lars stepped away from the other men and into the light. He was short-
er than most of the men there, but stocky, shoulders broadened in hard work
on a farm lost to the Depression. He stared at the man in the truck until the
man nodded, and then he climbed into the truck's box. The others followed.
The bet was on.

The truck carved its way through the Arctic air, and the men tried to turn
themselves inside out. The cold played with them as a small child might play
with a kitten, not realizing the cruelty of poking fingers into bright eyes. Icy
fingers reached under their collars, stinging their faces and turning their ears
numb. They tried not to pay attention to the cold. They had work for the
day—all or nothing.

The truck stopped and the men dropped to the ground. Hard as concrete
it was and unyielding as poverty and hunger. Other trucks were there, the
red dots of glowing cigarettes the only sign of life in their cabs.

"Get at it," growled the boss man, and the men danced in the trucks'
headlights, bowing to the beets, pirouetting as they threw the frozen roots to
the beds of the trucks. When they slowed, when the cold and the pain of

their backs made them hesitate a moment, the son of a bitch leaned out the window of the truck's heated cab, yelling at them as he might exhort horses to pit their muscles against a stubborn cottonwood stump.

First light gave them hope. Maybe the day would warm. Maybe the old man would see that they could break, too, just like the beet picker slumped at the edge of the field, its steel back broken by frozen gumbo.

But the old man drove them as he had driven the beet picker, and they broke too, slumping into the snow covering the field. Some lay too exhausted to move. Others twitched as the muscle spasms twisted their backs. The son of a bitch left them lying where they fell, leaking out their warmth into the snow.

All or nothing, the son of a bitch had said when he leaned out of the truck window and into the morning's darkness. All or nothing.

The casualties stiffened the resolve of the remaining farmers and clerks and barkeeps and bankers. They would show him that the Depression hadn't brittled their backs. They would show that son of a bitch, and ease the knot in their bellies where breakfast should have been.

But as the morning drew on, more men fell. Walking casualties rose then from the smoking fires at the edges of the field to help. The rescuers had no words to share, just a shoulder to cling to as the fallen made their way to the fires.

At noon the women came. They moved among the men, fueling them with soup steaming feebly in the cold. Mostly water, it was, with an occasional piece of potato or a slice of carrot swimming in the tepid water. Still, Lars felt guilty drinking it, knowing that Inga would likely have nothing, saving what little they had for dinner.

Lars stared at the ground as he ate his soup, not wanting to catch the eyes of the men watching from the edges of the field. He didn't want them to share their shame with him. All or nothing, it was, and they had nothing.

He dropped his chin to his chest, easing the muscles of his neck. He rose, swaying a little on the uneven ground. He carried his bowl of soup to a group huddled around a little campfire at the edge of the field, offering his bowl to the men. A young man took the soup, his hands shaking with the cold or his need for nourishment.

The son of a bitch screamed from the cab of the truck. "I am not feeding those men."

Lars turned to stare at the truck. "I am."

The son of a bitch's eyes roved over the field, measuring the number of men still on the field. He muttered something that Lars couldn't hear, and his head disappeared behind the rising window.

Lars stepped back into the field. "We came here to work," he shouted at the truck. "Let us work."

His hands died sometime that afternoon, his fingers giving up to the cold and going away. So he pressed his dead hands against the beets with the strength of his shoulders, throwing the roots awkwardly into the bed of the trucks.

He thought he might die that afternoon, abandoning the Earth as the sun had. But he would have to stop working to die, and he couldn't do that. Not with that son of a bitch watching him through the truck window, not with Inga waiting in the cabin.

Then in the darkness, the trucks stopped. He lined up with the other men to walk past the black truck, past the thin arm reaching into the darkness. He stared into the eyes of the son of a bitch as he took the silver dollars, and the son of a bitch looked away, muttering that there would be half a day's work tomorrow.

He didn't remember the ride back to the Board of Trade Cafe. He must have fallen asleep, hands shoved under his arms so that the warmth of his body would drive the frost away.

The dollars felt heavy in his pocket as he walked along the lane toward their home. They were hundred-pound sacks of potatoes and flour. They were a little bacon and maybe a doctor for Inga.

The door scuffed as he opened it, and the heat from the Majestic felt like the kiss of the summer sun. Inga was standing beside the table, a pan of soup in her hand.

"You found work," she said, as she might whisper a prayer in church.

Lars nodded. "Two dollars," he said, reaching into his pockets with fingers sore still from frostbite.

She reached behind her for the tin can on the back of the stove. He dropped the coins into the can one at a time, enjoying the delight on his wife's face.

"You feel better?"

She nodded.

"You don't look so yellow."

"Yellow jaundice. Mrs. Smith said I had yellow jaundice. She said it would go away."

"Now that we have the money, I think you should see the doctor."

She shook her head. Lars stood at the stove, washing his hands and face and neck, trying to get the stain of the day off him.

The two settled into the table, taking each other's hands, and he said, "*Takk for maten*," thanking God for the food He had placed on their table.

Shadows Moving Light

by Virginia Tranel

An Iowa native, **Virginia Tranel** has published essays, poetry, and short stories and recently completed a novel, *Against the Grain,* set in contemporary Montana. She is currently working on a book of essays focused on her family and is an accomplished painter. In May, 2000, she and her husband celebrated the graduation of the last of their ten children from college.

I'm packing up. For the eighteenth time in twice as many years, we're moving. Between boxes, I remind myself that this number represents, not basic shiftlessness, but all the back and forths of graduate school, internships, and summer jobs.

Every move is different. One swaggers with certitude and optimism; another wavers with doubt and backward glances. This 18th move simply makes sense. We've decided to consolidate two part-time houses into one full-time home. We're clearing out of our country place, jammed with a 15-year buildup of memories and things, and out of a house in town where we've lived the last five winters. It was here that I gradually established the first "room of my own." Tentatively at first, I gathered my books, set up a space for writing, invested in my first computer. Emboldened, I deposed the washer and dryer to the basement and transformed the main floor laundry room into my art space. An easel supplanted the Speed Queen. Oil paints landed in cupboards intended for Tide and Clorox. I worry about these innovations. Another shift, even into a dream house that overlooks the city of Billings, might squelch them for good.

"There's so much to be done," I moan, surveying three sets of washers and dryers, two eight-foot dining room tables with twenty chairs, two red velvet living room chairs and three more in blue cotton, a gold plush sofa, a huge, over-stuffed chair with a clunky ottoman, both upholstered in a gaudy orange flame-stitch. I dozed in that unlikely monster while our youngest child sat on my lap and patiently waited to learn the fate of Sam-I-Am.

My husband, Ned, doesn't share my hand-wringing approach to a new address. We've got the procedure down pat, he reminds me. We can box up efficiently. Unpack swiftly. We're good at the mundane chore of getting from here to there. He dismisses the gloomy list of life stressors that puts moving just below death and divorce. And I dismiss the strenuous optimism that compels him toward light. He's bound to come back in his next life as a sunflower, even though he claims he wants to be a bull bison in Yellowstone's Hayden Valley. "With 50 cows," he adds, straight-faced.

His cheery attitude doesn't mend mine. I lie awake nights fretting. I picture the cacophony of color about to clash on the teal carpet in our new home. I worry about the laundry room's proximity to the kitchen. I imagine myself falling prey to appliances again, tossing a load into the washer at random moments, doing menial work at the expense of all true, ardent, creative work, committing what Brenda Ueland calls in her book, *If You Want to Write,* a "sin against the Holy Ghost." Stubbornly, I renew my vow to shun sin and seek virtue.

By day I linger in front of basement shelves and read intriguing labels on bulging boxes:

Mike's stuff. I know what's in here. You don't need to.

Paul's law books—SAVE (I might go back)

Monica's high school scrap books: STAY OUT!!!

Jennie's letters (PERSONAL!)

Other boxes hold the things I cling to. Frayed books with broken spines, my children's favorite stories, *Little Bear, The Tall Book of Make Believe, Uncle Wiggily.* Collections of first-grade art work, a drawing labeled "Mom" that bears a dismaying resemblance to a Willem De Kooning woman. Two wedding gowns, one mine, one my daughter's. Long underwear, sizes 4 to 40, all mysteriously the same length. Parkas, multi-colored scarves, hand-knit caps, mittens without partners. A mothering habit, I suspect, this guarding against the cold of empty closets.

I unearth a packet of letters addressed to me and re-read one. In it, a young man generously acknowledges my concern about his impending trip to Alaska with my daughter. In fact, he says, he can even understand it, but he nevertheless insists that their decision is "sensible and right." I smirk. Within a week, my daughter had returned and left him shivering in the dark.

The daunting task at hand immobilizes me. What to keep, what to throw away. Moving lays bare every psychic cranny. It opens up dark thoughts, aggravates basic tendencies, dramatizes differences. Focused on the stress rating—death, divorce, moving—I brace for the impact. Insistently cheerful, Ned shrugs and lifts his petals upward. "Take it all," he smiles. "We'll go through it later at our leisure."

"We?" This is a job the two of us will turn to on a lazy Sunday afternoon? Even as I argue against unedited moving, I decide sorting is gender-connected. After all, it is work women know. Sorting closets for outgrown clothes, laundry for color, a five-year-old's chatter for the phrase that matters, ideas for direction, socks for pairs, adolescent lassitude for the fierce caring beneath.

I begin. The process is tedious and unproductive. Plunging my hand into the dark insides of a box labeled "costume possibilities," I recognize the contents—the slithery polyester evening gown, lush fake-fur stole, sleek satin oriental jacket. I lift a flat, battered box from the shelf and dump it out. There's the newspaper my mother urged me to save. "Victory! The End of World War II," the headline proclaims. I loosen the ribbon around a two-inch stack of prom programs and open one to a handwritten promise: "I will never forget you. John." I've forgotten John's last name. I pick up a glossy white matchbook with *Rick and Janet* embossed in gold. An easy toss. They're no longer married and I no longer smoke.

I open another box. Five saucers and three cups, rose flowered, silver-rimmed remnants of my childhood. I make three sets to give to my children. I envision eclectic Thanksgiving tables, generations connected by dishes handed down. I have no solution for the two left-over saucers.

Quickly, I sort through a closet full of unwanted coats and box them up to give away. The off-white wool confounds me. Seldom worn, but expensive, it testifies to a tendency I dislike in myself: hanging onto mistakes as a way to justify them. Chastened, I fold the coat into the give-away box.

A larger decision looms. How to transport our things. We make a deal with our nineteen-year-old son and his friend. They'll supply the brawn, a prospect that fits their rampaging testosterone and dismal bank accounts. With those exuberant muscles at our disposal, Ned fantasizes eliminating entirely the ordeal of boxing-up. "We can use the flatbed truck from the ranch," he proposes and "just set our stuff on the back."

I imagine dressers tipping over and sliding into the ravine as the truck winds up the short, steep hill to our new home. I see china bouncing into smithereens along the rutted roads of our country home. My gloom is rooted in the memory of the rainy day of Move Number 12: the pickup pulling in with soaked lamp shades and drowned rugs.

The next day I call Hertz and reserve a 26-foot truck. Armed with the receipt, I convince my husband of the practicality of a large enclosed vehicle. At the prospect of this macho mobility, my son and his friend flex their muscles and dub themselves "The Happy Movers."

Difficulties surface. Monstrous paperwork, pesky delays, missed deadlines, aggravating reversals. I'm discouraged and ambivalent. I want to stay here in this house with the room called mine and the neighbor who calls me by name. No, I want to move back to the country, where space vibrates with memories of children and the busy comfort of their constant care. I crave sure terrain, where my fingers track light switches in the dark and my ears understand every sigh and creak the house utters.

Ned appears undaunted by these shadows dropping across our days. He sifts patiently through nitpicking forms, financial questions, endless details. This is work he knows. "We'd be sorry in a year if we gave up now," he says simply.

Perhaps my edgy attitude is generating a self-fulfilling prophecy. I assess our predicament from the vantage point of a year and glimpse a truth: no matter how deep I plant my roots in a place, I must move through time.

We keep on. Rearranging furniture and habits. Finally, the boxes are closed, the van loaded, the hill climbed, the ruts navigated, the van unloaded. Two sweaty nineteen-year-olds hang around just long enough to collect their due.

Alone now, Ned and I stand on the problematical teal carpet. From the window of this new place set high above the city, we can look across Yellowstone Valley to the Beartooth Mountains beyond. An eagle soars nearby, its shadow swift against the amber sandstone cliff. I watch my husband watching it. He touches my arm. "In my next life," he begins, and I ready myself for the bull bison wish. Instead, he points toward the sky. "In my next life, I think I'll come back as an eagle."

I follow the move of wings through space, the rush and gliding. My heart stirs with envy at his bird. I want to soar, not sort. My husband is focused on the future and the light ahead. I hover over the past, raking through it for connections between place and time.

"An eagle?" I taunt, easily imagining this spouse of mine landing contentedly in one of those enormous messy nests. "So you really would like to live in a nest of accumulated debris?"

"No, not debris!" comes his shocked response. "Eagles gather that stuff carefully. Branches, twigs, bark. One piece at a time. They mate for life. And build their nests to last."

I wait in smug silence for the analogy to hit. But he is busy pondering the bird's flight through light, its high circling toward that piecemeal throne. I slant my gaze toward the ground and follow the shadowed dance of wings on rock. They vanish with a sudden cloud that slides across the sun. But in a moment, a shaft of impatient light breaks loose.

I sense something. Sorting is a cover-up. The real shift happens inside. Paring down demands honesty. Do I have the courage to cast off what is no longer useful? Is function the sole gauge of an object's worth? Does sentiment justify hauling along ragged bedtime animals, first grade report cards, high school letter jackets? How do we decide what history to take and what to leave behind?

Moving is a critical juncture, a merging of past and future. Coming here to this house with a view has shown me something. The things I treasure, wish to take along, are made of transient moments when sunshine and shadow merge. Perhaps our differences, after all, are what give us heart to move on.

The Womenfolk

by Julie Welle Verzuh

Born in Minnesota to a large German-American family, **Julie Welle Verzuh** has lived in Billings since 1969. She teaches German at both public and private elementary schools. While establishing an art career by exhibiting and selling her paintings, she has simultaneously pursued creative writing. In 1983 she published her first work of fiction, a collection of short stories titled *From the Heart of Lizzie.*

When Caroline was almost sixteen and of marriageable age, Niki spoke to her father about courting her. Until then he had to be content to dance with her at socials, or bid for her box lunch, or carry on a conversation here and there, which delighted him the most, as she was always full of stories, exaggerating everything she knew or heard. At first her father was reluctant to allow the courtship, as Niki was a common laborer. "A man should own some land, as land is a promise of wealth," he stated solemnly, like a preacher. "My sons and I value a good trade and a good day's work, but my only daughter should have a husband who can profit from the working of the land." Since he would have Caroline at all costs, Niki promised to rent a farm, which he would try to buy as soon as possible, and Papa Fromm saw the young man was in earnest and gave his blessing.

At first, since the farmhouse was dilapidated and uninhabitable, Niki and Caroline began their married life with the Fromm family, but after two months passed, Niki startled his wife by announcing in their closed bedroom upstairs, "I have fixed the leaks in the roof and have bought a cook stove that can be used as well for heat. Oh, the bedroom will be cold, but we will have each other," he teased, a little less seriously. "Tomorrow we move to our own place."

"But who will cook for Papa and the boys? Or sweep their house? Or scrub their shirts?" she asked innocently.

Niki had to bite his teeth hard to control his anger. "Jake and Frank are fixing to get married soon anyway, and the rest will just have to cook their own beans...or get a housekeeper who can," he said emphatically.

"Whatever you say, *Liebling*." She nodded and gave him her disarming smile. She prayed every day that she would be a good and obedient wife as the nuns had taught her, even though she was sometimes very tired from all the lovemaking he required. But now she would not have to work so hard, and she was grateful to God for her husband standing up like a man.

In no time, Niki had her working with him side by side—milking the cows, planting the garden, riding the horse in front of the plow, and on days when she brought him an afternoon lunch in the fields, she came with a blanket so they could make love outdoors on their own land.

poetry by Tom Whittle

Montana native **Tom Whittle** lives with his family near Shepherd, where they raise their own beef, keep a horse or two, and share their place with chickens, rabbits, and a cowdog named Bocephus. He received his degree from MSU-Bozeman and retired from the Army Reserve with the rank of captain. The following poem is based on an actual experience at Billings Rendering.

Fast Times at Billings Rendering

As a new guy at Billings Rendering, my job was to pick up the dead.
The note said, "Stop at the Custer Bar. They'll tell you where to head."
What type of critter didn't matter, be it horse, sheep, goat or steer.
Soon it'd be in the back of my truck—on that it was perfectly clear!
The barmaid had smelled me coming, handing me directions out the side door.
She jerked her thumb toward the two-lane and said, "It's an old bull, no good anymore."
Ten miles straight to a pen on the left: a white muley goat and a bull.
The beast'd been shot that morning, a bad eye having made him a cull.
Well, the goat, his buddy, was standing guard over the bovine form,
As I backed into position to throw a chain around his mossy old horn.
While I hooked up the chain, I thought to myself, "The boss'll surely be pleased,
For this critter was a 'skinnable.'" He smelled fresh on that afternoon breeze!
I was taking slack out of the cable to pull him on up to the gate,
When he come back alive with a beller—in his good eye, a look of pure hate!
He loaded his-self and quickly, the truck finally stopping his run.
So I lifted and chained the tailgate, and wished I'd a' carried a gun!
My next stop—Doc Michaels in Worden—would surely lend me his piece,
I mused as the bull in the back started hooking dead sheep, making fleece!
But Doc Michaels was plumb out of ammo, his arm in a cow, wouldn't you know.
So I jumped in my bellerin' truck once again: There was only one place to go!

To the skinner's dock at the Rendering Plant I did go with considerable haste.
I dropped the tailgate and got out of the way—time I did not waste!
Now Clark, the skinner, was good at his trade. There's nothing he couldn't
    skin.
But he usually preferred them lying down before he'd stick his knife in!
So when that bull hit the end of the chain, swapped ends and broke his neck,
Clark calmly stropped his blade once or twice, started skinning, said, "What
    the heck.
This is the freshest thing that I've ever had the opportunity to get near.
So after work tonight, I'm going to buy you a beer!"

poetry by Wilbur Wood

Poet and journalist **Wilbur Wood** is a third-generation Montana writer
based in Roundup. He has taught creative writing extensively in Billings and
surrounding communities. He writes articles, stories, and poems about his
Montana heritage, his neighbors and his ancestors. Wood is also well-known
as an essayist on NPR's *High Plains News Service*.

WHITE MAN

we come from cold country stock. had to
kill animals for meat, keep warm in winter.

in houses
all that time on our hands
no wonder we invent books and movies
    the rational mind

but the wolves howling outside.
the coyote crossing the road in our headlights,
the wind
    blowing snow through the barnyard

fire in the house
    whiskey-fire in the belly
we don't easily pass the pipe among friends
    in the flickering light
each of us has his own pipe
    his own glass. we tell stories
of the deer

LAST LIGHT

Night
does not drop
from the sky but rises

out of the Earth
where I stand grazing
the last light,

watching the powerlines
melt into forest,

feeling my eyes
seep into the view.

Downriver: A Yellowstone Journey

by Dean Krakel II

Born in Wyoming in 1952, **Dean Krakel II** is an award-winning photographer and writer. His article "The Untamed Yellowstone" appeared in *National Geographic Magazine* in August, 1981. He is currently assistant director of photography at *The Rocky Mountain News* in Denver. In addition to *Downriver,* he has published *Season of the Elk* and *Krakel's West.*

Pulling past the Columbus Bridge I nod to a pair of fishermen baiting their hooks. With a sweet sense of relief I row on. The river's picking up speed, gathering itself tighter. Waves, where there are waves, have a sense of power about them, rolling beneath the boat like muscles.

When most of the river veers toward open country, I take a sliver going south, a stream barely wide enough for the raft. To squeeze beneath an undercut rock, I swing the oars in, resting the blades on the bow. Beyond the rock we twist down a roaring chute, skid through shallows, oar blades scraping gravel on either side. Twice I have to get out and walk, sloshing along in my hip boots, leading the raft by the bowline until the channel's deep enough for it to float.

Brown sandstone walls several hundred feet high on the right bank, pocked with thousands of holes utilized by nesting swallows. Geese flush ahead of the boat and wheel against the cliffs, beating themselves into long floating lines. Deer tracks in the sand. Cottonwood boughs stretch over the channel, the outermost leaves almost touching the cliffs, forming a golden canopy. Shafts of sunlight fall onto the water. The river steams where it's touched by sun. Steam and shadow, shadow and steam. Droplets from my oar blades ripple still pools in arcs as I row. An eagle sitting on a tree limb ruffles himself in the sunlight, shuffles his yellow feet, cocks his head, excretes a white stream halfway across the river, gives me the eye.

In a pool I cast for trout with a spinner, letting it slap against rocks and topple down, water clear enough that I can follow it, sinking, for several feet. A few minutes later I've two medium-sized rainbow trout—frying pan size.

Resisting the temptation to nap, I opt for a swim, one dive that brings me quickly to surface and back ashore to stand in the sun and dry in the wind while two redtail hawks circle overhead.

Past Keyser Creek, Brown, Hensley, Tutt, Tucker, Allen, Cow, Tilden, Cole, Valley and Bellion.

...Civilization greets us with sirens, helicopters, car horns, beacons, towers, and dark dirty water. It's Billings, Montana, population 57,000, largest city in the basin. Down past the KOA campground (the nation's first) and the power plant (Reddy Kil-o-Watt blinking a neon hello), I drop the oars and drift beneath Sacrifice Cliff.

The Crow called this the Place of Skulls. You hear a number of stories, and varying reasons, but here some Crow warriors blindfolded their horses and rode off the cliff singing their death songs. Some say it was a grieving war party that returned from a raid to find their village decimated by smallpox. Others say it was done to drive the disease away.

In June of 1875 the steamer *Josephine* docked here, at the highest point anyone had brought, or would ever bring, a steamer up the Yellowstone. Her captain, Grant Marsh, carved her name and the date in a cottonwood trunk.

Grant Marsh had run away from Pittsburgh in 1845 to work as a cabin boy on the Allegheny. He was a roustabout on the Ohio, the Mississippi, and the lower Missouri; then a mate carrying the wounded from Shiloh Church to St. Louis in 1862 on the *John J. Roe,* "a boat so slow," Mark Twain wrote, "that when she sank it took the owners five years to discover it."

Marsh took his first steamer up the Missouri to Fort Benton in 1867, carrying miners to the Montana goldfields. Such was the flurry of activity—all those Civil War veterans trying to make a new start—that steamers were docked for a half mile above and below the landing. Other pilots discharged their cargo and went south; Marsh kept his boat at Fort Benton until autumn and took the miners back to St. Louis to spend their earnings. In doing so he risked getting iced in or stranded by low water, but as luck would have it, he succeeded, gaining a fortune....

Dark forces me to a beach next to the railroad tracks a few miles from town, exhausted, depressed, the stench of city in my lungs and clothes. Seven white-tailed deer flush out of my campsite, a sandy wash among three trees. I gather firewood from the largest log jam yet. Soon after supper, rain drives me into the tent.

I make a mistake this morning in lingering over pancakes and have to pack the boat in a storm. As soon as we're on the water, the wind begins, strong and cold, forcing me into a poncho. To move at all I must row with my back downstream, looking over my shoulder to see where we're going. Rain pelts the water like buckshot. The wind creates waves a foot high. Stryder curls up on the floor. Ahhhh for the life of a dog—just let ol' massa take care of things.

Over the sound of the wind and water and flapping poncho I listen for the telltale roar of Huntley Dam, the second largest diversion on the Yellowstone. The dam waters an irrigation project, in season allowing pumps to suck up 4500 gallons of water a second. The dam is poorly marked and has killed ten people—high school kids and fishermen who get drunk or daring and think it can be run.

There's a channel going around the dam on the left that appears to go all the way through, but I get out, tie the boat, and go for a look anyway. The dam extends across the river's main channel, dropping water over an eight-foot-high ledge, transforming it into foam; a tree caught out in the middle rolls over and over in the current.

The channel around the dam is passable and sheltered, but when I leave it the wind shoves me across the river and pins me against shore. I must wade, pulling the boat by the bowline, until I've got water deep enough to get purchase with the oars. Then I heave back out into the current.

Another mile and I stop at the town of Huntley, born of the irrigation dreams behind the dam, snug the boat to a piece of concrete riprap, and walk in on main street. At the general store I buy a sweet roll and hang out by the wood stove, my trench coat dripping onto the wooden floor.

"Lord," says the counter matron, "what would a body be doin' out on that river today?" I have no answer.

At the filling station I ask an eighty-year-old jack of all mechanics if he's any kerosene for my lantern. He shakes his head no.

"Number-one heatin' oil'll do the same," he says and takes me around back to a 1936 tank truck from which he pumps a quart jar of the same. When I ask what I owe, he says, "No charge to a fool."

In the Red Dog saloon I have a shot of whiskey to warm up with and another for luck. Cheers to a fat, red-cheeked beet farmer and the barmaid, both watching TV. The newscaster's talking about drought. Barges are already unable to navigate the Mississippi sandbars. Each day a million gallons of water seep out of the New York City sewers. Some restaurants are using disposable plates so they won't have to wash and serving water only if it's requested. "In fifty years," says the newsman, "the Great Plains will be a dustbowl." He's conserving by taking only two showers a day.

"Anyone heard the weather?" I ask.

"You're going to get stormed on," says the barmaid and the farmer's hard "Hoo hoo hraw" laughter chases me out the door into the rain.

Past the Huntley Bridge I hug the dirt bluffs on the left, but am forced, in seeking deep enough water, to get back out into the main. By midafternoon the rain has become snow, blowing so hard that the river's a blur. My arms hurt from rowing, each pull sending pain through my shoulders, hands growing numb from holding on to the oar handles so tightly. The moment I let up we're blown toward shore or blown back upriver. Every hour I stop and walk to warm my feet. Hundreds of ducks in the air, passing me like bullets. More ducks flush from each point, twisting and circling overhead, landing again after I've passed. The temptation to shoot costs me eight shells.

I find a camping place in a secluded wooded spot on the left bank. Only eight miles since dawn. Willows and young cottonwoods are as thick as porcupine quills; dense stands of cane and yellow marsh grass, and green reeds higher than my head. To find a decent place to sleep that's not marsh or thorn thicket or stone, I must walk several hundred yards inland. Since I expect to be here several nights, I carry most of the gear up from the raft: the kitchen box, camera gear, clothing bag, shotgun, books, dog food, tent, sleeping bag, and water jugs. While carrying the cooler across a slough, I'm startled by a pheasant flying up under my feet, trip over a beaver-chewed log, ages old, and fall into a muddy hole—spilling the cooler and all its contents into the water. Lying there, feeling the wind and snow pounding my back, I want to give up and fade away, to dissolve and awaken in some other place. But I pick myself up, take off my gloves and overcoat, and begin groping around in the water until my hands are too cold to feel anything.

The tent is wet before I get it pitched, and the rain fly is torn out of my hands twice by the wind. I've misplaced the tent stakes and must use sticks to anchor the corners. Somehow even the sleeping bag's soaked. While I boil oatmeal, droplets of water sizzle on the fire ring.

Taking a walk, trying to settle down and think, I find that this isn't the mainland, but an island. Its interior, beneath the cottonwoods, is a jungle of rosebushes; its edges are all willow. I wander up one sandy wash after another until it's dark and I'm lost. Stryder takes off after something and doesn't return when I call. The deer trails are too dim to follow and everything looks the same. Stumbling and cursing through the willows and rosebushes, I walk crosscountry until I hit a beach, follow it, knowing eventually I'll find the boat, nearly falling over it when I do.

Across the river are the lights of Huntley, and not far away the glow of Billings. It must be all of six, I think. People over there are in snug houses, watching the news, sitting down to supper. I could row across the river, cache the equipment, and hike to town. Go home. That's exactly what I'll do tomorrow, I promise myself. Enough of this.

Back at camp the fire's dead. A wind torn bough has crushed the tent. The sleeping bag, though wet, is passably comfortable, and I draw up beneath a willow, drape ponchos all around and sit zipped up with my back against the tree.

"Happy birthday," I say aloud. "Happy birthday."

A Month of Sundays—The Best of Rick O'Shay and Hipshot

by Stan Lynde

See page 191 for biographical information.

Reprint Information: Written permissions on file.

Aadland, Dan. "White Shorts and Tennis Shoes" in Sketches from the Ranch: A Montana Memoir. New York: Howell Book House, 1998: 120-124.

Abbott, E.C. ("Teddy Blue") and Helena Huntington Smith. We Pointed Them North: Recollections of a Cowpuncher. New York: Farrar & Rinehart, Inc., 1939: 91-94.

Abbott, Newton Carl. "Billings" from Montana in the Making. Billings MT: The Gazette Printing Company, 12th edition, 1959: 435-437.

Allard, Louis, M.D. "Laurel" and "Coulson" from Laurel's Story: A Montana Heritage. Laurel, MT: Elsie P. Johnston, 1979: 11-12.

Baker, Don. "Railroads: The Northern Pacific" and "Junction (and the Musselshell Trail)" from Ghost Towns of the Montana Prairie. Boulder, CO: Fred Pruett Books, 1997: 3-4, 43.

Banfill, W. H. "Junction City, Haven of Bullwhackers, Trappers and Soldiers, Witnessed Many Dramatic Episodes" from The Billings Gazette, February 1, 1931: Page 1 Second Section.

Billings, Frederick. The Speeches: Verbatim Report of What Was Said by Billings, Evarts, Grant and Villard at Billings from the Billings Herald, September 15, 1883: Page 1.

Billings, Parmly. Transcript of Dec. 4, 1886 letter to his father, Frederick Billings. Billings Family, 1884 photo. Courtesy of the Woodstock Foundation, P.O. Box 489 Woodstock, VT 05091.

Boden, Anneke-Jan. Billings: The First 100 Years, A Pictorial History. Norfolk/Virginia Beach: Donning Company/Publishers, 1981: 95. Text ©1981: Anneke-Jan Boden; drawing by Ben Steele.

Bragg, Addison. "Becoming History: Of Della Mae, nothing but good..." Commentary by Addison Bragg from The Billings Gazette, April 26, 2000: Page 1D.

Cade, Leland. Well, I Guess I Was Just Lucky!! Billings, MT: Leland P. Cade, 1992: 107-108.

Chapple, Steve. "Home" from Kayaking the Full Moon: A Journey Down the Yellowstone River to the Soul of Montana. New York: HarperCollins, 1993: 156-157, 159-163.

Charter, Anne G. Cowboys Don't Walk: A Tale of Two. Billings, MT: Western Organization of Resource Councils, 1999: 137, 141-143, 145-146.

Clark, William. "Clark's Exploration of the Yellowstone" excerpts reprinted from the Journals of the Lewis and Clark Expedition, Volume 8, edited by Gary E. Moulton by permission of the University of Nebraska Press. Copyright © 1993 by the University of Nebraska Press. 212, 217-219, 225-226, 283-285.

Clawson, Roger. "Chicken Guts and a Royal Coachman" from Yellowstone Reflections. Billings, MT: The Prose Works, 1991: 80-83.

Clawson, Roger and Katherine A. Shandera. "Calamity Jane" from Billings: The City and the People. 102-103. This text by Shandera © 1993. The Billings Gazette and ©1993: American & World Geographic Publishing.

Coleman, Julie. Golden Opportunities: A Biographical History of Montana's Jewish Communities. Billings, MT: Julie L. Coleman, 1994: 77-80.

Collins, Mabel. "Parmly Billings Memorial Library" from Billings, Montana: Metropolis of the Great Yellowstone Valley. Published under the Auspices of the Chamber of Commerce, January First, Nineteen Hundred and Nine.

Conner, Stuart. Ethnographic material excerpted from "Archaeology of the Crow Indian Vision Quest" published in Archaeology in Montana Vol. 23, No. 3, 1982: 85-86.

Cooper, Myrtle. "1901" from Tent Town to City: A Chronological History of Billings, Montana 1882-1935. Billings, MT: Myrtle E .Cooper, 1981: 36-37.

Crummett, Michael. Sun Dance: The 50th Anniversary Crow Indian Sun Dance. Helena & Billings, MT: Falcon Press, 1993: 1-5.

Davis, Donna. "March" appeared in Surviving the Western State of Mind, a companion to the Montana Writers' Daybook. Up the Creek Publishing 1997; "In the Days of Rock 'n' Roll," appeared in InterMountain Woman, July, 1998, first place winner for poetry in The Woman's Voice Awards contest; "Resolutions for the Coming Millennium" appeared under the title "Resolutions for the Millennium" in Inspiring Times January 2000.

Davis, Jean: "Coulson" from Shallow Diggin's: Tales from Montana's Ghost Towns. Caldwell, ID: Caxton Printers, 1963: 359-364.

DeCosse, Mildred Dover. The Man of Dover's Island. New York: Carlton Press, 1973: 7-8.

DeRosier, Arthur Jr. "Foreword" to Pioneer Trails West Don Worcester, editor. Caldwell, ID: Caxton Printers, 1985.

DeRosier, Linda. "Nature's Graces to Gathering Places" in Creeker: a Woman's Journey. Lexington, KY: University Press of Kentucky, 1999: 93-94, 99-100, 223-224.

Doig, Ivan. Reprinted with the permission of Scribner, a Division of Simon & Schuster from Ride with Me, Mariah Montana by Ivan Doig. Copyright 1990 by Doig: 265, 268-269, 275-279.

Doyle, Susan Badger, editor. From "Ellen Gordon Fletcher, Diary and Letters, 1866" in Journeys to the Land of Gold: Emigrant Diaries from the Bozeman Trail, 1863-1866 Volume Two. Helena, MT: Montana Historical Society Press, 2000: 487-488, 515-517.

Egan, Ken, Jr. "Montana Apocalypse: Extremism and Hope in the American West" from Western Futures: Perspectives on the Humanities at the Millennium Stephen Tchudi, ed. Reno: Nevada Humanities Committee/University of Nevada Press, 2000: 25-29.

Eunson, Dale. Up on the Rim. New York: Farrar, Straus And Giroux, 1970: 162-167.

Fedullo, Mick. Light of the Feather: Pathways through Contemporary Indian America. New York: William Morrow and Company, Inc., 1992: 96, 195.

Feldman, Catherine. Mathilda. ©1995 by Catherine M. Feldman. Pages 62-63.

Feyhl, Kenneth J. "Chief Joseph Inscription" published in Archaeology in Montana Vol. 28, No. 2, 1987: 61-63.

Forbes, Donna. "Isabelle Johnson" from the exhibition catalog: Isabelle Johnson: A Life's Work. Billings, MT: Yellowstone Art Center, 1992.

Gilliland, Hap with William Walters. "The Muggers" from Flint's Rock. Boulder, CO: Roberts Rinehart, 1996: 44-49.

Greene, Jerome A. "Canyon Creek" from Nez Perce Summer 1877: The U.S. Army and the Nee-Me-Poo Crisis. Helena, MT: Montana Historical Society Press, 2000: 226-227.

Grosskopf, Linda with Rick Newby. On Flatwillow Creek: The Story of Montana's N Bar Ranch. Los Alamos, NM: Exceptional Books, Ltd., 1991: 1-3.

Gulick, Walter B. "Placed and Dis-Placed in Montana: Finding Home in Memory and Locale." Early 1990s. No page numbers. Poetry: see Gwendolen Haste.

Haaland, Tami. "11:05" from 5AM, Number 12 (March 2000); "August" in Cowboy Poetry Matters: From Abilene to Mainstream, Robert McDowell, ed. Ashland, OR: Story Line Press, 2000.

Hamilton, Alice O. "Why a Book on High Plains" from Gardening in the Northern High Plains. Billings, MT: Alice O. Hamilton, 1986: 2-3, 5.

Harris, Ed. Billings: My City, My Home. © 1977 First Northwestern National Bank of Billings Montana. Reprint permission granted by Wells Fargo Bank Montana.

Hart, Sue. "Hemingway Treated at Saint Vincent Hospital" from The Call to Care 1898-1998, Saint Vincent Hospital and Health Center, the First 100 Years of Service. Billings, MT: Sue Hart SCLA, 1998: 51-52. Hemingway photo from the Allard Collection, courtesy Western Heritage Center of Billings, MT.

Haste, Gwendolen. "The Stoic" from Young Land. New York: Coward McCann, 1930. Used in the Gulick piece: "The Ranch in the Coulee" and "Horizons."

Hatheway, Flora. "Chief Plenty Coups" from Plenty Coups: Great Chief of the Crow Indian People. ©1971: Flora Hatheway. Revised edition, 1995: 5-13.

Heidenreich, C. Adrian. "The Crow Indian Delegation to Washington, D.C., in 1880" published in Montana The Magazine of Western History Spring 1981: 59-61.

Henckel, Mark. "'My Fish!' In this kids' game, an adult never catches anything." Published in The Billings Gazette April 12, 1990: Page 1D.

Huntington, William "Bill." "Harvesting Ice on the Yellowstone" from Both Feet in the Stirrups. Billings, MT: Western Livestock Reporter, 1959: 170-172.

Huntley Project History Committee. "Foreword" to Sod 'n Seed 'n Tumbleweed: A History of the Huntley Project. Ballantine, MT: The Huntley Project History Committee, 1977: 3.

Irving, Washington. The Adventures of Captain Bonneville U.S.A. in the Rocky Mountains and the Far West: digested from his journal. Norman, OK: University of Oklahoma Press, 1961; originally published in 1837. 164-165.

James, Will. Excerpt from "Bad Lands and Lions" in The Dark Horse. Original © 1939 Will James. 100-108. Handwritten dedication in the Parmly Billings Library's copy of The Dark Horse. Will James drawings, untitled (cowboy creeping up on a horse) n.d. carbon pencil on paper; The Return of the Prodigal 1921 pen and ink. Yellowstone Art Museum Permanent Collection, Gift of Virginia Snook. Reprint permissions granted by Will James Art Company, Yellowstone Art Museum, Parmly Billings Library.

Jensen, Joyce. "James Webb Memorial Drinking Fountain" from Pieces & Places of Billings History: Local Markers and Sites. Billings, MT: Western Heritage Press, Western Heritage Center; 1994: 78-79.

Jensen, Margaret. "Float the Yellowstone" published in Outdoors, the Magazine of Outdoor Recreation May 1968: 7-10.

Johnson, Isabelle. Old Willows, Winter, 1948, oil on linen. Billings, MT: Yellowstone Art Museum Permanent Collection, Gift of the Estate of Isabelle Johnson.

Johnston, Terry C. Wind Walker. New York: Bantam Books, 2001: 395-398.

Jones, Danell. "One Forward, Two Back" published in Beyond Bread, Summer 1998.

Jones, Keith. "No Queen Mary" from Reaching Port. New York: St. Martin's Press, 1983: 3-5.

Karnos, David. "At the End of the Rainbow's Run Lies a Memory of Gold." Published in Alkali Flats No. 1 (Billings, 1982): 14-18.

Keenan, Jerry. "The Old Scout Returns: The Interment of Yellowstone Kelly on the Rimrocks." From a forthcoming biography.

Kelly, Luther S. "Yellowstone Kelly": The Memoirs of Luther S. Kelly edited by M. M. Quaife. New Haven: Yale University Press, 1926: selections from 121-122, 146-147, 176-177.

Kirkpatrick, Jay F. Into the Wind: Wild Horses of North America. Minocqua, WI: NorthWord Press, 1994: 77-79, 108-113, 119.

Krakel, Dean II. Downriver: A Yellowstone Journey. San Francisco: Sierra Club Books, 1987: 116-117, 120-121, 124-129.

Landmarks. "Yellowstone County" from Landmarks Vol III reprint of 1883 City Directory; Billings, Montana Territory. Page 10.

Larson, Dorothy Weston. "Foreword" to As Shadows on the Hills. Billings, MT: Sandstone Publishing, 1978.

Lauson, Spencer Norman with Dolores W. Boyles. "Adventure: The Beginning" from Montana Bill. Billings, MT: Spencer Norman Lauson, 1983: 11-14.

Lee, J. Brock. "Newman School" from Cornerstones of Knowledge. Billings, MT: J. Brock Lee, 1982: 8.

Lehman, Tim. "Prairie Pastoralism and Predators: 'Keeping the Wolf from the Door'" presented to the American Society for Environmental History 1997 Biennial Meeting.

Leppart, Gary. "Pompeys Pillar: Signature Rock on the Yellowstone" published in Montana Magazine July/Aug 1995: 32-34. Western Meadowlark photo.

Linderman, Frank B. Pretty-Shield: Medicine Woman of the Crows. (Originally Red Mother. New York: The John Day Co., 1932) Lincoln: University of Nebraska Press, 1974: 9-11, 21-26.

Loendorf, Lawrence L. "Rock Painting of Shield Warriors at Pictograph Cave, Montana." New Mexico State University; published in La Pintura 2000-2001: 4-7.

Lundborg, Louis B. "A One-Class Society" from Up To Now. New York: W. W. Norton & Co, Inc., 1978: 77-80.

Lynde, Eleanor. "A Trip after Cough Medicine" from Daylight in the Canyon: The Memoirs of Eleanor Lynde. Spokane, WA: TypeCraft, 1993: 120-121.

Lynde, Stan. Two panels from A Month of Sundays—The Best of Rick O'Shay and Hipshot. Kalispell, MT: Cottonwood Graphics, Inc., 1993: no page numbers. Reprinted by permission of Tribune Media Services and Stan Lynde.

Mayer, Larry. "The Comet Hale-Bopp Photographed over the Billings Rimrocks on March 25, 1997." Published in The Billings Gazette, Mar. 26, 1997. Cover Photograph.

McClendon, Lise. "Prologue" to The Bluejay Shaman. New York: Walker and Company, 1994.

McLane, Wallace C. "Bobby Brooks Kramer: One of a Rare Breed" published in Ketchpen Spring, 2001: 16-18.

Mercier, Laurie. "Creating a New Community in the North: Mexican Americans of the Yellowstone Valley" in Stories from an Open Country: Essays on the Yellowstone River Valley edited by William Lang. Billings, MT: Western Heritage Press, Western Heritage Center, 1995: 127-131.

Medicine Crow. Illustrations (ledger art) drawn from memory of trip to Washington D.C, 1880. 1930.20— drawings of three trains by Medicine Crow. Crow. ca. 1880 Barstow Collection, Special Collections, Library, Montana State University-Billings.

Meyers, Bruce K. "A Poem," "Newton's Toes," and "The Naz as Green Grocer" from Ventriloquist in the Rain. Cody, WY: ConAmore Publishing, 1992: xii, 4, 50.

Meyers, Christene Cosgriffe. "Seasonal Change" from Cats as Gravity. Number 3 in the Oxalis Poetry Chapbook Series. Billings, MT: Shaun Higgins, Publisher, 1977: 18.

Morrison, Robert C. "The Frontier Myth" from Rocky Mountain Review, Vol. IV no. 2, 1967. Billings, MT: Rocky Mountain College Press: 4-6.

Murray, Earl. "Visions of Reno Crossing" from Ghosts of the Old West. New York: A Tor Book, Tom Doherty Associates, Inc., 1988, 1994: 19-24.

Nabokov, Peter. Two Leggings: The Making of a Crow Warrior based on a field manuscript prepared by William Wildschut for the Museum of the American Indian, Heye Foundation. New York: HarperCollins, copyright 1967 by Peter Nabokov; Lincoln: University of Nebraska Press, Bison Book 1982: 116-118. Reprinted by permission of HarperCollins.

O'Brien, Kathy Mosdal. "Hard Red Winter," published in Surviving the Western State of Mind, Gennie Nord, ed., 1996; "Helen," published in Owen Wister Review, fall 1988, University of Wyoming.

O'Donnell, I. D. "Parmly Billings 1884" by I. D. O'Donnell and "How Liver Eating Got His Name" by Judge J. R. Goss from Montana Monographs compiled by I. D. O'Donnell. No ©, no page numbers.

Old Coyote, Sally. ":SUMMER IN MY CHILDHOOD" published in Hip Huggin' Levis and Bib Overalls. ©1995 Charles William Brandal & Elnora A. Old Coyote.

Oravsky, Ken & Rich Pittsley. "A Park for All People: Chief Plenty Coups State Park" published in Montana Outdoors May/June 1994: 22-27.

Ping, Margaret. Looking Back—Moving Forward: The History of the Billings YWCA 1907-1988. Billings, MT: Margaret Ping, 1991: 2-5.

Polk, Loujincy. "The Devil on Barnett Creek" published in Bits of Sage 1957: 36-37.

Popovich, John. "Incident along the Yellowstone: The Story of the Immell-Jones Massacre" published in Hoofprints from the Yellowstone Corral of the Westerners Vol. 12, No. 1, Spring/Summer 1982: 9-12, 26-27.

Popovich, John. The Voice of the Curlew: J. K. Ralston's Story of His Life. Billings, MT: The J. K. Ralston Studio Inc., 1986: 112-114.

Potter, John. "Bough Down to Spirit of Christmas." Published in The Billings Gazette December 2, 2000: Page 4A.

Powers, Don. Model of the Josephine donated to the Montana Room of the Parmly Billings Library in the 1980s. Photo courtesy of Don Miller.

The Progressive Cookbook for the First M. E. Church, of Billings, Montana, 1893, edited by Alice Lloyd Free. Billings, MT: First United Methodist Church, 2000: 15, 88.

Prowell, Sandra West. When Wallflowers Die: A Phoebe Siegel Mystery. New York: Walker and Company, 1996: 1-7.

Ralston, J. K. "Horses Round the Bend," The Hawkins Collection.

Rostad, Lee. Fourteen Cents & Seven Green Apples: The Life and Times of Charles Bair. Great Falls, MT: C. M. Russell Museum, 1992: 91-92.

Ruble, Sheila. "Weaning" published in InterMountain Woman July, 1997.

Ryniker, Alice Durland. Eagle Feather for a Crow. Oklahoma City: National Cowboy Hall of Fame and Western Heritage Center, 1980: preface, 61-63.

Sample, Michael. "Tracks, Yellowstone River at Billings," cover photograph.

Scherer, Bonnie. Benjy's New Home. Billings, MT: text by Bonnie Scherer, art by Bill McCracken, 1989.

Schwidde, Jess. "Arcadian Idyll" published in Montana Sketchbook, Montana Institute of the Arts, 1989.

Seddon, Andrew M. Excerpt from the forthcoming book Alien Seas.

Shepherd Historical Book Committee. "Prologue" and "Billings & Central Montana Railroad" from "Lest We Forget..." Shepherd, MT: Luella DeVries, Sharon Wolske, Nell Kinghorn, & Marguerite Gerringa, 1976: 7-8, 43-44.

Shuart, Benjamin. Transcript of "Reminiscences of a Home Missionary 1882-1883," compiled in the 1930s. Billings, MT: First Congregational United Church of Christ: Our First Hundred Years 1882-1982, 1982: 27-30.

Small, Aaron P. The Remora. Pittsburgh: Dorrance Publishing Co., Inc., 1999: 52-54.

Small, Lawrence F. "Between the Wars" from A Century of Politics on the Yellowstone. Billings, MT: Rocky Mountain College, 1983: 61-65.

Spang, Bently. "A Northern Cheyenne Morning" from the exhibition catalog: Material Culture: Innovation in Native Art. Great Falls, MT: Paris Gibson Square Museum of Art, 2000: 8-30.

Spencer, Mrs. William. Excerpts from "Diary of a Homesteader's Wife, 1913-1916" in North of the Yellowstone, South of the Bulls, compiled by Marjorie (Jim) Barnard, John & Willora Brown, Rosella Johanson, Ida Sherrodd; ©1978 Northside Historical Committee: 266-294.

Steele, Ben. "Line Camp" a drawing first in Horizons O'er the Musselshell..., 1974; and "The Drive" a drawing from the Ben Steele Christmas Card Collection, the Ben Steele Gallery, Billings Deaconess Clinic.

Steele, Shirley. "Monuments" published in Pierian Spring Brandon, Manitoba, Canada: Brandon University: 1980 and "My Father Danced" published in Yokoi 1991 and in Alkali Flats III 1992.

Stevens, Karen D. & Dee Ann Redman. "Tunnels" from Billings A to Z. Billings, MT: The Friends of the Library, Parmly Billings Library, 2000: 106-107.

Strong, David. Crazy Mountains: Learning from Wilderness to Weigh Technology. Albany: State University of New York Press, 1995: 3, 8-9, 111-118.

Svee, Gary D. "All or Nothing" from Tales of the American West, Richard S. Wheeler, ed. New American Library [NAL], 2000: 185-189.

Throssel, Richard. Photo accompanying Zimmerman article courtesy of the Western Heritage Center, Billings, MT.

Tranel, Virginia. "Shadows Moving Light" by permission of author.

Van Sky, Thelma. "Antelope Stage Station" from Broadview in Review: 80 Years along the Buffalo Trail, second printing, 1992: 1, epigraph.

Verzuh, Julie Welle. The Womenfolk. ©1997 Julie Welle Verzuh; 154-155.

Vontver, May. "The Kiskis." First published in Frontier March, 1929.

Wagner, Glendolin Damon. Old Neutriment. First published Boston, 1934: 98-100.

Wagner, Glendolin Damon and Dr. William A. Allen. "Pretty Eagle's Story" from Blankets and Moccasins: Plenty Coups and His People, the Crows. Caldwell, ID: Caxton Printers Ltd. 1933: 21, 31-32, 40, 45-47.

Weldon, Monica. "River Crossings: South Bridges" from Trails & Tales South of the Yellowstone. Billings, MT: Trails and Tales Historical Committee, 1983: 696-697.

West, Carroll Van. Capitalism on the Frontier: Billings and the Yellowstone Valley in the Nineteenth Century. Lincoln: University of Nebraska Press, 1993: 156. Images of Billings: A Photographic History. Billings, MT: Western Heritage Press, Western Heritage Center; 1990: 26.

Whittle, Tom. "Fast Times at Billings Rendering" published in Rural Montana Sept. 1998.

Wildschut, W. [Willem]. Excerpt from "My First Journey to Washington," in Exploits of Plenty-Coups Chief of the Crows reprinted by permission of the National Museum of the American Indian Archives OC 265, folder 9, W. Wildschut [William was used for the publications in 1959 and 1960], pages 146-151 only.

Willard, John. "The Josephine—War Horse and River Queen: Freight Hauler and Servant to the Military" published in Hoofprints from the Yellowstone Corral of the Westerners Vol. 23 No. 1, Spring-Summer 1993: 3-4.

Wood, Wilbur. "White Man" published in Montana Gothic No. 5 (Blackstone Press; Missoula, MT) Winter 1977; "Last Light" published in Alkali Flats No. 2 (Billings, MT) 1985.

Wright, Bob & Kathryn. "Rustlers and Wrap-Up" from Montana—Territory of Treasures: People, Places, Events. Billings, MT: Bob & Kathryn Wright, 1964: 79-80.

Wright, Kathryn. "Lucky Diamond" from Billings: The Magic City and How It Grew. Billings, MT: Kathryn Wright, 1953: 23-27.

Zimmerman, Charles. "Building the Zimmerman Trail" from Along the Zimmerman Trail. Billings, MT: Charles Zimmerman, 1977: 13.

INDEX

Aadland, Dan 192
Abbott, E.C. "Teddy Blue" 115
Abbott, Newton Carl 141
Acton, Montana 160
Airplane 92-93, 264
Alderson, John 127
Allard, Dr. Louis 88-90, 129
Allen, Dr. William 109
Alling, Flora Amna 132
American Indians (see Battle, Crow, Northern Cheyenne Reservation) 11, 19, 25, 32, 33, 60, 68, 73, 109-111, 118, 123, 132, 220, 227, 240-242, 247
Animals/Wildlife (see Buffalo, Rabbit, Wolf) 8, 11, 13, 73, 109, 193, 217, 227, 240-242, 247, 288
Arapooish (Chief) 7-9
Audubon, John James 242
Automobile 80, 88, 174-175, 176-178, 219, 243
Bair, Mr. & Mrs. Charles 91, 157
Baker, Don 133
Banfill, W. H. William 124, 128-129
Bass, Rick 217
Battle (see Little Bighorn, Nez Perce) 15, 32, 34-43, 60-61, 110, 220
Beartooth Mountains 54-55, 148
Benteen, Capt. Fredrick 34-35, 39
Bernardis, Tim 36-37
Big Day, Heywood & Marylou 22, 202-204
Big Horn River xx-xxi, 9, 114, 123, 134, 224, 229
Billings Family Archives, Woodstock Foundation 144-146
Billings, Frederick and family (see Billings, Parmly) xix, 133, 140, 142, 145, 154-156, 198
Billings Gazette 57, 70, 84-87, 94, 132, 153, 156-157, 159-161, 223, 256
Billings, Montana xx-xxi, 55-57, 76-77, 79, 97, 109, 126, 128, 131, 136-147, 155-156, 196, 211, 261, 265, 286, 289
Billings, Parmly (see Parmly Billings Library) xix, 67-68, 145-146, 154-156, 198
Boats (canoes, sailboat, steamboats, Titanic,) 9-12, 73, 114, 126, 134, 161, 200, 226-229, 235-237, 285-289

Boden, Anneke-Jan 195
Boothill Cemetery 77, 127, 131, 148
Bozeman Trail 112-114, 190
Bradley, Lt. James 33
Bragg, Addison 83
Brewery/Beer 128-129, 131
Briceno, Severo "Sal" 180-181
Bridges 58-59, 62, 288
Bridger, Jim 60, 230-231
Broadview, Montana 57
Buffalo (see Animals) 9-11, 68, 75, 109, 127, 175, 227, 240-242, 278
Bull Mountains xxi, 29, 60, 62, 143, 147, 183-185, 272
Burkman, John 34
Businesses (see Farm, Ranch) 57-58, 61, 63, 124, 129, 131, 137, 153-154, 158-160, 179-182, 212, 283, 286
Cade, Leland P. & Family 63, 65
Calamity Jane (Canary, Martha Jane) 40, 70-71
Candy 171-173, 220-223
Canyon Creek 38-42, 70-72
Car (see Automobile)
Catlin, George 242
Cattle (see Cowboy, Ranch) xxi, 25, 57, 61, 63, 115-121, 127, 131, 134-135, 141, 191-195, 220, 259-260
Cemetery (see Boothill, Funeral) 78, 94
Chapple, Henry, James, Charles, or Wreford 154, 196-198
Chapple, Steve 196
Charter, Anne Goddard 182
Christmas 176, 178, 252-254
Church (see Religious, Shuart) 62, 135-141, 165
Clark, Capt. William 9, 15, 33, 41, 60, 123, 227, 242
Clarks Fork River 9, 11, 41, 55, 114
Clawson, Roger 199
Coal xxi, 62-63, 65, 134, 143, 182-185, 210
Coleman, Julie 94
Collins, Mabel xvii, 154
Colonia 180-182
Columbus, Montana 130
Congregational Church (see First Congregational) 135, 141-142, 148, 196
Conner, Stuart W. 105
Cookbook 149